The Invention of Dante's *Commedia*

The Invention of

Dante's *Commedia*

John G. Demaray

New Haven and London, Yale University Press

1974

Designed by John O. C. McCrillis
and set in Bodoni Book type.
Printed in the United States of America by
The Vail-Ballou Press, Inc., Binghamton, N.Y.

Published in Great Britain, Europe, and Africa by
Yale University Press, Ltd., London.
Distributed in Latin America by Kaiman & Polon,
Inc., New York City; in Australasia and Southeast
Asia by John Wiley & Sons Australasia Pty. Ltd.,
Sydney; in India by UBS Publishers' Distributors Pvt.,
Ltd., Delhi; in Japan by John Weatherhill, Inc., Tokyo.

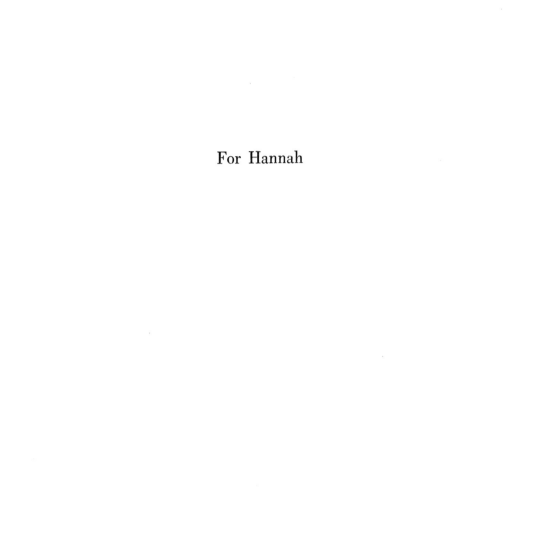

For Hannah

E quasi peregrin che si ricrea
nel tempio del suo voto riguardando,
e spera già ridir com' ello stea,
    su per la viva luce passeggiando,
menava ïo li occhi. . . .
            [*Paradiso* XXXI, 43–47]

    As a pilgrim who is refreshed
in the temple of his vow when he gazes,
and already hopes to tell how it is there,
    so, moving through the living light,
I cast my eyes. . . .

Contents

List of Illustrations

Acknowledgments

Portions of chapters that have appeared elsewhere are reprinted here with revisions by permission of the original publishers. "Pilgrim Text Models for Dante's *Purgatorio*" was first published in *Studies in Philology* (January 1969), pp. 1–25; "The Pilgrim Texts and Dante's Three Beasts, *Inferno* I," in *Italica* (Winter 1969), pp. 233–241; and "Patterns of Earthly Pilgrimage in Dante's *Commedia:* Palmers, Romers, and the Great Circle Journey," in *Romance Philology* (November 1970), pp. 239–258. Permission has also been granted by A. Mondadori to quote from Giorgio Petrocchi's authoritative edition of *La Divina Commedia secondo l'antica vulgata*, published in 4 vols. for the Società Dantesca Italiana; by Oxford University Press to quote from *Le Opere di Dante Alighieri*, edited by Edward Moore and revised by Paget Toynbee, and from William Jackson's English translation in *Dante's Convivio;* and by J. M. Dent and Sons to quote from the Temple Classics edition of the *Commedia*.

I am deeply indebted to the American University of Beirut for Cultural Studies and Honorarium Grants, together with a leave of absence in the winter of 1969–70, that made possible the completion of parts of this book in Egypt and Europe. Grateful acknowledgment is also made of a Hays-Fulbright Fellowship to the Near East that facilitated research on the present work in 1965–66. The finished studies were prepared for publication by using a grant kindly provided by the Research Council of Rutgers University.

To numerous colleagues, students, and friends, I owe many unnamed debts for suggestions and criticism. I am especially obligated to Dr. O. F. A. Meinardus, formerly of the American University in Cairo, for generous aid in obtaining information about, and for sharing his firsthand acquaintance with, medieval pilgrimage routes and monastic establishments in Egypt and Sinai. Thanks for assistance are due Dr. Antonio Carile of the Venice-and-the-Orient Institute, San Giorgio Maggiore; Dr. Olga Regusa of Columbia University; Dr. Bernard Blackstone of the American University of Beirut; Dr. Yakov Malkiel of the University of California; and Miss Hanan Mikhail and Dr. Richard Bevis. Individual staff members of the French Oriental Institute, Cairo; the Franciscan and Dominican Biblical Libraries, Jerusalem; the Vatican Library; the Vittorio Emanuele II Libraries, Florence and Rome; the American University Library, Beirut; and the New York Public Library, provided help that has been much appreciated. But it is to my wife Hannah Disinger Demaray, who through her research and journeys knows well the world of medieval pilgrimage, that I owe the greatest debt of all for constant encouragement, scholarly aid, and perceptive criticism. Because I fell ill on the purgatorial mountain of the Exodus pilgrimage in that "land beyond the sea," it was she who ascended the full length of the mountain's ancient stone stairs, passed through a gate of confession, and came to that summit where the pilgrims believed earth was joined to Heaven.

The Invention of Dante's *Commedia*

Introduction

Dante Alighieri's *Commedia* projects before the reader images of such vividness and power that they attain at once a strange familiarity. The blighted and idealized landscapes, the legions of dead souls, the angels, demons, beasts, and sacred guardians, all emerge before the reader, like bright-edged hallucinations, with a clarity so intense that the intellect, imagination, and memory are immediately engaged. Still, the eternal world depicted in the poem is never completely alien. The despairing souls in the *Inferno* remind one of individuals personally known. The dead that labor up Mt. Purgatory and the souls that sing and dance among the celestial spheres are recognizable men and women. The cities, woods, ice-fields, deserts, and rocky hills of the realm beyond, however extraordinary, remain vaguely reminiscent of actual locales upon earth. Even Dante's experiences during a pilgrimage beyond stir memories of one's own different yet comparable experiences during a journey through this life; the reader like the poet turns inward in reflection while moving spiritually toward God.

Medievalists have long understood the poetic devices employed by Dante to create this air of familiarity. It is now a commonplace of serious scholarship to assert that the eternal world of the *Commedia* reflects earthly events and persons recorded in two great medieval source books: the Book of God's Works, the existent universe; and the Book of God's Words, the Holy Bible. These two volumes, as read and interpreted by Dante and his contemporaries in the late Middle Ages, served as compendiums of truth filled with inscriptions pointing to the most significant persons, episodes, objects, and geographic sites in human history. Recently Arturo Graf, Karl Vossler, Edward Moore, Charles Singleton, Erich Auerbach, and numerous others have written extensive appraisals of how the medieval world and biblical events are mirrored in Dante's poem.

It is nevertheless an underlying premise of this study that many once-famous markings on ancient pilgrimage routes, key "words" in God's Worldly Book, have been overlooked by modern commentators, and that many persons and episodes shadowed in the eternal realm of the *Commedia* have been left unread. Certain

momentous biblical occurrences similarly reflected in the poem, it
is further maintained, have never been identified or examined in
the manner that they deserve. To illuminate the *Commedia* more
fully, the Books of God's Words and Works require additional explication.

Close readings of the *Vita Nuova, Commedia,* and epistle x to
Can Grande della Scala; an examination of early *mappaemundi,*
regional maps, sea charts, and many volumes of medieval pilgrimage and devotional literature; an inspection of a chain of
pilgrimage stations still in existence in Egypt, Palestine, Syria, the
Levant, and Italy; an analysis of Dante's techniques of figural
representation; and a study of the poet's dependence on the World
and the Bible as source books—these investigations suggest that
Dante's long pilgrimage throughout the *Commedia* is an imitation
of an earthly pilgrimage made by countless medieval Christians
to holy stations located in the Near East and Italy. And because
the sequence of inscribed sites in the Book of the World comple-
ments markings in the Book of God's Words, a knowledge of these
pilgrimage stations affords insight into biblical events that will
be shown to give basic form to Dante's poem.

That certain important "words" in God's Worldly Book and in
the Bible have been neglected by scholars and critics is under-
standable. It is a curious fact that the strength and weakness of
traditional commentary on Dante's writings—excepting research
into Islamic and Arabic influences—consists in its general con-
finement within the matrix of the classical-biblical culture of Latin
Christendom. As a medieval Italian Roman Catholic from Florence,
however, Dante Alighieri's cultural perspectives would in some
ways have been more sweeping than those of modern readers.

Today the Latin Church remains formally separated, as it has
been for centuries, from the Eastern Greek Orthodox, Syriac,
Ethiopian, and Coptic denominations which control pilgrimage
sites in remote regions of the Holy Land. A detailed knowledge of
some unique "words" in God's Worldly Book has accordingly
been lost to general Latin culture, for no longer do devout pilgrims
return to the West with stories of these places. But in Dante's period Latin Christians, trudging from the shrine of one sect to that
of another, opening church doors and frontier barriers with a

steady trickle of golden coins, bridged the gulf between Eastern and Latin religious denominations and left accounts of a Worldly Book that has now passed from memory. These accounts focus interest as well upon certain notable passages in the Bible.

To gain a renewed and authoritative acquaintance with special "words" in God's two Books, I have followed the ancient pathways of the pilgrims to all of the important Italian and Near Eastern holy sites mentioned in this study; the present book was in fact researched and written over a period of years in those cities and religious establishments that in the Middle Ages were centers of a bustling pilgrimage traffic between Europe and the Holy Land: Florence, Venice, Cairo, the Mt. Sinai monastery, Jerusalem, Damascus, Beirut, Rome, and Vatican City. But I have made a deliberate attempt not to intrude extraneous personal comment into the text. Medieval writers, pilgrims, and clerics have been allowed to speak for themselves and to reveal directly the two great source books of God.

If the early Christians' faith in the historicity of sacred markings in God's Worldly Book today seems embarrassingly literal-minded, it has only to be recalled that in past eras crusaders, artists, laymen, patristic fathers, monks and, indeed, Dante himself believed with equal literal-mindedness in the authenticity and instructive value of the holy places. At the present time a few monks, living in seldom-visited monasteries on the Egyptian, Sinai, and Arabian deserts, continue to guard and to revere the markings as true "words" in the Book of God's Works. But it was in the Middle Ages that Christendom was drawn to the sacred inscriptions as to points of supernatural light. Origin, Cyril of Alexandria, Clement of Alexandria, Philo, Eusebius of Caesaria, Paulus Orosius, and St. Augustine are a few among the many early church fathers who passed most of their lives in close proximity to the holy places. St. Jerome produced the Latin Vulgate version of the Bible in a cave at the site of the Nativity. In arid wastelands the first Christian hermits clustered in caves and hovels near the sacred writings; monasteries, shrines, and chapels were erected around the sites. In cities and towns the holy places were sheltered within round and octagonal chambers, structures incorporated into the earliest Christian basilicas so that crowds of pilgrims might circle

the "words" at their leisure. To secure militarily such sacred inscriptions in the homelands of Islam, hosts of crusaders joined with
the pilgrims in journeying to the Near East.

Because Dante's *Commedia* is created in part as an imitation of
certain of Christianity's most holy religious sites, the poem has
much in common with other artistic and architectual works of the
Middle Ages. These were regularly produced as types for distant
Holy Land stations; and they served to inspire Christians, who
remained comfortably in their home cities, to act out spiritually
and *in figura* journeys that they could not otherwise take in person.
In the fourteenth century, for example, Christians in Bruges,
Belgium, could act out a pilgrimage to the Holy Sepulchre in
Jerusalem by visiting a figural recreation of the Church of the
Holy Sepulchre in their native city. Another typological recreation
of the Church of the Holy Sepulchre was built at Fabriano, Italy,
by Peter and John Becket, supposed relatives of the martyred
Thomas Becket of Canterbury. The Basilica of the Nativity in
Bethlehem is believed to have been copied as a type in the
churches of Sta Croce and Sta Maria Maggiore in Rome, and in the
Church of the Anastasis in Istanbul, although this last church
eventually came to be identified with the virgin martyr St. Anas-
tasia. At the fifth-century monastery of San Stefano in Bologna,
seven buildings were situated so as to reproduce in figural pattern
important stations in the Holy Land. In the West, moreover, shrines
and churches were filled with relics from the Promised Land; and
often art works, such as the famous fifth-century mosaic in the apse
of Sta Pudenziana, Rome, mirrored in pictorial form distant
pilgrimage sites.

Though their modes and genres of expression differed, writers
in Dante's period and in later decades also celebrated the holy
places or introduced pilgrimage themes into their works. Petrarch
praises the peregrinations of Christians in his familiar epistles;
similar praise is offered by the anonymous English author of
The Stacions of Rome. The action of Chaucer's *The Canterbury
Tales* unfolds upon a local English pilgrimage route, one minor
link in a chain of routes that carried the Wife of Bath three times
to Jerusalem and the Knight once to St. James's shrine in Spain.
And Edmund Spenser in *The Faerie Queene* writes of a Red Cross
Knight and a Palmer who wend their way through allegorical,

fairyland backgrounds that on occasion reflect Holy Land sites also depicted in Tasso's *Jerusalem Delivered*. But it was Dante Alighieri who mirrored centrally in the *Commedia* the oldest, longest, and most famous pilgrimage in Christendom.

In this study a recurrent pattern of interrelated *figura,* appearing in the World and the Bible as well as in Dante's poem, will be examined from varying points of view. It is hoped that readers will discern from the following chapters how the Books of God's Words and Works were comprehended in the poet's period; how the divers structural and poetic elements in the *Commedia* were invented and disposed as figural imitations of markings in God's two Books; and how the literal sense of the poem, upon which all other meanings depend, obtains a historicity by reflecting *in figura* objects and episodes on earth. Yet amid the myriad surfaces and dimensions of the *Commedia,* it is all too easy to leave the straight path; therefore, only limited attention will be given to the seemingly inexhaustible shadings of meaning arising from the literal sense. By concentrating rather upon the primary and shadowed *figura* of the literal sense, an attempt will be made to disclose the basis of the poet's symbolism and allegory, and to uncover fundamental components of the poem's structure.

1

Pilgrimage in the Source Book of the World

There are three acts in a man's life which no one ought
either to advise another to do or not to do. The first is to con-
tract matrimony, the second is to go to the wars, the third is
to visit the Holy Sepulchre. I say that these three acts are good
in themselves, but they may easily turn out ill. [A warning addressed to Felix Fabri from Count Eberhart of Württenburg,
The Book of the Wanderings of Brother Felix Fabri]

When in the Middle Ages and early Renaissance the various
geographic areas of the world were commonly thought to contain
different degrees of innate spiritual perfection, Christendom held
as a passionate corollary of faith that one land above all others was
supreme in virtue and blessedness.

"The land beyond the sea, that is to say, the Holy Land,"
writes the author of a fourteenth-century pilgrimage book ex-
pressing the general view, ". . . passing all other lands, is the
most worthy land, most excellent, and lady and sovereign of all
other lands." It is, the author continues, "the heart and middle of
the world." Christ himself is said to have chosen this land as his
own because "he that will publish any thing to make it openly
known, he will cause it to be cried and proclaimed in the middle
place of a town; so that each thing that is proclaimed and pro-
nounced may equally reach to all parts; right so, he that was
creator of all the world would suffer for us at Jerusalem, that is
the middle of the world, to the end and intent that his passion and
his death, which was published there, might be known equally to
all parts of the world." [1]

1. See *The Book of Sir John Maundeville* reprinted in *Early Travels in Palestine*,
ed. Thomas Wright (London, 1848), pp. 127–128. The writer calling himself Maundeville, according to his own account, set out from England in 1322, traveled through
the Holy Land to the regions ruled by "Prester John," and returned to the west in
1356. Shortly thereafter, *The Book of Sir John Maundeville* appeared in French,
Latin, and English versions (*Early Travels*, pp. viii, 129).
The book has long been recognized as a curious compendium of fact and fiction
perhaps actually written by Jean de Bourgogne and Jean d'Outremeuse. A detailed
analysis of the case for various authors, together with arguments suggesting that at
least one of the authors really visited Palestine, can be found in *The Buke of John*

This praise of the "land beyond the sea" is a late reflection of the spiritual ardor that, from the time of the fourth-century pilgrimage of St. Jerome, the Byzantine Empress Helena, St. Silvia, and others, inspired Christians to believe that sins might be forgiven and the soul perfected through a journey to the holy places. To myriads of Christians the Holy Sepulchre in Jerusalem was a spiritual center of the world, a place where one experienced the most profound of religious griefs and joys. Here in A.D. 386 the Roman matron Paula, in the account of St. Jerome, "kissed 'the very place of the body' on which the Lord had lain, as one who thirsts drinks long-desired waters. What tears, what groans, what sorrow she displayed, all Hierusalem is witness, and the Lord Himself whom she called upon." [2] Here in later years pilgrims excitedly claimed to have witnessed Holy Fire descending from Heaven during Holy Week. And here in the year A.D. 1094, according to a widely circulated medieval story, Peter the Hermit was first urged by Christ, who appeared in a vision, to call for a crusade.[3]

Another city, however, challenged Jerusalem for supremacy as a center for medieval pilgrimage. The monuments, relics, and basilicas in the eternal city of Rome, seat of the Latin Church, attracted throngs of worshipers who there made the "rounds" of the holy sites. Francesco Petrarch, a participant in a Jubilee pilgrimage to the eternal city in 1350, enthusiastically summed up in a familiar letter the benefits of such peregrinations:

> How well it is for the Christian soul to behold the city which is like a heaven on earth, full of the sacred bones and relics of the martyrs, and bedewed with the precious blood of these witnesses for truth; to look upon the image of our Saviour, venerable to all the world, to mark the footprints in the solid stone forever worthy of the worship of the nations, wherein is verified to the letter and clearer

Maundevill, ed. with French text, notes, and intro. by George F. Warner (London, 1889), pp. xv–xvii. For other discussions of the book and its authorship see C. Raymond Beazley, *The Dawn of Modern Geography* (Oxford, 1906), 3 : 319–324; Arthur Perceival Newton, *Travel and Travellers of the Middle Ages* (New York, 1926), pp. 160–163; and George H. T. Kimble, *Geography in the Middle Ages* (London, 1938), pp. 95–98.

2. *The Pilgrimage of the Holy Paula*, trans. Aubrey Stewart, notes C. W. Wilson (London, 1887), pp. 5–6.

3. See Edwin James King, *The Knights Hospitallers in The Holy Land* (London, 1931), p. 14.

than the day the word of Isaiah, "And the children of them that afflict thee shall come bowing down to thee, and all that slandered thee shall worship the steps of thy feet"; to roam from tomb to tomb rich with memories of the saints, to wander at will through the Basilicas of the Apostles with no other company than good thoughts.[4]

Some western pilgrims and crusaders, after arduous trips in the Holy Land, visited the sacred places of Rome as did Petrarch.

The general outline of the Great Circle journey is well illustrated in the itinerary of Bernard the Wise (ca. 870). In Rome Bernard and his companions "gained the desired permission to set forth," and after arranging ship passage on the Italian coast, "were conveyed to the port of Alexandria, the voyage lasting thirty days." On the River Nile the pilgrims "sailed southward six days and came to the city of Babylonia in Egypt, where once King Pharaoh ruled, under whom Joseph built seven granaries [the pyramids], which yet remain." Moving from Babylon (Old Cairo) to the city of "Damiate" on the coast and then to the perimeter of the Sinai deserts, Bernard and his group took advantage of the "camels . . . for hire for the desert passage." Unlike many Christians on long pilgrimage, they did not turn south into the Sinai wastes to visit one of the most isolated of sacred sites, the ancient "ring" of stations at St. Catherine's monastery at Mt. Sinai; instead, they passed along the coast to Gaza and then on to Jerusalem. While venerating sacred places on a special "ring" of stations in the Holy City, Bernard, speaking of the four structures comprising the Church of the Holy Sepulchre at Calvary and Christ's tomb, writes that "four churches, not to speak of others, are notable, joined to each other by partition walls which they have in common"; one of the four he calls "Constantine's Basilica." Bernard adds that "between the above four churches there is an unroofed court, the walls of which blaze with gold, the pavement is made of the most precious stone." Leaving Jerusalem, the pilgrims "came to the sea. And embarking we sailed for sixty days . . . to Mount Aureus." Bernard then tells of the journey's end: "Coming from Mount Aureus we arrived in Rome. In this city on the eastern side, in the place called the Lateran, is a well-built

4. *Epistole Familiares* (Venezia, 1942), Book II, Letter 9. The English trans. is by Fr. Herbert Thurston in his *The Holy Year of Jubilee* (London, 1900), p. 139. An account of Petrarch's pilgrimage to Rome in 1350 can be found in Ernest Hatch Wilkins, *Life of Petrarch* (Chicago, 1961), pp. 93–95.

church in honour of St. John the Baptist, where is the proper seat of the successors of the Apostles. There every night are the keys of the whole city brought to the successor of the Apostles. On the western side is the church of blessed Peter, the chief of the Apostles, where his body rests. In size there is no church like it on the whole earth." Bernard briefly remarks, "it contains also various ornaments." [5]

In going to Jerusalem and often to Mt. Sinai as well, palmers left familiar countries in Europe to sail across what they conceived to be the earth's single inland sea of truly vast dimensions, the *Mare Internum* or Mediterranean Sea. The pilgrim Felix Fabri in the fifteenth century writes,

> It is called "the Mediterranean" because it flows through the midst of the earth, from the west even unto the east, seeing that it lies between the principal parts of the world, namely, Europe, Asia, and Africa, and divides and marks off each of them from the other by itself and its arms. For on the west and north it has Europe, on the east Asia, on the south Africa. Wherefore the pilgrim who goes to St. Catherine's touches by sea at each one of these three parts of the world. He begins his voyage in Europe; at Crete, Rhodes, and Cyprus he reaches Asia, and when he arrives at Alexandria in Egypt he will be in Africa.[6]

In the view of the palmers, their arrival at the one land having supreme spiritual value, that "land beyond the sea," placed them in a geographical position near or at the center of the earth. If the earth were a globe, as some thought, then it followed that they were uplifted to a high position near the top. The author of *The Book of Sir John Maundeville,* for example, informs his western readers that they must "go upward" over the globe to reach Jerusalem because it is at "the middle of the world; and that may be proved and shown there by a spear which is fixed in the earth at the hour of midday, when it is equinoxial, which gives no shadow on any side" (pp. 220–221).

Carrying guide books, breviaries, and copies of the Bible, many Christians sailed directly to the Near Eastern ports of Joppa (modern Jaffa) or Berytus (modern Beirut) and traveled over-

5. *The Itinerary of Bernard the Wise,* trans. J. H. Bernard (London, 1893), pp. 3–10.

6. *The Book of the Wanderings of Brother Felix Fabri,* trans. Aubrey Stewart (London, 1896), vol. 1, part 1, p. 115.

land to the Holy City. But the most intrepid of the palmers, following generally in the course of Bernard the Wise, took what might
be termed the famous six-month to four-year "Venetian tour,"
usually boarding ship before the Doge's Palace off St. Mark's
Square and debarking at Alexandria or Damietta on the Egyptian
delta, proceeding south along the River Nile to Babylon, turning
east in the approximate path of the Exodus to the Red Sea, and
then, under the leadership of pagan guides, riding by camel across
the deserts of the Sinai peninsula to the individual "ring" of
stations on Mt. Sinai.[7] Greek Orthodox monks at St. Catherine's

7. In the introduction to *Canon Pietro Casola's Pilgrimage to Jerusalem*, trans., ed.,
and notes M. Margaret Newett (Manchester, 1907), pp. 36–113, M. Newett provides
a detailed account of the statutes regulating pilgrim traffic from the Italian ports.
She points out that the archives of Venice alone show that in the late fourteenth
century, the period of her special interest, over three hundred pilgrims sailed from
this city to the Holy Land in A.D. 1382, three hundred thirty in A.D. 1383, over six
hundred in A.D. 1384, three hundred eighty in A.D. 1385, three hundred forty in
A.D. 1386, three hundred twenty-three in A.D. 1387, and three hundred ninety in
A.D. 1388. From the eleventh through the thirteenth centuries, when the crusades were
at their height, thousands of pilgrims and crusaders, of whom no individual record
remains in Venice, passed through this port on their way to that land beyond the
sea. The distinction between the pilgrim and the crusader, however, is difficult to
make; for some crusaders considered themselves pilgrims forced to take up arms.
See in particular Richard of Devizes, Geoffrey de Vinsauf, and Lord John de Join-
ville, *Chronicles of the Crusades*, ed. Henry G. Bohn (London, 1848).

As early as the sixth century, the Italian city of Amalfi regularly dispatched ships
carrying pilgrims and merchants to the ports of Berytus (modern Beirut) and
Alexandria, and a number of the Italian cities soon joined in the Near Eastern com-
merce. Pisa was very prominent in the twelfth century; then following Pisa's defeat
in 1284, Genoa rose as a major power engaged in Near Eastern shipping. Venice attained its preeminence as a pilgrim port in the period of the crusades (*Casola's
Pilgrimage*, pp. 5–6).

For a discussion of the usual itineraries and activities of Holy Land pilgrims, see
Thomas Wright, ed., *Early Travels in Palestine*, pp. 1f., 136–142; Lina Eckenstein,
A History of Sinai (London and New York, 1921), pp. 154–164; Niccolò of Poggi-
bonsi, *A Voyage Beyond the Seas*, trans. Fr. Theophilus Bellorini and Fr. Eugene
Hoade, intro. Fr. Bellarmino Bagatti (Jerusalem, 1954), pp. vii–xlvii; Leonardo
Frescobaldi, Georgio Gucci, and Simone Sigoli, *Visit to the Holy Places*, trans. Fr.
Theophilus Bellorini and Fr. Eugene Hoade, preface and notes Fr. Bellarmino Bagatti
(Jerusalem, 1948), pp. 1–28; Mahfouz Labib, *Pèlerins et Voyageurs au Mont Sinaï*
(Cairo, 1961), pp. 1–42; Malcolm Letts, *Sir John Mandeville: The Man and His
Book* (London, 1949), pp. 32f.; and Elinor A. Moore, *The Ancient Churches of Old
Jerusalem: The Evidence of the Pilgrims* (Beirut, 1961), pp. 20–74. Aziz Suryal
Atiya has admirably summarized a wide range of Holy Land narratives, particularly
those of the fourteenth century, in *The Crusade in the Later Middle Ages* (London,
1938), pp. 155–186. Individual narratives are recorded in *Itinéraires à Jérusalem et
Descriptions de la Terre Sainte*, ed. Henri Michelant and Gaston Raynaud (Genève,

monastery guided pilgrims over this Holy Circle, gave them communion in the monastery church, and saw them off to Jerusalem. The Latin pilgrims accepted these ministrations gladly, for the monks were renowned for their exceptional piety and their special relationship to God.[8]

Most palmers after leaving St. Catherine's had no wish to venture deeply inland into the Orient. Following ancient routes to Gaza and Palestine, they regularly stopped at the arid basin cradling the Dead Sea, a place reputed to be a mouth of Hell; and there they gazed upon smoke-like mists and observed the sites of Sodom and Gomorrah. Further on they bathed in the sacred stream that empties into the Dead Sea—the River Jordan—their actions symbolizing baptism and spiritual cleansing. Then after "taking the palm" at nearby Jericho and wrapping it around their staffs, they moved forward, brandishing this outward emblem of their spiritual purity, to the Holy Sepulchre within the city of Jerusalem.[9]

1882) ; *Itinera Hierosolymitana et Descriptiones Terrae Sanctae*, ed. Titus Tobler and Augustus Molinier (Osnabruck, 1966) ; *Itinéraires Russes en Orient*, ed. Mme. B. De Khitrowo (Osnabruck, 1966) ; and *Deutsche Pilgerreisen nach dem Heiligen Lande*, ed. Reinhold Rohricht (Osnabruck, 1967). See also the Holy Land narratives of Augustin Jacques de Vérone (ca. 1335) and Nicolas de Martoni (ca. 1394) in *Revue de L'Orient Latin*, (Paris, 1895), 3 : 155–302, 566–610.

Possibly the writings of numerous Palestine pilgrims have been neglected by Dante scholars because these texts have been published individually in the 1890's under the auspices of the British-controlled Palestine Exploration Fund; later the Fund collected the works in fourteen volumes as *The Palestine Pilgrim Texts* (London, 1890–1897). One would expect these texts to contain much geographical and scientific information; instead, such positivistic comment as one can find is highly colored by the pilgrims' excited accounts of a series of religious stops or stations. The texts really belong to the literature of "spiritual travel."

8. See Eckenstein, pp. 121–133; William Farid Bassili, *Sinai and the Monastery of St. Catherine* (Cairo, 1962), pp. 33–84; and H. Rabino, *Le monastère de Sainte Catherine du Mont Sinai* (Cairo, 1938). For accounts of medieval monastic establishments on the Exodus route that are still in existence today see O. F. A. Meinardus, *Monks and Monasteries of the Egyptian Deserts* (Cairo, 1951), and *Christian Egypt, Ancient and Modern*, (Cairo, 1965), pp. 135–185, 349–497.

9. *The Book of Sir John Maundeville* provides a succinct summary of this overland Exodus route: "From Alexandria we go to Babylon, where the Sultan dwells, which is situated also on the river Nile." This is the river in which "are found many precious stones, and much also of lignum aloes, a kind of wood that comes from out of terrestrial Paradise. . . . From Babylon to Mont Sinai, where St. Catherine lieth, you must pass by the desert of Arabia, by which Moses led the people of Israel." The author states that this trip "from Babylon to Mt. Sinai is twelve good days

No recounting of comparable modern travels can adequately re-capture the miraculous nature of that earlier Exodus pilgrimage. In the Holy Land the mysteriousness of the extensive Asiatic and African regions became apparent to pilgrims from the odd persons and things to be seen: camels, elephants, silks, exotic perfumes, watery "manna," paradisaic fruits, strange birds, delicate fountains, gigantic pyramids, turbaned Saracens, and domed and towered mosques. Unfamiliar scenes passed before the eyes of the pilgrims as they wandered through the palm groves and villages of the Egyptian delta, over the barren deserts, and on to the green and rolling hills of the Promised Land. To the east stretched relatively unknown realms reputed to be populated by other Oriental peoples, mythological beasts, and even devils. And farther east still, at the point of the morning sunrise possibly in an ocean, was said to rise a peak surmounted by the Terrestrial Paradise, its fountains watering underground streams that burst forth in various parts of the world to form the Ganges, Tigris, Euphrates, and Nile Rivers. Surrounding the circular landmass of the earth was the Great Ocean which extended horizontally into unexplored spaces or, if the world were a globe, covered the vast southern hemisphere.[10]

The surviving writings dating from the fourth to the fifteenth

---

journey, and some make it more; and some haste them, and thus make it less." Pilgrims, the author explains, "from Babylon go by the Red Sea, which is an arm of the ocean. There Moses passed with the children of Israel across the sea all day, when Pharaoh, king of Egypt, pursued him. . . . Then we go by desert to the vale of Elim, and thence to Mt. Sinai" (p. 156–157). Following the desert passage to Gaza and the walk through green lands to Jerusalem, pilgrims made trips, according to the author, to the River Jordan and the adjoining Dead Sea. "And you shall understand," he writes, "that the river Jordan runs into the Dead Sea, and there it dies, for it runs no further. . . . Some call that sea the Lake Dasfetidcc; some, the River of Devils; and some the river that is ever stinking. Into that sea, by the wrath of God, sank the five cities, Sodom, Gomorrah, Aldama, Seboym, and Segor, for the abominable sin that reigned in them." From this "River of Devils" pilgrims are said to return again to Jerusalem (p. 179).

10. The curious blend of fact and fiction that was medieval geography is well documented by Ferdinand Denis, *Le Monde Enchanté: Cosmographie et Histoire Naturelle Fantastiques du Moyen Age* (New York and Paris, 1845); in chapters III and IV of this work, there is a discussion of Brunetto Latini's *Tesoretto* and its influence upon Dante (pp. 48–106). See also George H. T. Kimble, *Geography in the Middle Ages*, pp. 97–102; W. L. Bevan, *Medieval Geography* (London, 1873), pp. 79–93; and John Kirkland Wright, *The Geographical Lore of the Time of the Crusades* (New York, 1925).

century which afford insight into the Exodus pilgrimage reveal a
remarkable resemblance in structure, content, and tone because
palmers generally recorded the same basic reactions to the same
places in the same order. During a tour of the Holy Land in A.D.
342, the Byzantine Empress Helena, displaying a unique talent for
divining the alleged sites on which numerous Old and New Testament events occurred, fixed most of the place stops along the
pilgrimage route. St. Silvia in A.D. 382 confirmed and added to
the established stops while traveling along and writing of the
Exodus path. Guide books and other pilgrim accounts of the
twelfth century categorized the stops into the Stations of the Exodus
and gave a general allegorical interpretation of their meaning, an
interpretation later to be echoed in Dante's epistle x to Can
Grande della Scala. "The significance of these stations [of the
Exodus], and a catalogue of them I have arranged so as to mention them in my works," writes Fetellus in a pilgrim guide book of
the twelfth century still in use in the seventeenth: "through them
the true Hebrew who hastens to pass from earth to heaven must
run his race, and, leaving the Egypt of the world, must enter the
land of promise, i.e., the heavenly father-land." [11] Anonymous
Pilgrim vi (Pseudo-Beda), also in the twelfth century, repeats the
words of Fetellus about "the meaning of the stations . . . ; it is
through them that the true Hebrew who is eager to make his way
from earth to heaven must pass, and leaving behind the Egypt of
this world, enter into the land of promise and his heavenly
home." [12]

All along the Stations-of-the-Exodus route from Egypt to Jerusalem, the written accounts reveal, the pilgrims on the great journey of their lives were often swept by intense emotion as they prepared themselves spiritually for entrance to the Holy City. They
sang and wept, confessed and repented; they reflected on the sins
and good actions of their past lives, read appropriate biblical

11. Fetellus, *Description of Jerusalem and the Holy Land,* trans. James Rose
MacPherson (London, 1892), p. 14. The translation is based mainly upon the Latin
manuscript (ca. 1130) now in the National Library of Paris (Imperial Library, Fonds
Latin, no. 5, p. 129). This Latin version was copied many times and was even published as late as 1653 by Leon Allatius under the name of Eugesippus.

12. *Anonymous Pilgrims, I–VIII,* trans. Aubrey Stewart (London, 1894), p. 40.
Stewart's translation is based upon the text published in *Oesterreichischer Viertel-
jahresschrift für Katholische Theologie,* notes V. Newmann (Vienna, 1868, 1870).

passages at venerated sites, listened to edifying *exempla* of their guides, and prayed before holy icons often arranged in story-groups depicting biblical events—the literal and spiritual experiences of the pilgrims paralleling those of souls in *Purgatorio*. They believed, moreover, that through confession and repentance of sin and the gaining of special Holy Land indulgences remitting the temporal punishments of Purgatory, they were in fact spiritually ascending toward Heaven as they trudged the lonely sand tracks, supposedly uphill over the globe, to a Holy City considered to be in the middle of the world.

Exactly what official Roman Catholic indulgences they were gaining is still something of an ecclesiastical and scholarly puzzle.[13] But in 1346–50 when Niccolò of Poggibonsi compiled the first, complete, unofficial list made by a pilgrim, he noted some twenty-six partial indulgences granting the full remission of all temporal punishment, and ninety-two partial indulgences granting a limited remission of temporal punishment. Not all of these indulgences were recognized by the Roman Church. In a very human way the palmers tended to exaggerate colossally the supposed benefits of the indulgences until in the fourteenth century references appear to indulgences remitting every sin, presumably past, present and future (*A Voyage*, p. xxiii). Yet those palmers who made the long pilgrimage to gain all possible indulgences, whatever they might be, were those fortunate few who could say that before death they had truly been both once to Sinai and once to the Holy City.

In Jerusalem a separate series of stops along the Holy Circle path of venerated places eventually became known as the Stations of the Cross after Franciscans, leading palmers to the places beginning in the fourteenth century, established a regular pattern of worship centering on the theme of Christ's death and resurrection.[14]

13. See Fr. Bellarmino Bagatti's exhaustive table of unofficial Holy Land indulgences as compiled from pilgrim texts and included in his introduction to Niccolò of Poggibonsi, *A Voyage*, pp. xl–xlviii. Fr. Bagatti compares the unofficial indulgences with those which the Roman Church, as far as can be ascertained, officially recognized (pp. xxii–xxvii). A list of what may possibly be official indulgences can be found in the "Table of Indulgences of Acre" reproduced in *Itinéraires à Jérusalem et Descriptions de la Terre Sainte*, pp. 235–236.

14. See Fr. Herbert Thurston, *The Stations of the Cross* (London, 1906), pp. 165f; and Michel Join-Lambert, *Jerusalem*, trans. Charlotte Haldane (London and New York, 1958), pp. 219–221. Fr. Bellarmino Bagatti in discussing the Holy Circle in

Priests and palmers from the Holy Land introduced the ritual of worshiping at the Stations of the Cross into Europe where it was adopted by the Roman Church, but the observances at the desert Stations of the Exodus and on the Mt. Sinai "ring," concentrating generally on the purgation of sin before entrance to the Holy City, were practiced by fewer persons and were forgotten. While certain pilgrim texts written after Dante's death are quoted for their detailed information about the stops on the desert, on Mt. Sinai, and in Jerusalem, one can be assured that these writings describe no new experiences or new places; they simply give more elaborate accounts of the familiar old ones.

The palmers remained in and around Jerusalem for varying periods of time, a few electing to stay for years. Those deciding to terminate their pilgrimages in Rome returned across the sea to the eternal city and there venerated at yet a third individual "ring" of stops. In the fourteenth century when the Latin Church held Jubilee pilgrimages in 1300 and 1350, these holy places, each one carrying special indulgences, became known as the Stations of Rome. Among the many churches, tombs, and relics included in this Holy Circle were two of particular importance: on the eastern edge of the city, pilgrims invariably visited the Lateran, the supposed mother church of Christianity and a palace of the popes; and crossing the city, they entered St. Peter's, the most magnificent of the city's basilicas. On certain feast days the pilgrims saw exhibited, either on the steps of St. Peter's or in the Veronica Chapel within, one of the most famed relics in all Christendom: the Veil of Veronica on which an image of Christ's face was reputed to be printed. So moved by the sight of the veil was Francesco Petrarch that he wrote a sonnet about an aged prilgrim who comes to view the relic as a final act in a long life:

> Movesi il vecchierel canuto e bianco
> Del dolce loco ov'ha sua età fornita,
> E da la famigliuola sbigottita
> Che vede il caro padre venir manco;
> Indi, traendo poi l'antiquo fianco
> Per l'estreme giornate di sua vita,
> Quando più po col buon voler s' aita,
> **Rotto da gli anni e dal cammino stanco;**

Jerusalem includes a table of the major stops compiled from the writings of pilgrims of the fourteenth century (*A Voyage*, pp. xvii–xix).

E viene a Roma, seguendo 'l desio,
  Per mirar la sembianza di colui
  Ch' ancor lassù nel ciel vedere spera.
Così, lasso! tal or vo cercand'io,
  Donna, quanto è possible, in altrui
  La disïata vostra forma vera.[15]

[The palmer bent, with locks of silver gray,
  Quits the sweet spot where he has pass'd his years,
  Quits his poor family, whose anxious fears
  Paint the loved father fainting on his way;
And trembling, on his aged limbs slow borne,
  In these last days that close his earthly course,
  He, in soul's strong purpose, finds new force,
  Though weak with age, though by long travel worn:
Thus reaching Rome, led on by pious love,
  He seeks the image of that Saviour Lord
  Whom soon he hopes to meet in bliss above:
So, oft in other forms I seek to trace
  Some charm, that to my heart may yet afford
  A faint resemblance of thy matchless grace.]

And like the aged man in Petrarch's poem, many Christians climaxed their pilgrimages by staring upon the supposed visage of Christ in an eternal city.

In ardently attempting to save their souls on pilgrimages to Mt. Sinai, Jerusalem, and Rome, Christians sought above all else to "read" spiritual truths from the iconographic Book of God's Works. They studied publications by God in the form of holy rocks, trees, rivers, mountains, hills, and caves; and these publications were elaborated into complex nests of icons by the artful markings of holy men. Cross-shaped churches were erected on venerated sites; within the churches individual chapels also commemorated the holy places; and within the chapels paintings, statues, and relics did the same—each structure and object comprising part of a most complicated "speaking picture." Thus in the fourteenth century Niccolò of Poggibonsi saw from a distance Mt. Sinai, a single stop on the Stations of the Exodus as listed in Fetellus's guide book. At the foot of the mountain he paused at the site of the Burning Bush, a separate station on the independent

15. *Le Rime di Francesco Petrarca*, notes Giosuè Carducci and Severino Ferrari (Firenze, 1946), sonnet XVI, pp. 17–18. The translation is by Dacre in *The Sonnets, Triumphs, and Other Poems of Petrarch*, intro. Thomas Campbell, trans. various persons (London, 1916), pp. 13–14.

Mt. Sinai "ring"; and this station was marked in turn by a church containing many chapels, paintings, and sacred objects.[16]

Christians on pilgrimages, moreover, learned by means of the processional method of education, a method later formalized by the Church in the Stations of the Cross worship and adopted by Dante for use in the *Commedia*. One or more persons were led by a guide from one instructive place to another and encouraged to stop, look, listen, sing, and pray. Allegorical meanings were then often associated with relics and actions at each station. For example, St. Jerome, writing of Paula's journey to the Holy Land, explains that this Roman matron stood near the River Jordan on the site of Christ's baptism and "as the sun rose, remembered the Son of righteousness." Paula is said to have been aware of "how, by His baptism, the Lord cleansed the waters, which had been defiled by the Flood and stained by His death" (*Holy Paula*, p. 12). The pilgrim's consciousness of the sun over the Jordan accordingly suggests Christ's entrance into the mind; and the pilgrim's baptism in Jordan waters cleansed by Christ would be understood to wash away the stain of past sin. Yet man can be saved from future sin, St. Jerome implies, by movement into the city of God. The church father states that Sion, here meaning Jerusalem, "signifies 'citadel' or 'watch tower'." The "gates of Sion" through which Paula passed suggest those "against which the infernal one prevaileth not, and through which the multitude of believers enter into Christ" (*Holy Paula*, p. 6). Just as baptism in the Jordan washes away the stain of past sin, St. Jerome asserts, so entrance into the Holy City signifies a final conversion of the soul to Christ; for it is in Jerusalem that Christ rose from the dead and gave man hope for future salvation. Through such interpretations did St. Jerome, like other pilgrims and their chroniclers, try to look beyond the veil of matter and to discern the spiritual meaning of the holy places.

As historians of cartography have shown, the pilgrims' recurrent descriptions and "readings" of iconographic places and objects provided source materials that influenced the shape and content of medieval *mappaemundi*. These world maps were regularly included in psalters and medieval geographic-religious works by writers such as Cosmos Indicopleustes, Sallust, Beatus, Macro-

---

16. Niccolò of Poggibonsi's precise description of Mt. Sinai, St. Catherine's monastery, and the chapels and icons in the monastery church is in *A Voyage*, pp. 104–111.

bius, and Brunetto Latini. Though many of the original maps accompanying manuscripts have been lost, a sufficient number of copies survive to suggest that their distribution in the Middle Ages was widespread. John Kirkland Wright, in a study of medieval geographical lore, believes that, when St. Augustine wrote *The City of God* and Paulus Orosius *The Seven Books of History Against the Pagans*, both authors penned geographical passages with *mappaemundi* before them; and Paolo Revelli cites specific maps that, he thinks, may have influenced Dante in creating the *Commedia*.[17]

Among the most detailed world maps of the Middle Ages were those apparently first drawn to illustrate either a passage in Sallust's *De bello Jugurthino* or a commentary on the Apocalypse by Beatus, a priest of the eighth century living in Spain. Maps of the Sallust and Beatus type took their general form from earlier and more primitive "T-O Maps" which concentrated upon a single representation of the world with its three known continents. On the "T-O Maps" the entire earth is depicted as a circle or oval within which is drawn the T-shaped mass of the *Mare Internum* or Mediterranean Sea. In these round maps the east lies toward the top of the page. The cross bar of the T runs therefore horizontally north and south across the middle of the circle, and the stroke of the T runs vertically east and west through the bottom half of the circle. The large landmass above the cross bar constitutes Asia; the lower left hand segment, Europe; and the lower right hand segment, Africa. The edges of the circle are marked to suggest the waters of a surrounding ocean. On "T-O Maps" legends are reduced to a minimum and decorative drawings uncommon.

Sallust and Beatus type maps adopted the T-O outline, but, after the tenth century, added a wealth of detail gleaned from biblical commentary, secular writings, and pilgrim texts. The Garden of Eden is drawn at the furthermost point east; evident as well are the four rivers of the Terrestrial Paradise flowing from the garden; various cities in all three continents are indicated; and Jerusalem is revealed as a circular city near or at the center of the earth.[18] On maps of this kind by Isidore of Seville,

17. See Wright's *The Geographical Lore of the Time of the Crusades*, pp. 103–104; and Revelli, *L'Italia nella Divina Commedia* (Milano, 1922).

18. See Leo Bagrow, *History of Cartography*, rev. and enl. R. A. Skelton, trans. D. L. Paisey (Cambridge, Mass., 1964), pp. 41–66; Walter Wilson Jervis, *The World*

Henry of Mainz, Richard of Haldingham, and the creator of the Epsdorf world chart—as on almost all *mappaemundi* after the tenth century—Rome is drawn as a walled town or castle in the lower half, the western sector, of the world. The city is placed on the shores of the *Mare Internum* midway between Jerusalem, near or at the center, and the Gates of Hercules (modern Gibraltar) at the western perimeter of the world. A palmer leaving from Rome on a Great Circle pilgrimage would, therefore, sail eastward up the vertical stroke of the T-shaped *Mare Internum* to Alexandria, Egypt, marked somewhat to the right on the crossbar of the T. After proceeding inland and moving north parallel to the crossbar to Jerusalem, the pilgrim would travel back to the coast and embark for home at Berytus or Joppa, located a little to the left on the crossbar. The return voyage would carry the palmer down the vertical stroke of the T and back to Europe.[19]

To obtain a geographical model for the physical earth in the *Commedia*, Dante had only to conclude that the three continents on the Sallust and Beatus type maps were located on the northern hemisphere of a globe with Jerusalem at the middle of the landmass. The ocean surrounding the land on the maps would be conceived as existing in the southern hemisphere. And the Terrestrial Paradise, marked always at the furthermost point east on the flat maps, would then be construed as situated opposite Jerusalem in the middle of the southern hemisphere's ocean. Dante in the *Commedia* is, after all, merely echoing views of the world held also by his teacher Brunetto Latini. In the *Tesoretto* Latini claims that the world is round, and a "T-O Map" is included in some manuscripts to disclose the accepted shape of the northern hemisphere.[20]

Dante conveniently provides geographical information in the *Purgatorio* by noting that, when there are three hours of daylight

---

in *Maps: A History of Ancient Geography*, 2 vols. (New York, 1959); and Raymond Beazley, *The Dawn of Modern Geography*. Reproductions of the different types of medieval maps can be found in the works cited and also in *Monumenta Cartographica Vaticana*, 2 vols. (Città del Vaticano, 1944); and *The world map by Richard of Haldingham in Hereford Cathedral*, intro. G. R. Crone (London, 1954).

19. In his introduction to *The world map by Richard of Haldingham in Hereford Cathedral*, G. R. Crone discusses how the accounts of pilgrims making the Holy Land journey influenced mapmakers' conception of the world.

20. These maps are reproduced in the French-language edition of *Li Libres Dou Trésor*, ed. Francis J. Carmody (Berkeley, 1948).

left at Mt. Purgatory, it is midnight in Italy; and the poet in another passage writes that the sun rises on Mt. Purgatory at the time of vespers, heard at three P.M. in Italy (*Purg.* xv, 1–6; III, 25). There is, in other words, a nine hour time difference between Rome and Mt. Purgatory and a twelve hour time difference between Jerusalem, at the middle of the earth, and Mt. Purgatory at the antipodes. Rome can then be placed one quarter of the way around the globe from the Holy City, its position on Sallust and Beatus type maps when interpreted as flat projections of a globular earth.

With this general knowledge of the medieval Book of the geographical World, one is better able to appreciate the outlook of that great company of early palmers who roamed the deserts and sailed the seas seeking spiritual fulfillment. A complete historical survey of their route and its wonders, as recounted by pilgrims from earliest times through the fourteenth century, is unnecessary here. It is enough, first, to observe the antiquity and particulars of the Mt. Sinai and Jerusalem "rings" of stations by turning to the earliest extant writings of the palmers; then pilgrim texts will be used to review the entire Great Circle journey as it was known to Christians in Dante's time.

St. Silvia in the fourth century was the first traveler to describe the Mt. Sinai "ring" and what she claimed were "all the places which the children of Israel had touched in going to or returning from the Mount of God." [21] The opening portion of St. Silvia's manuscript is missing, but the part which remains begins dramatically at the moment when this pilgrim and her companions saw "a great valley, very flat and extremely beautiful; and beyond the valley appeared Sinai, the holy Mount of God" (*St. Silvia,* p. 11). They advanced to "the valley at the head of which was the place where holy Moses was when he fed the flocks of his father-in-law, where God spake to him from the Burning Bush"; that is, to the present-day Wády ed Deir which has St. Catherine's monastery and the site of the Burning Bush at its narrow end. But the pilgrims, traveling southeast, did not turn left into the Wády; rather,

---

21. *The Pilgrimage of St. Silvia of Aquitania to the Holy Places,* intro., notes, trans. John H. Bernard (London, 1891), p. 19. Correct directional points—north, south, east, and west—as established by modern geographers will hereafter be used in describing the movements of St. Silvia and medieval pilgrims.

they crossed "through the middle of the head of the valley, and so came round to the Mount of God." In so doing they followed the present-day Wády el Lejá southeast to that locale, on the opposite side of the mountain from St. Catherine's, where then as now stands what St. Silvia identified as "a certain monastery" with "kindly monks" and a "church" (pp. 12–13). This establishment was known in the Middle Ages as St. Mary of Mercy.

St. Silvia and her party, guided by monks from the monastery, spent a full day arduously laboring up and down the desolate pathways on Mt. Sinai. "Now, our route," St. Silvia writes, "was first to ascend the Mount of God at the side from which we were approaching, because the ascent here was easier; and then to descend at the head of the valley where the Bush was, this being the easier way of descent from the Mount of God" (p. 12). In short, the pilgrims climbed from the monastery at the mouth of Wády el Lejá to the summit of Mt. Sinai, and then went down the other side to St. Catherine's monastery in Wády ed Deir. In following centuries it became traditional for pilgrims to negotiate the Mt. Sinai "ring" on the same pathway used by St. Silvia and her companions; but later travelers began their ascent at St. Catherine's in the "valley where the Bush was," rather than at Wády el Lejá, and so moved in a direction opposite to that taken by St. Silvia's group.

Four hours were spent by St. Silvia and her party struggling upward to the mountain's peak over terrain characterized as "all rocky, so that it has not a bush on it." "Although the labour was great," St. Silvia comments, "I did not feel it. To that extent the labour was not felt, because I saw that the desire which I had was being fulfilled by the command of God" (pp. 12–13). Upon reaching the summit, St. Silvia was awed by what seemed the enormous height of Mt. Sinai: "those mountains which we had at first ascended with difficulty were like little hills in comparison with that central one on which we were standing. And yet they were so enormous that I should think I had never seen higher, did not this central one overtop them by so much. Egypt and Palestine and the Red Sea and the Parthenian Sea [the eastern part of the *Mare Internum*] which leads to Alexandria, also the boundless territories of the Saracens, we saw below us, hard though it is to believe; all which things those holy men pointed out to us" (p. 15).[22] On Mt. Sinai's peak St. Silvia visited a small chapel and the place where Moses received the Law, and during the descent to St. Catherine's monastery another stop was made at the cave of Elijah. Passing the evening within St. Catherine's monastery at the mountain's base, the pilgrims rose "early on the next day" and inspected that place in Wády ed Deir "where it rained manna and quails" (p. 18). They continued on their way along Wády ed Deir to the "spot where we came back again to our road," the place from which they had first glimpsed Mt. Sinai.

St. Silvia and her party next took a very long route to the Holy Land by venturing over stations on the Exodus path, first, northwest to the Red Sea, then north to the "city of Arabia," and finally east along the coast to Palestine. "Thence our return journey," St. Silvia writes, "was by the route that we had taken going" (p. 20). The pilgrims passed their first night on "the desert of Faran"— probably at Wády Feirán about twenty miles northwest of Mt. Sinai—where they "came at length to the station." The next day the travelers "arrived at the station which is over the sea" at a point where "there is an exit from the mountains" and "the deserts are quite sandy." At this station, as at other stops on the path, St. Silvia reflects upon the Exodus: "The children of Israel also, returning to Sinai, the Mount of God, returned by the way that they had gone to that very place where we came out among the mountains, and finally approached the Red Sea" (pp. 19–20). Turning to the north, the party followed the route "from the Red Sea . . . to the city of Arabia" passing by "four stations" (p. 20). The group remained only for a short time in Egypt; soon they struck out for the Promised Land. This last segment of their pil-

22. This description of the view from Mt. Sinai is not just "hard . . . to believe"; it is inaccurate and cannot be believed. The Red Sea, the Mediterranean Sea, and Palestine are not visible from the summit of Mt. Sinai. However, the brilliant play of light in the region does sometimes give a bluish cast to the horizon; and on the Mt. Sinai complex of mountains in 1963, a monk from St. Catherine's monastery pointed out to this writer hazy blue areas on the horizon and claimed that the Mediterranean and Red Seas were visible. In writing of the summit view in an appendix to his edition of *The Pilgrimage of St. Silvia of Aquitania to the Holy Places*, John H. Bernard rightly comments: "There can be little doubt that S. Silvia was misinformed by her guides, as travellers and pilgrims often are at the present day" (p. 140). But early Christians apparently wished to believe that Mt. Sinai, as a mark of its importance, was far higher than other mountains; and descriptions of the kind recorded by St. Silvia gave rise to the conviction that the mountain towered almost to the sphere of the moon. See the statements of pilgrim Felix Fabri quoted in chapter v, pp. 156–157.

grimage is but briefly mentioned in St. Silvia's chronicle: "Again making our route through several stations in Egypt by which we had formerly taken our course, I arrived at the borders of Palestine; and thence in the name of Christ our God, again making my stations through Palestine, I returned to Aelia—that is, Jerusalem" (p. 24).

The Mountain of God gained new prominence in the years following St. Silvia's visit, for in the sixth century the Emperor Justinian, recognizing the importance of Mt. Sinai both as a religious site and a possible military base, erected structures that became part of the famous "ring." Procopius of Caesarea (ca. 560) notes that a "church" dedicated to the Virgin was built on the slopes of the mountain "a long way below" the summit, and fortifications were constructed to protect the main monastery. "At the foot of the mountain," Procopius writes, "our Emperor also built a very strong fort, and placed in it a very considerable garrison of soldiers, in order that the barbarian Saracens might not from that point, the country being, as I have said, a desert, secretly invade Palestine." [23]

Pilgrims during this period marched to Mt. Sinai, not only by way of Egypt as did St. Silvia, but sometimes straight from Jerusalem across Palestine and the Sinai deserts. Commenting on the stages of the journey to the holy Mountain of God, Theodosius (ca. 530) writes, "From Jerusalem to Elusa there are 3 stages; from Glutiarinalia 7 stages, which Alexander the Great of Macedon built. From thence to Mt. Sinai there are 8 stages, if you are willing to go the short way through the desert, but if you go through Egypt there are 25 stages." [24]

The wonders of the Mt. Sinai "ring" in the sixth century are recorded by Antoninus Martyr (Antoninus of Piacenza). "Journeying through the desert," Antoninus Martyr says of his party's advance from Gaza, "on the eighth day, we came to the place where Moses brought forth water from the rock; and after that we came to the mountain of God, Horeb, from which place we removed, that we might ascend Mount Sinai." [25] The newly fortified monas-

23. *Of the Buildings of Justinian,* trans. Aubrey Stewart, notes C. W. Wilson and T. Hayter Lewis, (London, 1896), pp. 146–147.

24. *On the Topography of the Holy Land,* trans. J. H. Bernard (London, 1893), p. 17.

25. *Of the Holy Places Visited,* trans. Aubrey Stewart, notes C. W. Wilson (London, 1887), p. 29.

tery and the monks within attracted the notice of this pilgrim: "The monastery is surrounded by walls, and in it are three abbots learned in tongues—that is to say, Latin, Greek, Syriac, Egyptian, and Persian—and many interpreters of each language. In it are the dwellings of the monks." In climbing to the peak of Mt. Sinai, Antoninus Martyr, like St. Silvia, remarks upon a sacred cave and the summit chapel, but the cave is given a new identification: "We ascended the mountain unceasingly for three miles, and came to the place of the cave in which Helias was hidden when he fled before Jezebel. . . . Thence we ascended unceasingly for three miles farther, to the topmost peak of the mountain, upon which is a small chapel, having six feet, more or less, in length and breadth. In this no one is permitted to pass the night; but after the sun has risen, the monks ascend thither and perform the Divine Office. In this place many, out of devotion, cut off their hair and beard, and throw them away; and there I also trimmed and cut my beard" (*Holy Places,* pp. 29–30).

Though the Mt. Sinai "ring" was widely celebrated, the other goal of pilgrimage on the Exodus route, Jerusalem, undoubtedly gained in renown when in the fourth century an extraordinary discovery was said to have been made in the Holy City. Excavations were then under way for a new basilica ordered by the Emperor Constantine. "And as one layer after another was laid bare," Eusebius reports in his *Life of Constantine* (ca. 330), "forthwith, contrary to all expectation, did the venerable and hallowed monument of our Saviour's resurrection become visible." [26] The site of Christ's tomb had purportedly been found, and Eusebius regarded the event as an emblem that might be read by all good Christians. At the moment of its unearthing, he writes, "the most holy cave received what was an exact emblem of His coming to life. For after its descent into darkness it again came forth into light, and afforded to those who came to see a clear insight into the history of its wonders which had there been wrought, testifying to the resurrection of the Saviour by deeds more eloquent than any voice could be" (p. 3).

Two buildings joined by a courtyard were eventually built at the sacred site. Within a round structure known as the Anastasis, Eusebius reports that twelve columns "equal in number to the

26. *Life of Constantine,* trans. John H. Bernard, intro. and notes T. Hayter Lewis (London, 1896), p. 3.

Apostles of the Saviour" formed a circle around the cave of Christ's tomb and supported a lofty ceiling "overlaid . . . with radiant gold" (pp. 8–9). To the east of the Anastasis was "a very large space of ground . . . open to the pure air of heaven; the floor of which a polished stone pavement adorned, bounded by long porticos which ran round continuously on three sides." Beyond this open space on "the site, opposite the cave, which looked towards the rising sun, the basilica was erected, an extraordinary work, reared to immense height, and of great extent both in length and breadth." The entrance to the basilica was through "three gates facing the rising sun" (pp. 7–8). Eusebius concludes with emphasis: "So on the monument of salvation itself was the new Jerusalem built, over against the one so famous of old, which, after the pollution caused by the murder of the Lord, experienced the last extremity of desolation;" and he speculates that "perhaps this was that strange new Jerusalem, proclaimed in the oracles of the prophets, to which long passages prophesying by the aid of the Divine spirit make countless allusions in song" (pp. 6–7).

The New Jerusalem was located on a height in the western quarter of the city where the present Church of the Holy Sepulchre stands, and it was approached from the east by walking uphill through Jerusalem over the slopes of Mt. Sion. Below in the city's southeastern quarter was the traditional site of Solomon's Temple, the place now occupied by the Dome of the Rock Mosque.

Pilgrim texts from the fourth through the sixth centuries again and again refer to these stations on the city tour, stations that were also mentioned by palmers in later periods. The earliest of the pilgrim writings, that of the anonymous Bordeaux pilgrim (ca. 333), begins with a list of distances on the extended overland journey from Bordeaux to Jerusalem by way of Constantinople; then primary attention is given to a narrative enumerating the places visited within the Holy City. The pilgrim first walks along the eastern side of Jerusalem. Stops are made at "two large pools" of Solomon "at the side of the temple"; at the "high tower" with the "pinnacle" in the Temple area; and at the place "where stood the temple which Solomon built." [27] Of this last locale the Bor-

---

27. *Itinerary from Bordeaux to Jerusalem*, trans. Aubrey Stewart, notes C. W. Wilson (London, 1887), pp. 19–21.

deaux pilgrim notes, "they say that the blood of Zacharias which was shed upon the stone pavement before the altar remains to this day. There are also to be seen the marks of the nails in the shoes of the soldiers who slew him, throughout the whole enclosure, so plain that you would think they were impressed upon wax" (p. 21).

Turning right, the pilgrim skirts the southern edge of the city, sometimes going outside the old walls, and progresses uphill from east to west in a line that approximates the path of the present King David Street. Not far from the site of the Temple, the pilgrim, as he climbs Mt. Sion, passes a miraculous "pool which is called siloe and has four porticoes; and there is another pool outside it. This spring runs for six days and nights, but on the seventh day, which is the Sabbath, it does not run at all, either by day or by night" (*Bordeaux to Jerusalem*, pp. 22–23). Arriving at the southwestern corner of the city, the pilgrim observes that "inside the wall of Sion, is seen the place where was David's palace." Near this palace is said to be "the little hill of Golgotha were the Lord was crucified. About a stone's throw from thence is a vault wherein His body was laid, and rose again on the third day. There, at present, by the command of the Emperor Constantine, has been built a basilica" (*Bordeaux to Jerusalem*, pp. 23–24). After visiting the basilica, this traveler leaves the city and so completes his "round."

The Bordeaux pilgrim's chronicle is striking in its revelation of how well established was the Jerusalem "ring" even in the fourth century. Stations used today are identified, and the direction of the Christian's progress is plainly indicated. Movement is south through the Temple area, the city's southeastern quarter, and then west and north to the Church of the Holy Sepulchre—a route often followed by pilgrims in later centuries.

Confirmation of the distinction of stations mentioned by the Bordeaux pilgrim is to be found in *The Epitome of St. Eucherius about Certain Holy Places* (ca. 440). While providing no personal narrative of a city tour, St. Eucherius gives a terse, pointed account of Jerusalem and its major stops. "The site of the city itself is almost circular," St. Eucherius writes, "enclosed within a circuit of walls of no small extent, whereby it now receives within itself Mount Sion, which was once outside, and which, lying on the

south side, overhangs the city like a citadel." [28] Of the Temple
and its "pinnacle" this commentator says, "The Temple, which
was situated in the lower part of the city near the city wall on the
east side and was splendidly built, was once a world's wonder,
but out of its ruins there stands only the pinnacle of one wall, the
rest being destroyed to their very foundations. A few cisterns . . .
to collect water are to be seen on the north side of the city in the
neighborhood of the Temple." Like the Bordeaux pilgrim, St.
Eucherius states that near the Temple there are "twin pools, one of
which is generally filled by winter rain, while the water of the
other is coloured red." And the commentator reaffirms the existence of a marvelous spring below the Temple: "On that side of
Mount Sion which looks from a precipitous rock . . . the fountain Siloam gushes forth, not running continuously, but on certain
days and hours welling through caverns in the rock" (pp. 9–10).
One stop above the others is emphasized in this text, for all princi-
pal streets are said to lead to the Church of the Holy Sepulchre,
the most sacred station of the Jerusalem "ring": "In consequence
of the direction of the streets, one must visit the basilica, which is
called the 'Martyrium' . . . built by Constantine with great
splendor. Adjacent to this, upon the west side are to be seen
Golgotha and the 'Anastasis'. . . . Now, the 'Anastasis' is at the
place of the Resurrection, and Golgotha, which is between the
'Anastasis' and the 'Martyrium,' is the place of the Lord's Passion,
wherein may be seen the very rock which once supported the cross
itself on which the Lord's body hung" (pp. 8–9).

In the following centuries many new wonders were reported in
Jerusalem. The anonymous author of the *Breviary or Short Description of Jerusalem* (ca. 530) discloses that in the Church of
the Holy Sepulchre was "the spear with which our Lord was
pierced, and of it a cross has been made, and it shines in the
night as does the sun in the heat of the day." [29] At an unspecified
place in the city, the pilgrim Arculf (ca. 670) saw a linen cloth
"which, as is said, St. Mary wove, and which, on that account, is
held in great reverence." [30] Holy stones with waxlike impressions

28. *The Epitome*, trans. Aubrey Stewart, notes C. W. Wilson (London, 1890), p. 8.
29. *Breviary*, trans. Aubrey Stewart, notes C. W. Wilson (London, 1890), p. 8.
30. *The Pilgrimage of Arculfus in the Holy Land*, trans. and notes James Rose
MacPherson (London, 1895), p. 16.

abounded. Theodosius in *On the Topography of the Holy Land* (ca. 530) speaks of the impressions left by Christ on the pillar of the scourging: "His arms, hands, and fingers sank into it, as if it were wax, and the marks appear to this day" (p. 11). Theodosius also writes that "On Mount Olivet the Lord placed His shoulders on a stone, and both His shoulders sank into the rock as if it were soft wax" (p. 15). More marvelous still, the Holy Grail itself was said to be on display in the Church of the Holy Sepulchre. The author of the *Breviary or Short Description of Jerusalem* mentions a "sanctuary of the basilica" containing "the cup which the Lord blessed and gave to His disciples to drink, saying 'This is My body and My blood' " (p. 15). In *Of the Holy Places Visited* Antoninus Martyr alludes also to a "cup of onyx, which our Lord blessed at the last supper" (p. 17). But a subsequent pilgrim tract, *Arculf's Narrative about the Holy Places, Written by Adamnan,* relates that this Holy Grail, now strangely transformed in its substance, is made "of silver, holding the measure of a French quart, and has two little handles placed on it, one on each side" (p. 11).

However numerous the relics in the Holy City, however diversified the tour from station to station, palmers through the centuries always trudged to those key stops initially identified by the Bordeaux pilgrim: they walked through the Harem area, gazed upon the site of Solomon's Temple and pools, looked down upon the spring of Siloam, climbed sloping city streets to Constantine's New Jerusalem, and with special ardor venerated Golgotha and Christ's tomb in the Church of the Holy Sepulchre. By the ninth century pilgrims at the New Jerusalem saw markers indicating that they had finally reached the geographical center of the world. In the courtyard separating the churches of the New Jerusalem, four chains "joined to each other by partition walls," as Bernard the Wise remarks, crossed in the center of this open area. "Here it is said," writes Bernard (ca. 870), "is the center of the world." [31]

To become acquainted with pilgrim tales of the kind current when the *Commedia* was first written and circulated, one has only to turn to the fourteenth-century reports of Niccolò of Poggibonsi, Leonardo Frescobaldi, Giorgio Gucci, and Simone Sigoli, all of whom were educated Christians from Florence or the vicinity. Gucci, who before his journey was a Prior of Florence and an am-

31. *The Itinerary of Bernard the Wise,* trans. J. H. Bernard (London, 1893), p. 8.

bassador from Florence to Rome, expressed concisely the several goals of his group in making the long pilgrimage: "We departed from Florence on the XII day of the month of August, in the year of Our Lord one thousand three hundred and eighty four, intent upon pursuing our voyage to St. Catherine's and Mount Sinai and to the sacred and holy Sepulchre of Christ and to the other devout and holy places" (*Visit*, p. 93). Niccolò of Poggibonsi, Frescobaldi, and Sigoli thirty-five years before had actually made this long pilgrimage. And how extraordinary are the four pilgrims' observations!

In Egypt, Frescobaldi, Sigoli, and Niccolò declared that in sailing up the River Nile they were floating on waters flowing from the Terrestrial Paradise. With all the boldness of authority, Sigoli insisted that the river "has of the best drinking water in the world" (*Visit*, p. 165). Moreover, Niccolò spied on the river banks numerous "Paradise birds." "They were a wonder to behold," he writes, "and when a person comes near to them, he cannot look on them so great the splendor reflected by their wings!" (*A Voyage*, p. 86). Sigoli tasted Paradise apples "on which our forefathers sinned. . . . In this fruit is seen a very great wonder, for when you divide it in any way either by its length or by its breadth, which ever way you cut it, the Crucifix is distinctly to be seen inside" (*Visit*, p. 161). Such was the past distinction of the banana.

Beasts almost as strange as those in Dante's *Inferno* roamed amid the palm trees and mud-hut villages of the Nile delta, creatures which alternately delighted and alarmed the pilgrims. In fact the travelers' descriptions of these curious animals, when passed on in written and verbal form throughout Europe, served as a source for the monsters rendered in medieval art works and in the empty spaces of *mappaemundi*. Niccolò found the camel "a very moody animal and when one wants them to walk fast, he plays some instrument, or sings something and then they go all out happy and content" (*A Voyage*, p. 99). The giraffe to Frescobaldi was "as corpulent as an ordinary camel; and as meek as a sheep, and has the hide of a stag." This eclectic creature had in addition a neck "about four braccia long" and a "head like that of a sucking heifer, and the horns covered with skin like those of a roebuck" (*Visit*, p. 49). Yet it was Niccolò who observed perhaps the oddest animal of all: "the head is very large and the eyes so very small and red that they frighten the looker; the teeth are long and out of the mouth several braccia in length; . . . the ears are fashioned like dragon wings; the tail is small; the feet are entirely round." This creature, "so big that he is a marvel to look at," was identified by the palmer as an elephant (*A Voyage*, p. 91).

In the great city of Babylon the din and confusion often appalled the pilgrims. This metropolis, as Niccolò knew, was the home of "infidels: Turks, Indians, Tartars, Jews, Samaritans, Saracens, Arabs, and Berbers" (*Visit*, p. 89). Crowds thronged the streets. "Nobody can walk freely and quickly," Niccolò reported, "on account of the encounters and pushing of the people" (*A Voyage*, p. 88). Tempers were frequently short. "The men of Egypt are the vilest," Frescobaldi declaims, ". . . and sometimes they quarrel so that it would seem to us they are about to cut one another to pieces, and when one cries '*ista furla*', they are at once pacified; '*ista furla*' is in our language, 'Peace, for God's sake' " (*Visit*, p. 48). The "priests" of these "vile" infidels contributed throughout the day to the general clamor. Sigoli tells how they appeared each morning on their towers "shouting at the top of their voices that it is nine, at the same time recounting something of the dishonest life of Mohammed and of his evil companions, who, they say, were his apostles. Then they shout: do such a thing, which would be dishonest to write down just as distinctly as they say it." The shouting is repeated "when the hour of Vespers comes, save that they stay on the tower to shout three times as much, recounting most dishonest things of luxury, which Mohammed did in his life, and they command each one that he should do them; and in this way they live like animals." Again at "Compline" the "shouting" is heard. "And likewise they do at night at Matins," Sigoli adds, "except that they shout more at Matins than at any other time of day, all the time recommending to them: increase and multiply" (*Visit*, p. 166).

Obviously, Egypt to the pilgrims was a place of luxury, worldliness, and worse. Even before landing near Alexandria, Niccolò was shaken by his first sight of Saracens in a nearby boat: "they looked like devils; may Jesus Christ be with us: and then I thought: if those of Egypt are all so made, how could we be safe among them?" (*A Voyage*, p. 84). In order that the pilgrims might be properly identified and not robbed or killed by these evil-looking people, the Christians, in Frescobaldi's words, were "registered and numbered like animals" (*Visit*, p. 38). And before entering Babylon the palmers had to pay a toll at a river stop with the ominous name of *"Satanus"* (*Visit*, p. 95). Under the circumstances, it is not hard to imagine what pilgrims thought of former Christians who permanently inhabited the great Saracen city; they were in Niccolò's view "miserable wretches who live in . . . damnation" (*A Voyage*, p. 89).

Outside the city of Babylon, all four pilgrims reported seeing, at the desert's edge, gigantic pyramids of stone, the reputed "granaries of Joseph." Niccolò explains that "Joseph, the son of Jacob, had them built, what time he was sold into Egypt to Pharaoh; on account of the want which he expected, according to Pharaoh's dream, he caused these granaries to be made, as is related in Holy Writ in the Old Testament" (*A Voyage*, pp. 96–97). Other structures in and around Babylon brought to the minds of the pilgrims memories of Moses and the Exodus. Frescobaldi learned that the Sultan's palace was constructed "exactly on the site . . . where Moses was given suck" (*Visit*, p. 45). And it was possible to see, as did Niccolò, the "tower where Moses spoke to God, when he sent him to Pharaoh, to tell him to allow the people of Israel to depart" (*A Voyage*, p. 97).

On the second stage of the long pilgrimage, the palmers left sinful Egypt and traveled in the course of the Exodus toward the Red Sea and the holy Mountain of God. Niccolò, in the spring of 1349, mentions being led over the deserts by a "good and loyal guide" named "Saetta," the European form for the name Said (*A Voyage*, p. 102). Some years later in 1384 Sigoli and his party were also guided by this now seventy-year-old Saracen, a man whom the pilgrims came to admire. "And he told me," Sigoli comments, "that in his life he had accompanied the pilgrims who went to St. Catherine's and the Holy Sepulchre sixty-seven times, excluding the present one" (*Visit*, p. 165).

The dangers and terrors of the desert were ever present to the palmers: Niccolò refers to the Sinai wastes as "the most perilous in the world, where nothing of good is found, where everything is barren and all is of sand, where one must needs bring all the necessaries of life as if traveling by sea" (*A Voyage*, p. 102). Grotesque creatures and devilish men were sometimes encountered.

Niccolò writes that at the Red Sea his "companion saw a fish which had a head like a man's, with face, mouth, teeth, nose, eyes, hair and likewise a bit of neck" (p. 100). Later during the journey Bedouin Arabs swooped down upon Niccolò's party, carrying off and holding the group's interpreter for two days. And shortly thereafter, Niccolò and his companions met a "frightening" band of shouting Saracens: "they carried a cloth piece before and after: others wore camel skins and their hair gathered on the top of the head like a hat" (*A Voyage*, p. 103).

It was with a sense of both elation and relief that the palmers came at last to St. Catherine's monastery. After their arrival the pilgrims climbed the "ring" of stations on Mt. Sinai to the holy place where Moses received the Law; and they ascended as well to the summit of neighboring Mt. St. Catherine to look upon the rock where the body of the saint was once supposed to have rested. "The rock itself made place for this blessed body," writes Frescobaldi, "and it made in it a form where the angels stood" (*Visit*, p. 63). Niccolò relates that his party "on the summit of the mount . . . sang in a loud voice *Salve Regina*" (*A Voyage*, p. 113). Upon returning to the monastery of St. Catherine, Niccolò collected "holy manna" that dripped from a relic on display in the main monastery church (*A Voyage*, p. 111).

In seeking that second goal of pilgrimage as set forth by Gucci, Christ's Sepulchre in the Promised Land, the palmers were inevitably drawn northward to the River Jordan, the symbolic and literal boundary separating the desert wastes from the Holy Land. The stop at the River Jordan, traditionally made at the place where John the Baptist was said to have baptized Christ, came at a dramatic moment in the pilgrimage. From this station on the river, palmers could look down into the low, misty depression that held the body of water alternately called the Mare Mortuum, the Asphaltic Sea, and the Devil's Sea. Into this sea, guides explained, the cities of Sodom and Gomorrah sank under the waves as a hail of fire and brimstone fell from Heaven. But only a few miles to the west was Jerusalem itself, and for Christians immersion in the Jordan was a necessary baptismal ritual before entry into the Holy City. Gucci explains that pilgrims "bathed in the said river, and some swam across, and some half the way and some held on to the willows there by the bank" (*Visit*, p. 134). Frescobaldi was among those who swam all the way across. "On the other side," he writes, "we sang *Te Deum Laudamus*, those responding from over there to those who remained on this side" (*Visit*, p. 78). Niccolò notes that at this place "each nation sings in its own tongue in the loudest voice" (*A Voyage*, p. 73).

Having arrived on Holy Land, the Christians marched on to Jericho; "here the pilgrims," Frescobaldi reports, "take the palm" (*Visit*, p. 79). With the long-stemmed reed wrapped around girdle or staff, they walked on to the Holy City. "While still far off," Gucci notes, "we took off our shoes and barefooted we went as far as the place where we were put up. . . . And as we went we recited psalms and other devout prayers" (*Visit*, p. 127). Many days were spent making the "rounds" of stations in Jerusalem; and within the Church of the Holy Sepulchre, a separate series of substations elicited the wonder of pilgrims at this center of the world. "Beneath Mount Calvary there is a chapel," writes Frescobaldi, "almost like a cellar, where was discovered the head of Adam, our first father, and it is called Golgotha. . . . And nearby is a chapel, where lots were cast on the vestments of Christ." The pilgrim remarks also upon "another chapel, where Christ appeared to Our Lady. . . . And there is also a chapel of St. Helena, entirely underground; and then you go down farther a stair of some twenty steps, and there below is where the holy Cross of Christ was found" (*Visit*, p. 77). In this same church Niccolò joyously records how on Good Friday he looked out of a window and "saw a dove coming, which alighted upon the chapel of the Holy Sepulchre: and then a great light appeared within the Holy Sepulchre, with a great brilliance, and then he feels himself the happier who can first get hold of that light . . . ; and so everybody takes his torch, or even candles, so that the church really seems afire from the great glow" (*A Voyage*, pp. 23–24).

Near the Sepulchre Niccolò saw a spot marked by "a round stone, with a hole in the middle" (*A Voyage*, p. 18). On this stone, Gucci was informed, "Christ placed his foot and said: There is the center of the world" (*Visit*, p. 127). Yet not all guides told the same story, for Frescobaldi learned that Christ marked this stone at the earth's middle "with his finger" (*Visit*, p. 76). The Exodus pilgrimage of the palmers had come to an end.

Details of the extended journey from Jerusalem back to Europe, as narrated by fourteenth-century Christians, need not be traced here, for no series of "stops" was established on the diversified routes of return comparable to the forty-two Stations of the Exodus on the Sinai peninsula, or to the "rings" of stations at Jerusalem and Mt. Sinai. Attention can rather be focused immediately upon the circuit of stations in Rome, the final goal of pilgrimage. Because the action of Dante's *Commedia* is set in 1300, and because the Golden Jubilee pilgrimage of that year is specifically mentioned in the poem (*Inf.* xviii, 28–30), it is helpful to review those events occurring in Rome in 1300 that led to the Church's formal recognition of stations in the eternal city.

On Christmas Eve, 1299, according to a treatise written at the time by Cardinal Stefaneschi,[32] a vast throng of foreigners and local persons congregated at St. Peter's for vespers, a throng attracted to the Holy City by conflicting and sometimes fantastic reports of great indulgences about to be bestowed during the first year of the new century. Some persons were reported to have claimed that a plenary indulgence would be granted to Christians praying at the tombs of Sts. Peter and Paul on the first of January; others asserted that the indulgence would be in effect on every day of the ensuing year; still others insisted that the grant would be in effect for only one hundred days, but that it might be extended if prayers were said in the tombs of the saints on every day of the new year. During Christmas week the reports became ever more confusing and extreme; the crowds of pilgrims in the city increased; and Pope Boniface viii at this time took an interest in the rumors.

On 17 January 1300, when the Veil of Veronica was exposed on the steps of St. Peter's before another huge assembly, Pope Boni-

32. Card. Iacopo Gaetano Stefaneschi, *De Centesimo seu Jubileo Anno Liber* printed in *Bibliotheca Patrum of La Bigne*, (Paris, 1610), 6 : 536f. The work has been reprinted under the title *L'anno santo del 1300: storia e bolle pontificie da un codice del sec. XIV del Card. Stefaneschi* (Roma, 1900). Another contemporaneous account of the Jubilee pilgrimage of 1300 was written by Giovanni Villani, *Villani's Chronicle*, trans. Rose E. Selfe, ed. Philip H. Wicksteed (London, 1906), section 36, pp. 320–321. For recent comments on the pilgrimage of 1300, see Herbert Thurston, *The Holy Year of Jubilee: An Account of the History and Ceremonial of the Roman Jubilee* (Westminster, Maryland, 1949), pp. 10–27; Constantine Carboni, *Il Giubileo di Bonifazio VIII e la Commedia di Dante* (Roma, 1901); Thomas Caldecot Chubb, *Dante and His World* (Boston and Toronto, 1966), p. 23–46; and Lonsdale Ragg, *Dante and His Italy* (New York and London, 1907), pp. 1–39.

face VIII, passing among the crowds before the basilica, halted to ask an aged Savoyard pilgrim about the reports. The pilgrim, who was said to be extremely old and who had to be carried by several of his sons, answered that in the first year of the previous century his father had gained great indulgences in Rome and that now he, the son, had come on the advice of his father to gain indulgences at the beginning of another century. Boniface next heard similar stories told by two elderly men from Beauvais who stood nearby, and aged pilgrims from different sections of Italy also spoke to the pope of the indulgences. Soon after, the pope commissioned some of his cardinals to investigate the authenticity of the accounts. Although the cardinals could find no written documents in support of the statements, they did inform the pope of a general belief among the people that special indulgences were to be granted during the new year. This was enough.

Boniface VIII issued a papal bull on 22 February 1300 that read in part:

> In order that the blessed Apostles Peter and Paul may be the more honoured as their Basilicas in this city shall be the more devoutly frequented by the faithful, and that the faithful themselves may feel that they have been replenished by an abundance of spiritual favours in approaching their tombs, We, confiding in the mercy of Almighty God, in the merits and power of these His Apostles, in the counsel of our brethren, and in the plenitude of the apostolic authority, grant to all who, being truly penitent, and confessing their sins, shall reverently visit these Basilicas in the present year 1300, which commenced with the festival of the Nativity of our Lord Jesus Christ which has just been celebrated, and to all who being truly penitent, shall confess their sins, and shall approach these Basilicas each succeeding hundredth year, not only a full and copious, but the most full pardon of all their sins.[33]

Evidence suggests that about this same time Boniface VIII issued a second papal bull granting lavish indulgences and quarantines to Christians going to the Holy Land and Jerusalem. The text of a surviving fifteenth-century manuscript, a translation into Spanish of fragments of a lost papal bull, indicates that the original bull was forwarded by the pope to Gandulph, the Dominican patriarch

33. English trans. of the Bull by Fr. Herbert Thurston in his *The Holy Year of Jubilee*, p. 14. The original Latin version is available in *L'anno santo del 1300: storia e bolle pontificie da un codice del sec. XIV del Card. Stefaneschi* (Roma, 1900), pp. 30–31.

of Jerusalem. And as the editor of the document, Fr. P. A. López, rightly notes, a rough dating of the manuscript can be adduced from the fact that Gandulph, also known as Radulph II and Landulph de Grandeville, was appointed to his post by Boniface VIII in 1295 and died while still in office in 1304.[34] A commentator on the document, Fr. Bellarmino Bagatti, who argues that "it cannot be seriously doubted but that the original Bull translated . . . in the XV century was authentic," believes that it is likely that the bull was issued in August 1304, when Boniface was vainly striving to launch a new Crusade;[35] but lacking evidence for an exact dating, it is equally possible that Boniface chose the Jubilee year of 1300 in which to make his proclamation.

Whatever the date of the original bull, the fifteenth-century manuscript reveals that twenty-nine partial indulgences, each ranging from one hundred years and one hundred quarantines to five thousand years and five thousand quarantines, and in one case a plenary indulgence, were attached to sacred sites associated with Old Testament events and the life of Christ. Holy Land indulgences of this kind were hardly new. In 1163 Pope Alexander III had proclaimed an "accustomed" one-year indulgence to Christians visiting the Holy Sepulchre; the medieval Table of Indulgences of Acre lists various spiritual blessings to be derived from visits to churches in the Holy Land; and in 1477 the Franciscan Cristoforo da Varese, in his collection of Holy Land bulls known as the *Bullarium,* reflects a popular tradition in stating that the first Holy Land indulgences were given "by St. Silvester at the request of Constantine and St. Helena."[36] But most important, the year in which Dante sets his pilgrimage in the *Commedia* is the same year in which exceptional indulgences were possibly granted for pilgrimages to the Holy Land and were definitely granted for pilgrimages to Rome.

The most complete fourteenth-century catalogue of the multifarious indulgences and stations in the eternal city can be found

34. "Antiguo Catálogo de Indulgencias" in *Archivos Iber.-Americano,* ed. Fr. P. A. Lopez (1918), pp. 458–460.

35. See Fr. Bagatti's comments on the bull and on Holy Land indulgences in *A Voyage,* pp. xxii–xxvii.

36. See *Itinéraires à Jerusalem et Descriptions de la Terre Sainte,* pp. 235–236; and Fr. Cristoforo da Varese's unfinished work in *Diarium Terrae Sanctae* (Jerusalem, 1908–1912).

in a curious poem in English, by an anonymous author, entitled *The Stacions of Rome.* No false modesty, no tendency toward restraint inhibits the author from expounding the superabundant blessings supposedly available in the eternal city. Listing forty-six key stations, but claiming the existence of many more, the author urges Christians to visit the holy sites and to enjoy basic indulgences totaling over thirty-two thousand years pardon for sin, indulgences that can be vastly augmented, the author insists, "withouten ende." [37] For the poem implies that supposed Holy Year indulgences remain permanently in effect. It was "Pope Bonefas," according to the text of *The Stacions of Rome,* who "gif men wuste grete and smale / the pardoun that is at grete Rome" (ll. 285–287). Because of the great number of pardons available in the eternal city, it is asserted that

> Hit were no neod to man in cristiante
> To passe in to the holy lond over the see
> To Jerusalem ne to kateryne
> To bringe mannes soule out of syne
> For pardoun there is with-outen ende
> Wel is him that thider may wende.

[ll. 289–294]

Thus the aim of the author is in part polemical: *The Stacions of Rome* seeks to convince Christians that, after Pope Boniface's formal declaration of indulgences in 1300, the complete Great Circle pilgrimage to St. Catherine's monastery, Jerusalem, and then to Rome does not have to be made; the stations in the eternal city are now said to provide the pilgrim with the greatest possible pardon for sins. Both at the beginning and end of the poem, the author takes care to stress the singular spiritual nature of the eternal city. The work opens with the words:

> Hose wole his soule teche
> Lustne to me I wol him teche
> Pardoun is thi soule bote
> At grete Rome, ther is the Roote.

[ll. 1–4]

And at the conclusion of the poem, readers are informed that

37. *The Stacions of Rome,* ed. Frederick J. Furnivall (London, 1867), p. 10, l. 293. This edition is based upon the Vernon manuscript in the British Museum.

In Rome is muche pardoun more
then I have told here bifore
Or telle schulde with al my miht.

[ll. 727–729]

This attempt to direct pilgrims to the eternal city, and to dis-
suade persons from making the Great Circle journey, suggests what
the pilgrim texts corroborate: that in the fourteenth century sizable
numbers of Christians still engaged in long tours to the Mt. Sinai
and Jerusalem "rings." In appealing particularly to these Christians and to those contemplating a Great Circle pilgrimage, the author of *The Stacions of Rome* liberally praises certain key stops
in the eternal city. Seven years pardon for sin, the author states
after a brief introduction, is given to devout pilgrims as they ascend or descend each step of the stairs before St. Peter's Basilica:

At seint peter we shul bi-ginne
to telle of pardoun that slaketh sinne
A feir Munstre men mai ther se
Ninene and twenti greces steps ther be.
As ofte as thou gost up or doun
bi cause of devocioun
thou schalt have at eche gre step
Mon or Wommon whether thou be
Sevene yer to pardoun.

[ll. 17–25]

Pilgrims are then advised to enter the basilica and to gain further indulgences by venerating before the altars of the Veil of Veronica, Mary, St. Simon and Jude, St. Andrew, St. Gregory, St.
Leo, and the Holy Cross. Special mention is next given to St.
Peter's altar, a place where an indulgence of "xxviii year" is
granted (l. 50). "At the Auter the peter is don / ," the author explains, "the pope Gregori gaf gret pardoun" (ll. 47–48).

Following devotions in St. Peter's, pilgrims, the author suggests,
should tread a circuit both within and beyond the city's confines
that includes stops at the churches of St. Paul's Outside the Walls,
St. Mary the Nunciate's, St. Fabian's and Bastian's, St. Thomas of
India, and finally St. John Lateran, the supposed Mother Church
of Christendom and palace of the popes. So that pilgrims might be
properly impressed by this famous church, a fabulous story about

its past is briefly summarized: "King Constantine," the author confidently asserts, suffered from leprosy, but was converted to Christianity and cured of his disease by Pope Silvester. In gratitude Constantine is said to have asked that Pope Silvester grant special blessings to all who might worship there (*Stacions of Rome*, ll. 241–248). The author states that, as a result, Christians in St. John Lateran will be the fortunate recipients of "alle maner clansing of sinne" as they venerate before a most unusual collection of relics (l. 282). In the papal palace of the basilica could be seen the two tablets of the Law, Aaron's rod, parts of the loaves and fishes, the tablecloth from the Last Supper, Christ's swaddling cloth, and even the infant Christ's foreskin (ll. 321–325). And the palace's "sancta sanctorum," the Chapel of St. Lawrence, contained wonders such as an icon of Christ made by other than human hands and the heads of St. Peter and St. Paul (ll. 349–366).

Wandering on through the eternal city, pilgrims made their way to the great domed Pantheon, a structure known to the author of the *Stacions* as "St. Mary in the Round." According to the author, this building once housed a gigantic statue of Neptune; and a brass cover, at one time placed on the statue's head, is said to have been blown away to St. Peter's. It is this seven-foot-high "cover," in the shape of a pine cone, that Dante in the *Inferno* compares in size to the face of the giant Nimrod (*Inf.* xxxi, 58–60).

Christians making their "round" in Rome also observed persons and places associated with pilgrimages of the past and present. The author of the *Stacions* asserts that they can see in the Pantheon a picture of the "holy pope Bonefas" who established the Golden Jubilee pilgrimage in 1300 (l. 637). English Christians, who had traveled at home on a local pilgrimage to the shrine of the martyred Thomas à Becket in Canterbury, no doubt would have been pleased to find their saint commemorated in the eternal city's "ring." Medieval tradition averred that this holy man had once been a teacher in Rome; and eight hundred years indulgence might be earned, the text of the *Stacions* states, by veneration at "Our Lady's Chapel wher Thomas / a Becket kept school" (ll. 716–719). Relics of the saint were said to be on display in the Basilica of St. Mary the Major:

> And an Arm men seyn is ther
> Of seint Thomas the holy Marter

> And a parti of the brayn.
> At Canterburi he was slayn.
>
> [ll. 496–499]

Neither could pilgrims on the "ring" in Rome be forgetful of St. Helena's past pilgrimage through the Holy Land in search of sacred sites. Her discovery of the true cross in a cave in Jerusalem, over which a part of the Church of the Holy Sepulchre was later erected, was commemorated in the eternal city by the Church of the Holy Rood. As the author of the *Stacions* makes clear, two hundred and fifty years pardon for sin could be gained through a visit to "a chapel for Elene" who is inaccurately described, not as Constantine's mother, but rather as his "daughter" (ll. 367–368).

However much the author might wish Rome to be the single center for pilgrimage, it is obvious even from the *Stacions* that other ancient cities and sites of pilgrimage continued to exercise their attraction over Christians. Special indulgences had been sanctioned by Boniface VIII covering both Holy Land sites and Rome, and pilgrims still plied their way over the Great Circle route to Egypt, Mt. Sinai, and Jerusalem.

Dante's Alighieri's intense interest in the holy relics and places of pilgrimage is unmistakable. The poet in his writings, as will be shown, clearly reveals his acquaintance with the main sites of Rome. Dante is known to have visited that city and, at the age of thirty-five, to have lived there while serving in an embassy sent by Florence to the papacy.[38] Then too the poet, in recording his reactions to troubling political and military events, displays a deep concern for the sacred places of the Holy Land.

In 1291 the last major crusading forces were driven from the mainland of Palestine and the Levant, and that land beyond the sea came completely under Moslem domination. Although Holy Land pilgrimages were permitted and most Christian establishments in the Holy Land protected by the Moslem rulers, a busy Pope Boniface VIII, in the Jubilee pilgrimage year of 1300, nevertheless called for a new crusade against the Saracens and levied a tithe on the whole of Christendom to support the military venture. But response to the appeal was weak. What interest there was

38. Michele Barbi, *Life of Dante*, trans. and ed. Paul G. Ruggiers (Berkeley and Los Angeles, 1954), p. 15. See also Thomas G. Bergin, *Dante* (Boston, 1965), p. 44.

in the crusade soon died when it was learned that the armies of the Khan of Tartary and the King of Armenia, then at war with Sultan Nasir Mohammed Ibn Qelaoun of Egypt and Palestine, had been crushed by the Sultan's forces. Under these circumstances, Boniface VIII again raised his voice in 1304 to announce a new crusade, and again his plea went largely unheeded.[39]

In the *Commedia* Dante gives expression to the fierce Christian desire to liberate the holy places. The damned soul of Guido da Montefeltro berates Boniface VIII for not taking sufficiently strong action against the infidel. The pope, says Guido, is

> Lo principe d'i novi Farisei,
> avendo guerra presso a Laterano,
> e non con Saracin né con Giudei,
>   ché ciascun suo nimico era Christiano,
> e nessun era stato a vincer Acri.[40]
>
> [*Inf.* XXVII, 85–89]

> [The Prince of the new Pharisees—
> waging war near to the Lateran,
> and not with Saracens or Jews;
>   for every enemy of his was Christian,
> and none had been to conquer Acre.]

And Dante in the *Paradiso* takes care to enshrine famous crusaders in a gigantic cross glowing in the fifth heaven. Among the lights in the cross is that of Godfrey de Bouillon, the first conqueror of Jerusalem (*Par.* XVIII, 47).

Dante's awareness of pilgrimage sites in Rome and abroad was

39. Fr. Thurston, *The Holy Year of Jubilee*, pp. 17–18.

40. The text of the *Commedia* used throughout is Dante Alighieri, *La Divina Commedia secondo l'antica vulgata*, ed. Giorgio Petrocchi, 4 vols. (Milano, A. Mandadori for the Società Dantesca Italiana, 1965–68), reprinted in Dante Alighieri, *La Divina Commedia*, ed. and notes C. H. Grandgent, rev. Charles S. Singleton (Cambridge, Mass., 1972). The quotation, *Inf.* XXVII, 85–89, is from the reprinted version, p. 240; and all passages quoted in this and the following chapters will also be from the reprinted version. The English translation follows that in the Temple Classics edition of the *Commedia*, rev. ed., 3 vols. (London, 1954), although on occasion words have been altered for reasons of clarity or accuracy. The Temple Classics edition of 1954 is a reprinting of three separate volumes: *The Inferno of Dante Alighieri*, trans. J. A. Carlyle and rev. H. Oelsner, notes H. Oelsner, rev. ed. (London, 1900) ; *The Purgatorio of Dante Alighieri*, trans. Thomas Okey, notes Philip H. Wicksteed, rev. ed. (London, 1901) ; and *The Paradisio of Dante Alighieri*, trans. Philip H. Wicksteed, notes H. Oelsner and Philip H. Wicksteed, rev. ed. (London, 1899).

doubtless gained from a variety of sources. An exile who traveled frequently on the roads of Europe, the poet could hardly have been unfamiliar with that very ancient oral tradition based upon the tales spread by pilgrims and crusaders as they passed through Italy and other western lands. In the manner of modern tourists, many travelers must have talked more than they wrote about their journeys. Medieval maps and charts showing that land beyond the sea, it has been noted, were available as a supplement to the oral tradition.

Further information could have been obtained by the poet from the Franciscan fathers, those Guardians of Mt. Sion about whom Dante wrote at length and under whom he may have studied. The Franciscans from the early thirteenth century to the present day have considered it their duty to maintain chains of houses in the Holy Land and to care for Holy Land pilgrims. A Franciscan hostel was in existence at Joppa in 1275, and in the thirteenth century others were founded at Nicosia and Famagusta. In 1296 the Friars Minor opened a convent at Rama (er-Ramieh) near modern Beirut; and by 1335 the Franciscans were firmly established in Jerusalem where they remain today.[41] According to Giovanni Villani, the poet was buried in the habit of a Franciscan brother.[42] In the *Paradiso* Dante refers to the thirteenth-century debate between St. Francis and the Sultan of Egypt which resulted, tradition holds, in St. Francis' being granted permission to make the pilgrimage to Jerusalem (*Par.* xi, 100–103). Dante is said to have made the trip from Egypt to the Holy City (*Par.* xxv, 52–57); and the poet's great-great-grandfather Cacciaguida is depicted in paradise, along with many martyred crusaders, because he died fighting to secure the Holy Land for just such journeys

41. See Girolamo Golubovich's *Serie cronologica dei Superiori di Terra Santa* (Jerusalem, 1899), pp. 204–205; and *Biblioteca bio-bibliografica della Terra Santa e dell' Oriente francescano* (Quaracchi, 1927), 2 : 372–387, 525–534. A brief discussion of the Franciscan order in Jerusalem appears in *A Voyage*, p. xvii.

42. Helmut Hatzfeld has summed up Dante criticism on the question of the poet's waistband in "Modern Literary Scholarship as Reflected in Dante Criticism," *American Critical Essays on The Divine Comedy*, ed. Robert J. Clements (New York and London, 1967), 205–207. An account of the types of persons and pilgrims Dante might have met on the road is available in Christopher Hare's *Dante, The Wayfarer* (New York, 1905), pp. 15–46; see also Arthur Percival Newton, *Travel and Travellers of the Middle Ages*.

(*Par.* xv, 91–96). That land beyond the sea, Cacciaguida ex-
claims, belongs by right to Christians such as Dante (*Par.* xv,
144).

From passages in the *Commedia* it is apparent that Dante, who
wrote so authoritatively in his poem of his own pilgrimage beyond,
was conscious of some works in a voluminous body of popular and
devotional literature describing pilgrimages to the Holy Land.
From Brunetto Latini's *Tesoretto*, a work mentioned by name in the
Inferno (xv, 119), Dante could have learned about Egypt, the
River Nile—said to flow from the Earthly Paradise at the farthest
point east—the Red Sea, the Sinai deserts, the Dead Sea, Sodom
and Gomorrah, the River Jordon, and Jerusalem. Latini locates
these places in Asiatic regions near the summit of the round
earth's northern hemisphere. Jerusalem is said to be at the middle
of the landmass covering the northern hemisphere, while the southern hemisphere is described as covered by a great ocean. In certain
early manuscripts Latini's lively comments are illustrated with a
zonal map of the world and, one should recall, with a T-O map of
the northern hemisphere.[43]

Because in the *Commedia* the venerable and holy "Beda" is discovered by Dante among theologians in the sphere of the sun (*Par.*
x, 131), possibly the poet was familiar with Bede's remarks on
Egypt and Palestine in *Concerning the Holy Places* (ca. 700). This
work describes primarily the details of sites in and around Jerusalem, including the River Jordan and the Dead Sea.[44]

In the sphere of the sun, Dante also espies a small glowing light
(*Par.* x, 118–20) traditionally identified by scholars as St. Augustine's companion Paulus Orosius, author of *The Seven Books of
History against the Pagans* (418).[45] This is the same Paulus Orosius who in life once carried a message from St. Augustine across
the Sinai deserts to St. Jerome, then studying and writing in Bethlehem; Orosius later returned to the Bishop of Hippo bearing St.
Jerome's reply. As one might anticipate, Orosius's history contains
specific remarks about the Exodus route. The author even speaks of
his inspection of ruts in the Red Sea shore supposedly left by the

43. See the French-language edition of *Li Livres Dou Trésor* (Berkeley, 1948).
44. *Concerning the Holy Places*, trans. and notes James Rose MacPherson (London,
1895), pp. 67–87.
45. *The Seven Books*, trans. Roy J. Deferrari, (Washington, 1964), pp. 6–35.

wheels of Pharaoh's chariots, an attraction still pointed out to any modern visitors now able to make the Exodus journey.

High above the sun in the Primum Mobile (*Par.* xxix, 37–39), Beatrice explains that St. Jerome, author of *The Pilgrimage of Holy Paula* (ca. 430), has produced works on the nature of angels and of creation. The saint in actual life, as previous remarks have revealed, tried to encourage pilgrimages to the Holy Land by writing of Jerusalem, Bethlehem, the River Jordan, the Dead Sea, and Egypt.

Dante, during an earlier lecture in Eden, listened to Beatrice talk about the life of Adam; she presented facts about Adam taken from a commentary by Eusebius, author of the famous *Life of Constantine* (*Purg.* xxxiii, 61–63). The *Life* contains accounts of the holy places in Jerusalem, the buildings at Mt. Sinai, and the holy sites found by St. Helena in Palestine and Sinai.

Of one point there can be no doubt: from even the slightest acquaintance with early maps, guidebooks, devotional writings, and oral pilgrimage tales; from only occasional conversations with knowledgeable clerics, pilgrims, diplomats, or teachers; from only a general interest in contemporaneous secular and Church politics involving the Holy Land; and from only a casual personal familiarity with the shrines and basilicas of Rome, Dante Alighieri would have garnered an immensely greater store of information about remote desert stations in Egypt, Sinai, and Palestine, and about more accessible stations in Jerusalem and Rome, than modern readers could learn from the available information about pilgrimage in works of Dante criticism and historical scholarship. Commentators have in general overlooked or ignored the Great Circle journey; yet the weight of evidence surely suggests that the poet, far from being incidentally concerned with the route, was deeply mindful of and influenced by the literature and lore of the long pilgrimage. But to measure the precise extent of that influence, one must turn to the texts of Dante's writings.

2

Invention from the Book of the World

*The whole of this fugitive life is divided into four periods:
the period of erring, or wandering from the way; the period
of renewal, or returning to the right way; the period of recon-
ciliation; and the period of pilgrimage.* [Opening statement by
Jacobus de Voragine in *The Golden Legend*]

During that mournful period in the spiritual life of Dante Alighieri
following the death of Beatrice, a seemingly chance encounter
with a group of Christians passing through Florence kindles in the
soul of the poet, as the *Vita Nuova* reveals, a premonition of the
journey he will someday record in the *Commedia*. The angelic
Beatrice has left the earth and is now in Heaven. And through her
city move a select few from among a larger band of pilgrims on
their way to view the Veil of Veronica at St. Peter's Basilica in
Rome. In chapter XLI the poet writes:

> Dopo questa tribolazione avvenne (in quel tempo che molta gente
> va per vedere quella imagine benedetta, la quale Gesù Cristo lasciò
> a noi per esempio della sua bellissima figura, in quale vede la mia
> donna gloriosamente), che alquanti peregrini passavano per una via,
> la quale è quasi mezzo della cittade, ove nacque e vivette e morío la
> gentilissima donna.
>
> [After this time of tribulation, it happened, during that season when
> many people go to see the blessed portrait left to us by Jesus Christ
> as a copy of his most beautiful face, which my lady gloriously
> beholds, that some pilgrims were passing down a street which is
> almost in the middle of the city where my most gracious lady was
> born, lived, and died.[1]]

Realizing that the worldly thoughts of the pilgrims are not of Beatrice but of other things, "forse pensano delli loro amici lontani"

---

1. *Le Opere di Dante Alighieri*, ed. E. Moore, rev. Paget Toynbee, 4th ed. (Oxford,
1924), pp. 231–232. As has been previously noted, Italian quotations from *La Vita
Nuova* and *Il Convivio* are from Moore's edition of Dante's works; Italian quotations
of the *Commedia* are from Giorgio Petrocchi's edition published for the Società
Dantesca Italiana and reprinted in the edition of C. H. Grandgent, rev. Charles S.
Singleton (Cambridge, Mass., 1972). The English translation of passages in the
Commedia is based upon the English text of the Temple Classics, revised edition.

("they perhaps are thinking of their friends far away"), Dante calls upon them in the sonnet "Deh peregrini" ("Ye pilgrim-folk") to think of his lady

> E le parole, ch' uom di lei può dire,
> Hanno virtù di far piangere altrui.

> [And those words which may be said of her
> Have the power of making others weep.]

This meeting with Christians going to Rome inspires Dante to conceive of a pilgrimage to Heaven. Before composing the final poem "Oltre la spera" ("Beyond the sphere") in the *Vita Nuova,* Dante remembers an earlier verse "Venite a intender li sospiri miei" ("Come to me and listen to my sighs"), which includes the words

> Voi udirete lor chiamar sovente
> La mia donna gentil, che se n' è gita
> Al secol degno della sua virtute.

[chapter XXXIII]

> [And you will hear my sighs calling often
> Upon my gracious lady who is gone
> Into a world most worthy of her virtue.]

New poetic associations are formed, and Dante now writes the last verse about his sigh, "Lo peregrino spirito" (chapter XLII; "the pilgrim spirit"), that soars beyond the Primum Mobile to Beatrice. Forging a new link between the poet on earth and his lady in Heaven, the sigh outlines the path that the poet will later follow, gazes upon the lady and the splendor surrounding her, and finally speaks within the thought of the poet in a manner that ultimately brings enlightenment.

Here is Dante's early development of a twofold pilgrimage to Beatrice, and the resulting illustration of the poet's figural technique could hardly be more graphic. Step by step the reader observes how a single earthly journey at one stage gives rise to a second and corresponding celestial voyage; what is foreshadowed here in the realm of the living is fulfilled there in the realm beyond. The actors in this world are pilgrims; their movement into Beatrice's city below prefigures the flight by Dante's sigh to Beatrice above. On this earth words of grace heard about the lady correspond figurally to the more fulfilling benefits of gazing upon

Beatrice in Heaven, yet the mundane pilgrims are committed to press on to the Veil of Veronica in the eternal city of Rome just as, by implication, the sigh beyond the sphere may soar to even greater visions in the realm of eternal bliss.

Other thoughts about pilgrimage stir the mind of Dante after his fortuitous meeting with Rome-bound Christians. In enumerating the kinds of travelers who could in a general sense be termed "peregrini," the poet in chapter XLI speaks of those Christians whose respective peregrinations when linked comprise the Great Circle pilgrimage:

> Chiamansi *Palmieri* in quanto vanno oltremare lá onde molte volte recano la palma.
>
> [They are called Palmers who go beyond the sea eastward, whence they often bring back palm-branches.]

The palmers, of course, moved beyond the sea to Egypt, then over the deserts to the Red Sea, Mt. Sinai, and Jerusalem. Among the other pilgrims mentioned by the poet are those called *"Romei in quanto vanno a Roma"* ("Romers in that they go to Rome"), and this group, it has been observed, regularly visited the Basilicas of the Lateran and St. Peter in the eternal city.[2]

In the following and last chapter (XLIII) of the *Vita Nuova*, Dante, shifting his interest from this world to the next, leaves no doubt about the central focus of his mind and soul: they are upon Beatrice beyond the sphere, and Beatrice is gazing upon God. Exposed through his sigh to the glories of Heaven, the poet announces that he has seen a wonderful vision, and he promises to record that vision in a future work honoring his lady.

> Appresso a questo sonetto apparve a me una mirabil visione, nella quale vidi cose, che mi fecero proporre di non dir più di questa benedetta, infino a tanto che io potessi più degnamenta trattare di lei. E di venire a ciò io studio quanto posso, si com' ella sa veracemente. Sicchè, se piacere sarà di Colui, a cui tutte le cose vivono, che la mia vita duri per alquanti anni, io spero di dire di lei quello che mai non fu detto d'alcuna. E poi piaccia a Colui, ch' è Sire della cortesia, che la mia anima se ne possa gire a vedere la gloria della sua donna, cioè di quella benedetta Beatrice, la quale gloriosamente mira nella faccia di Colui, *qui est per omnia saecula benedictus.*

2. See chapter, I, pp. 11–12.

[After writing this sonnet, there appeared to me a very wonderful vision in which I saw things that made me resolve to say nothing further of this most blessed one, until a time when I could discourse more worthily about her. And to achieve this I am laboring all that I can, as she well knows. So that, if it be His pleasure through whom all life flourishes, that my life continue for a few years, I hope that I shall yet write of her what has never before been written of any other woman. And then may it please Him who is the Master of Grace, that my soul should go to behold the glory of its lady, that is, of that blessed Beatrice who now gazes continually on the countenance of the One *who is blessed through all ages*.]

Despite their many differences, recent commentators seeking to demonstrate how Dante gave poetic reality to his "wonderful vision" tend to be in agreement on at least one issue involving the typology of the *Commedia:* that the poet's interior spiritual pilgrimage beyond the grave shadows mortal man's spiritual pilgrimage in this life; the progressive illumination of Dante's soul mirrors the secular, intellectual, and mystical experience of a few saintly Christians during their earthly existence. Yet once correspondences between spiritual states in the mortal and immortal regions are drawn, commentators encounter difficulty in identifying any other pattern of events here that appear to be reflected in all stages of the sojourn there; only certain parts of Dante's unique peregrination to God have been shown to contain episodes shadowing those on earth.

The journey beyond has been read as a figure for the historical Exodus of the Israelites, yet detailed expositions of the parallel patterns have been largely focused upon the *Purgatorio* and the first two cantos of the *Inferno*. Similarly, parallels discovered between Dante's ascent of Mt. Purgatory and Roman Catholic Easter liturgy, which contains allusions to the Exodus, have been confined largely to the *Purgatorio*. The poet's references to the Golden Jubilee pilgrimage to Rome in 1300, while frequently cited by critics, are scattered in the *Inferno* and *Paradiso* and do not in themselves constitute an inclusive counterpart to Dante's movements through the other world.[3]

3. Close readings of the journey beyond in relation to the Exodus in this world have been advanced by Charles Singleton in *Dante Studies 1: "Commedia": Elements of Structure* (Cambridge, Mass., 1954); *Dante Studies 2: Journey to Beatrice* (Cambridge, Mass., 1958); and "'In Exitu Israel de Aegypto'," *Seventy-Eighth Annual*

However, in emphasizing the historical Egypt-to-Jerusalem Exodus of the past, the Easter liturgy with its stress upon the Exodus, and the Golden Jubilee pilgrimage to Rome in 1300, the body of relevant Dante criticism, when combined and elaborated, points to an inclusive earthly model for the poet's journey beyond, a model here on earth that has yet to be fully disclosed. For when Dante attempted to write of his own passage through the immortal regions, he turned for guidance to the most immediately accessible and directly related source: the actual trips made by "true Hebrews," not just to Rome in his own time or from Egypt to Jerusalem in the distant past, but to both Jerusalem and Rome in the Golden Jubilee pilgrimage year of 1300.

Certainly, an enormous body of early secular and religious writings appears also to have influenced Dante, among them, numerous Moslem legends about the otherworld. In the *Risalat al-Ghufram*

Report of the Dante Society (Boston, 1960), pp. 1–24. Elaborated accounts of possible Exodus and pilgrimage references in the second canto of the *Inferno* can be found in Singleton's "'Sulla fiumana ove 'l mar non ha vanto'," *The Romanic Review* 39 (December, 1948) : 269–277; and John Freccero's "The River of Death: *Inferno* II, 108," in *The World of Dante: Six Studies in Language and Thought,* ed. S. Bernard Chandler and J. A. Molinaro (Toronto, 1966), pp. 26–41. For early and very general comments on the Exodus pattern in the *Commedia* see Benvenuto da Imola, *Benvenuti de Rambaldis de Imola Commentum Super Dantis Alligherii Comoediam,* (Florence, 1837), 3 : 63–64; and the remarks of Dante's relative in *Petri Alligherii Dantis Ipsius Genitoris Comoediam Commentarium* (Florence, 1845), p. 540.

Allusions in the *Commedia* to the Easter liturgy have been examined by Lizette Andrews Fisher, *The Mystic Vision in the Grail Legend and in the Divine Comedy* (New York, 1917), pp. 87–116; and by Fr. Dunstan J. Tucker, "'In Exitu Israel de Aegypto'; *The Divine Comedy* in the Light of the Easter Liturgy," *The American Benedictine Review* 11 (March–June, 1960) : 43–61.

N. Zingarelli in *Dante e Roma* (Roma, 1895), and C. Carboni in *Il Giubileo di Bonifazio VIII e la Commedia di Dante* (Roma, 1901) present moderately detailed readings of references to the Rome pilgrimage of 1300. Fr. Herbert Thurston's *The Holy Year of Jubilee* (Westminster, Maryland, 1949) has specific information about the early Golden Jubilee pilgrimages. See also Arsenio Frugoni, "Il Giubileo di Bonifacio VIII," *Bull. dell' Ist stor. Ital.* 62 (1950) : 1–121. The significance of the city of Rome in Dante's work has been studied by Fritz Kern, *Humana Civilitas,* Mittelalterliche Studien, vol. I, no. 1 (Leipsig, 1913) ; Konrad Burdach, "Dante und das Problem der Renaissance," *Deutsche Rundschau* 198 (Jan.–Mar., 1924) : 129–154, 260–277; L. Pietrobono, "Dante e Roma," *Giornale Dantesco* 33 (1930) : 1–24; Nancy Lenkeith, *Dante and the Legend of Rome,* medieval and Renaissance Studies, supplement II (London, 1952) ; and Charles Till Davis, *Dante and the Idea of Rome* (Oxford, 1957). A recent analysis of allusions to Rome in the *Commedia* appears in Arsenio Frugoni's "Dante e la Roma del suo Tempo," *Dante e Roma* (Florence, 1965), pp. 73–113.

Abu-l-Ala al-Ma'arri depicts Christian and other poets tortured remorselessly in Hell along with the fettered *Iblis* (Satan); in the same tale a *houri* or beautiful lady, acting as a guide, meets the narrator at the entrance to paradise. Ibn Arabi in *Al-Futuhat-al-makkiza* pictures nine levels each in both Hell and Heaven, writes of the voyage of a philosopher and theologian through the spheres to paradise, and then describes both a celestial mystic rose and angels circling the Divine Light. The Koran too is richly strewn with the terrible details of Satan's abode and the sensuous delights of paradise; and many medieval Moslem *Miraj* (ascension) and *Isra* (night journey) stories take up and elaborate the account, in Surah VII of the Koran, telling of Mohammed's night flight amid the spheres to the Seventh Heaven. Because by the thirteenth century few if any of these Arabic tales had been translated into any language that Dante could have read, the case for possible influence rests largely upon oral tradition.[4]

Visions of the joys and horrors of the region beyond were more directly available to the poet in Christian, classical, and pseudo-classical works, the most familiar being Aeneas's descent to the underworld in the sixth book of Virgil's *Aeneid*, and St. Paul's supposed tour of Hell as narrated in medieval legend and particularly in the twelfth-century writings of Adam de Ros. Pseudo-Dionysius' *The Heavenly Hierarchy* provided a very famous description of the spheres, angelic orders, and Heaven. And in Dante's time Joachim of Floris added his apocalyptic voice to the chorus of visionary travelers by penning the tale of his personal descent to Hell and ascent to Heaven.[5]

4. Possible Arabic influences are traced in Miguel Asín Palacios' *Islam and the Divine Comedy*, trans. Harold Sunderland (London, 1926); E. Blochet's *Les sources orientales de la Divine comédia* (Paris, 1901); Enrico Cerulli's *Il "Libro della Scala" e la questione delle fonti arabo-spagnole della Divina Commedia* (Città del Vaticano, 1949); Leonardo Olschki's "Mohammedan Eschatology and Dante's Other World," *Comparative Literature* 3 (1951): 1–17; and in Giuseppe Macaluso's *Dante e Maometto* (Roma, 1951). The visions and heresies of the Franciscan "Spirituals" are taken up by Macaluso in the same work, p. 75 ff.

5. Medieval legends about the world beyond are carefully analyzed in Arturo Graf's *Miti, leggende e superstizioni del medio evo* (Turin, 1892), 1 : 5 ff.; and *La Leggenda del Paradiso Terrestre* (Turin, 1878). Karl Vossler in *Medieval Culture: An Introduction to Dante and His Times*, trans. William Cranston Lawton (New York, 1958), vol. 1, cites a number of possible sources for Dante's otherworld. See also G. Busnelli's *La Concezione del Purgatorio dantesco* and *L'ordinamento morale del Purgatorio dantesco* (Roma, 1906, 1908); R. Palgen's *Das mittelalterliche Gesicht der Göttlichen*

From a fusion and imaginative transformation of elements in this plethora of medieval otherworldly literature and legend, Dante in part developed his extraordinarily precise and lucid conception of what lay beyond the grave. And from the works of theologians and mystics such as St. Thomas Aquinas, St. Augustine, St. Bonaventura, and St. Bernard of Clairvaux, the poet derived insights into the various stages of spiritual experience possible to man upon earth, stages of experience that could be shadowed in Dante's own spiritual growth in the region beyond.[6] But further to relate the otherworld to this mortal realm, to disclose extended figural correspondences between the region there and the world of the living here, Dante looked for instruction to the holiest "pages" in God's Book of the World: the iconographic cities, landscapes, holy sites, and even persons on the Egypt-Jerusalem-Rome pilgrimage route.

Some understanding of how profoundly the Great Circle pilgrimage influenced Dante in his invention of the *Commedia* can best be gained by first drawing a few rather obvious implications from the relation of pilgrimage references in the *Vita Nuova*, epistle x to Can Grande, and the *Commedia*. The complete general outline of the twofold pilgrimage in the *Commedia* will thus quickly come into view, and the perspective afforded will be helpful later in making close readings of specific passages in their figural contexts.

Key route information comes early in the *Commedia*—in the very first canto—and one must carefully heed stated directions. Dante, having met Virgil on a desert, listens as the Mantuan offers to act as a guide among the underworld's eternally suffering souls and then among souls stirred by hope (*Inf.* I, 112–120). A worthier spirit or "anima" (*Inf.* I, 122), Virgil asserts, will conduct the poet through realms of the blessed controlled by "quello imperador che là sù regna" (*Inf.* I, 124: "that Emperor who reigns above"). Says the Mantuan: "quivi è la sua città e l'alto seggio" (*Inf.* I, 128: "There is his city, and his high seat").

Dante now declaims at the end of the canto upon the goal of his tour:

Kommödie (Heidelberg, 1935) ; and Howard Roland Patch's recent study, *The Other World According to Descriptions in Medieval Literature* (Cambridge, Mass., 1950).

6. Edmund G. Gardner, *Dante and the Mystics* (London, 1913).

"che tu mi meni là dov' or dicesti,
sì ch'io veggia la porta di san Pietro
e color cui tu fai cotanto mesti".
    Allor si mosse, e io li tenni dietro.

[*Inf.* i, 133–136]

["lead me where you have said,
so that I may see St. Peter's Gate,
and those whom you have made so sad."
    Then he moved on; and I kept close behind him.]

Dante is going with Virgil to the underworld of the *Inferno*; but
the poet eventually wishes to arrive at a Gate of St. Peter which,
the Mantuan's preceding remarks imply, exists in Heaven. The
Gate can in fact be associated with the celestial city's threshold
where Dante is stopped and examined by St. Peter, holder of the
keys to eternity (*Par.* xxiv, xxviii), after having been led through
the spheres by Beatrice, a most worthy guide. Given the recurrent
motifs implicit in the poem, however, the reference to the Gate
also embraces on a lower spiritual level the "porta" on Mt. Purgatory guarded by an angel wielding a sword and two keys (*Purg.* ix,
76–129).

Before setting out for that very holy Gate of St. Peter located
at an imperial city above, Dante in canto ii calls attention to an
imperial city on earth. The poet is aware that he must follow in
the footsteps of Aeneas and St. Paul, both of whom were thought
to have traveled through the otherworld before eventually arriving
in the eternal city of Rome. Of Aeneas, Dante comments:

ch'e' fu de l'alma Roma e di suo impero
ne l'empireo ciel per padre eletto:
    la quale e 'l quale, a voler dir lo vero,
fu stabilita per lo loco santo
    u' siede il successor del maggior Piero.
    Per quest' andata onde li dai tu vanto,
intese cose che furon cagione
di sua vittoria e del papale ammanto.

[*Inf.* ii, 20–27]

[for in the empyreal heaven, he was chosen
to be the father of glorious Rome, and of her Empire;
    both these, to say the truth,
were established as the holy place
where the Successor of the greatest Peter sits.

By this journey, for which you honor him,
he learned things that were the causes
of his victory, and of the Papal Mantle.]

Now the "loco santo" or holy place where the Papal successors
of the greatest Peter regularly sat in state was, of course, St.
Peter's Basilica in Rome. And to establish securely that "loco
santo," it was first necessary for Aeneas to tour mortal and immortal regions and finally, in coming to his destination, to achieve
victory by becoming the "padre" of Rome and its empire. The
"Chosen Vessel" St. Paul, Dante adds, brought confirmation of
the faith by afterwards making a similar journey (*Inf.* ii, 28–29),
and now it is obviously Dante's turn to progress in some fashion
over the general path charted by the pagan hero and the Christian
saint. Even in these opening cantos it would appear that the poet is
commencing a journey both here on earth and there beyond life.
Although Dante is to head toward a Gate of St. Peter at a heavenly
city wherein sits the Emperor of the universe, his movements will
also carry him *in figura* toward a Gate of St. Peter at imperial
Rome wherein sits the Emperor of the Church.

Somewhere on this twofold progress to an eternal city, however, Dante *in figura* also wanders over desert trails used by the
palmers as they converted their souls on hopeful marches toward
the rising sun; this much one unmistakably learns from Beatrice
during her conversation with St. James in the realm of the fixed
stars. The theological virtue of Hope, so the poet's lady declares,
enabled Dante Alighieri to make the long journey from Egypt to
Jerusalem to see, and her words certainly cannot be taken lightly:

> "La Chiesa militante alcun figliuolo
> non ha con più speranza, com' è scritto
> nel Sol che raggia tutto nostro stuolo:
>   però li è conceduto che d'Egitto
> vegna in Ierusalemme per vedere,
> anzi che 'l militar li sia prescritto."

[*Par.* xxv, 52–57]

> ["Church militant has not a child
> more full of hope, as is written
> in the sun which beams rays on all our host;

therefore, he was allowed to come from Egypt
to Jerusalem to see
before his life's warfare was over."]

Such allusions to a shadowed Great Circle pilgrimage—and many others will soon be discussed—become increasingly fascinating when examined against passages in epistle x to Can Grande and the *Vita Nuova*. In writing to his patron, Dante in epistle x urges that the allegory of the *Commedia*, for its better manifestation ("ut melius pateat"), can be considered by reference to a verse from Psalm 114 (113 in the Vulgate):

> "In exitu Israel de Aegypto, domus Iacob de populo barbaro, facta est Iudaea santificatio eius, Israel potestas eius." [7]

> ["When Israel came out of Egypt, and the house of Jacob from a people of strange speech, Judaea became his sanctification, Israel his power."]

A long and perhaps wearisome familiarity with the letter has taught readers the kind of multifold interpretation that the author of the *Commedia* intended be applied to such a spiritual pilgrimage. The Exodus from Egypt to the Holy Land, Dante explains, need not be understood simply as a literal journey. In an allegorical sense, the Exodus signifies the redemption of man by Christ; in a moral sense, the conversion of the soul from sin to the state of grace; and in an anagogical sense, the departure of the soul from the imprisonment of mortal corruption to the liberty of eternal glory. And these views represent a sophisticated restatement of the customary allegorical interpretation given both to Exodus passages in the Bible and to pilgrimage literature about the Egypt-to-Jerusalem journey of the Israelites and their fellow "true Hebrews." The remarks of the twelfth-century writer Fetellus about the actual Stations of the Exodus on the Sinai peninsula, for example, might again be recalled: "through them the true Hebrew who hastens to pass from earth to heaven must run his race, and, leaving the Egypt of this world, must enter the land of promise, i.e., the heavenly fatherland." [8]

7. All quotations from the letter x to Can Grande are from *Le Opere di Dante Alighieri*, ed. E. Moore, rev. Paget Toynbee, 4th ed. (Oxford, 1924), pp. 414–416.

8. *Description of Jerusalem and the Holy Land*, trans. James Rose MacPherson (London, 1892), p. 14.

While Dante's letter with its accent upon the historical Exodus has been used by critics as a gloss upon the Egypt-to-Jerusalem pilgrimage typology in the *Purgatorio*, it is an "after-the-fact" document written as an explanation of a completed segment of the poem. The letter mentions an event on earth and supplies meanings to reveal its significance. On the other hand, the *Vita Nuova*, produced before the letter and the *Commedia*, outlines in verse and prose a twofold pilgrimage here and beyond and implies spiritual meanings for both. Now the biblical Exodus cited in the letter has been called the "master pattern that guided the poet's hand as he staged *conversio*" in the *Commedia*.[9] Ignored is the striking fact that, when Dante first depicted a twofold tour in the *Vita Nuova*, it was a worldly passage toward Rome and Christ's image on the Veronica, rather than toward Jerusalem, that prefigures the celestial flight of the poet's sigh toward Beatrice and God. Only upon completion of the sigh's ascent does the poet, with spiritual energies rejuvenated and directed upon Beatrice beyond the sphere, speak of enjoying the "wonderful vision" that inspires him to labor as much as he can on another work in praise of his lady.

Clearly, the celestial voyage to Beatrice projected into the *Paradiso* canticle of the new work-in-progress indirectly has as its original model the solemn progress of Romers on their way to the eternal city, and Dante might be expected to introduce into his new poem a correspondence between earthly and heavenly travels to Rome. It has been alleged, nevertheless, that in the *Paradiso* a collective pilgrimage in this world cannot mirror a collective pilgrimage to Heaven. In the *Purgatorio*, the pattern of a biblical Exodus signifying the conversion of the soul has been discovered, and it has been pointed out that on Mount Purgatory, which exists in a realm of time and change, dead souls can move toward God as in pilgrimage; but in the timeless, changeless *Paradiso*, dead souls remain relatively motionless within an eternal hierarchy and so cannot figure the forward progression of pilgrims.[10]

9. Charles Singleton, " 'In Exitu Israel de Aegypto'," *Seventy-Eighth Annual Report of the Dante Society* (Boston, 1960), p. 5.

10. Singleton in his essay " 'In Exitu Israel de Aegypto'," p. 14, writes that in hell "souls may not be seen as 'pilgrims' eternally *fixed* in their places as they are. Nor may souls in Paradise be thought of as being 'in via,' for they have reached the *patria*. But Purgatory, as Dante chose to picture that realm of the Afterlife, can lend

The argument is sound, yet it overlooks Dante's own movements through *Paradiso*. In the poet's individual journey can be figured an earthly pilgrimage of a different kind from that involving the collective conversion of many souls from sin to grace. The poet's aim in the *Paradiso* is not the conversion of the soul to the Creator, but the union with God through mystical vision of an already converted soul. And in Christian tradition it was thought to be the common lot of man on earth to sin and to repent, but it was believed to be the lot of very few individuals—of a Moses, St. Paul, or St. Bernard—to have mystical visions of the Almighty. A pilgrimage of conversion in the *Purgatorio* would carry a man in the company of other men from Egypt to Jerusalem, but a pilgrimage of vision in the *Paradiso* could carry an individual man from Jerusalem to that place before the Gate of St. Peter where the image of God was displayed.

In inventing the basic narrative of the *Paradiso*, Dante, then, had only to elaborate in great detail the twofold Rome-Heaven pilgrimage of vision already introduced in the *Vita Nuova*. For the *Purgatorio* a preparatory journey of a lower spiritual order was

---

itself especially to the metaphor of pilgrimage. . . . The whole of Purgatory, in hope and aspiration if not in fact, is a place where a forward movement towards a 'promised land' takes place, and always with a sense that such a movement is group movement: entire groups of souls become pilgrims, along with Dante and Virgil there." See also Singleton's statements in *Dante Studies 1: Elements of Structure*, pp. 22–24.

Thomas M. Greene in "Dramas of Selfhood in the Comedy," in *From Time to Eternity: Essays on Dante's Divine Comedy*, ed. Thomas C. Bergin (New Haven, London, 1967), p. 120, makes a similar point in observing that on Mt. Purgatory the dead figures "are creatures in transition, acutely conscious of the transition. We do not, to be sure, actually see any soul transformed before our eyes; only Dante the pilgrim changes as we read, and for our purposes he is irrelevant, being alive. But even if the souls are static as we meet them, they are in upward movement from the perspective of God, and Dante could not have permitted himself to regard them as finally perfected or fulfilled." Greene continues: "In the *Inferno* selfhood is fixed; in the *Purgatorio*, refined. For the *Paradiso*, one must have recourse to a word Dante coined: there, the self is 'trasumanato.' It is 'transhumanized'; it passes beyond humanity. In heaven, the individual finds the place of rest which defines him for eternity . . ." (p. 131).

Greene, however, calls attention to the *Commedia*'s "two subjects—one, the dynamic, involving a process, redemption, and the other, the static subject, the state of souls after death" (p. 117), and he offers sophisticated qualifications of interpretations by Auerbach that deal exclusively with the static subject. For a recent reading affording insights into the static structure of the *Commedia*, see Enrico De' Negri, "Tema e Iconografia del 'Purgatorio'," *The Romantic Review* 49 (April, 1958) : 81–104.

required, a journey that could insure the conversion of the pilgrim's soul from sin to grace prior to mystic vision. The letter to Can Grande, written after the *Vita Nuova,* discloses that the poet thought of the biblical Exodus from Egypt to Jerusalem as the type for such a journey; and the *Vita Nuova* itself, that Dante was aware of the travels of contemporary palmers over the Exodus path. To devise a lower-order journey, it was only necessary greatly to extend the trip toward Rome and Heaven by preceding it in the *Purgatorio* with a figured pilgrimage from the Egypt of this world to the Jerusalem of the Earthly Paradise, the entire twofold movement taking place in the year of the first Golden Jubilee pilgrimage to the eternal city. A descent into Hell to gain rational understanding, however, certainly would have been an inappropriate introduction to a poem essentially about an ascent to the see of St. Peter and God. A prologue was needed to suggest the opening but unsuccessful stages of an Egypt-to-Jerusalem journey; after the prologue the narrative could be broken off and the traveler next pictured at the gate of Hell ready to make his descent.[11]

11. Whatever the order in which Dante actually wrote the canticles and cantos of the *Commedia,* studies by Erich Auerbach and Helen Dunbar suggest the possibility that the poet may have first conceived of his work beginning with the *Paradiso.* In comparing Thomas Aquinas's *Summa Theologica* and the *Commedia,* Erich Auerbach in *Dante: Poet of the Secular World* (Chicago, 1961) notes that the poet, by placing the *Inferno* prior in sequence to the *Paradiso,* reversed the order in which persons trained in scholastic philosophy usually viewed the hierarchy of creation. Auerbach writes that the *Summa Theologica* "employs the method of listing and classifying, beginning with God" and then proceeding to lesser beings. "Thus, by reversing the order of the *Summa,*" writes Auerbach, "Dante discloses divine truth as human destiny, as the element of Being in the consciousness of erring man, who participates only inadequately in divine Being and is in need of completion and fulfillment" (p. 94). Helen Dunbar in *Symbolism in Medieval Thought* (New York, 1961) asserts that Dante's epistle x, along with including remarks on allegory and the Exodus, contains as well an introduction to the *Paradiso* revealing that canticle as the logical "inceptive cause" of the *Commedia.* "The scene of the first two canticles is time and space," she writes, "whereas that of the third is eternity. Dante's comment [in epistle x], beginning with his third canticle, began at the beginning, since for the Middle Ages the beginning was in eternity, not in time and space; and only in eternity was the real truth of the time-space universe contained. Indeed, the final cause is logically, though not temporally, the inceptive cause." She adds, "Logical as it may seem to begin with the first canticle in the interpretation of the medieval masterpiece, modern thought beginning with time and space makes of its attempted progress to eternity an endless puzzle resembling the old antinomy of Achilles and the tortoise . . ." (p. 29). Miss Dunbar accordingly examines the canticles in re-

A few moments reflection brings to mind the possible figural pattern of action and visual imagery in a poem so conceived. In the prologue and middle canticle would be mirrored the landscape of the Exodus: the desert separating Egypt from Jerusalem with Mt. Sinai jutting upward from the wastes; and following the prologue in the first canticle, images of a debased earthly region and corrupt human society figuring worldly Egypt. Finally, in the last canticle would appear the great sea separating Jerusalem from the eternal city of Rome, a sea sometimes clouded with mists and fired with the light of planets, sun, and stars.

The figured Christian in the prologue would fail to cross the Exodus landscape; he would be driven back among the heretics and sinners of worldly Egypt; but in the second canticle, the pilgrim would successfully move over the Exodus landscape to a most holy place; and in the last canticle, he would sail beneath the lambent lights of Heaven, upon a sea surface reflecting Heaven's images, to a distant shore and the eternal city of Rome.

And in turning to the *Commedia*, one finds there in the first two cantos of the *Inferno* a haunting landscape that is shadowed again in the first two cantos of the *Purgatorio*; one discovers an empty strand, a "gran diserto" (*Inf.* I, 64) stretching inland from the strand, and on the desert a "bel monte" (*Inf.* II, 120). There in the poem's opening cantos is Dante resting on the shore, crossing the desert, seeking to climb the slope at the mountain's base. But he is halted by a leopard, frightened by a lion, and driven backward and downward by a she-wolf to a place where the sun "tace," is silent (*Inf.* I, 60). And there at the beginning of the *Purgatorio* is Dante, after having passed through the pit of Hell, again moving from a shore over a desert, attempting to climb a mountain; but this time the beasts have vanished, and the poet is able to begin his ascent to an Eden resting on the mountain's summit. Lastly in the *Paradiso* one observes the poet swiftly and effortlessly soaring from the peak of the mountain through "lo gran mar" or the great sea (*Par.* I, 113) of the celestial universe, arriving on a "riva" or shore of right love (*Par.* XXVI, 63) that is the Primum Mobile, and gazing upon a heavenly "città" (*Par.* XXX, 130) formed as a rose in which Beatrice is enthroned.

verse order on the assumption that "the basis for complete interpretation is to be found in the *Paradiso*" (p. 30).

But do Dante's otherworldly movements in fact figure an Egypt-Jerusalem-Rome pilgrimage of a kind suggested by the *Vita Nuova* and the letter? Can one discover in the *Commedia* a prolonged, twofold series of concrete, explicitly defined, almost identical episodes in which the region beyond mirrors earthly events here?

A reasonably complete answer to these questions must come after extended analysis and so be postponed to the last chapter. But at this point one should recognize that the possible depiction and configuration of reflected events here on earth would obviously depend on how the literal sense of the poem is developed and defined there in Hell, Purgatory, and Heaven. And the precise character of the literal sense there—its landscapes, persons, dramatic incidents—has been the subject of a number of recent essays that have considerably advanced Dante criticism.

Rejecting the long held opinion that the literal sense is a beautiful fiction, an artificial and insubstantial veil of imaginative images drawing their existence from the concealed ideas they represent, commentators have argued that objects and figures in the other world have their own literal identities and exist in themselves. Étienne Gilson, reacting against the opinion that Virgil must represent only Reason and Beatrice only Theology, has noted how in the realm beyond life each of these characters has an individualized existence and can symbolize a variety of meanings. Erich Auerbach has advanced detailed readings demonstrating that the full identities of persons are continued beyond the grave, but in the other world character traits are further actualized and intensified against the background of the eternal. The actions of persons, their conversations, even certain landscapes against which they are seen—all are disclosed as intensified, morally ordered, and somewhat transformed continuations of situations and scenes on earth. The compelling immediacy and realism of Dante's other world are thus explained as a distillation of the essential being of this world, the whole of the *Commedia* acting as an ordered arrangement of exemplary types or figures pointing back to earth. According to Charles Singleton, Dante intended the *Commedia* as an "allegory of the theologians" with an historically true literal sense that mirrors other senses.[12]

12. Étienne Gilson's comments on Dante's allegory in *Dante the Philosopher*, trans. David Moore (London, 1948), pp. 287–289, are more limited in scope than those of

After all that modern criticism has affirmed about the concreteness and existential reality of literal events there, it would seem

---

Erich Auerbach and Charles Singleton. In maintaining that characters such as Virgil
should be regarded in the *Commedia* as living figures, Gilson writes, "we should
always proceed from what Virgil says and does to what he symbolizes, and not *vice
versa*. In the *Commedia*, then, he is the supreme poet, but not Poetry; a wise man, but
not Wisdom; an illustrious representative of the natural virtues or moral prudence,
but not Philosophy. If we seek to obtain a one-word answer, as we may expect to do
when mere poetical fictions are involved, we find that the question 'what does
Virgil symbolize' does not admit of any answer" (pp. 294–295). Gilson further states,
"We are told that Dante symbolizes *homo viator*, man in his pilgrimage through life.
This is undoubtedly true, but he does so because, in reality, that is what he is"
(p. 293).

Erich Auerbach in *Dante, Poet of the Secular World*, trans. Ralph Manheim
(Chicago, 1961), insists that all being in the world beyond exists in itself and yet
reflects being on earth. "Thus in truth the *Comedy*," he writes, "is a picture of
earthly life. The human world in all its breadth and depth is gathered into the structure of the hereafter and there it stands: complete, unfalsified, yet encompassed in an
eternal order; the confusion of earthly affairs is not concealed or attenuated or im-
materialized but preserved in full evidence and grounded in a plan which embraces it
and raises it above all contingency" (p. 133). Auerbach defines this kind of
typological allegory in "Figura," *Archivum Romanicum* 22 (1938): 436–489, reprinted
with changes in *Neue Dantestudien* (Istanbul, 1944). See also Auerbach's "Typological Symbolism in Medieval Literature," *Yale French Studies* 9 (1952): 3 10. Joseph
Anthony Mazzeo writes of a specific example of typology in the *Commedia* in "Dante
and Epicurus: The Making of a Type," in *Medieval Cultural Tradition in Dante's
Comedy* (Ithaca, 1960), pp. 174–204.

In defending the view that all persons and things in the world beyond have an
existence in themselves, Charles Singleton writes, "if we take the allegory of the
Divine Comedy to be the allegory of the theologians, we shall expect to find in the
poem a first literal meaning presented as a meaning which is not fictive but true,
because the words which give that meaning point to events which are seen as historically true. And we shall see these events themselves reflecting a second meaning
because their author, who is God, can use events as men use words. *But*, we shall not
demand at every moment that the event signified by the words be in its turn as a
word, because this is not the case in Holy Scripture" (*Elements of Structure*, p. 90).
Singleton finds that "in the poem, as in the mode of scriptural allegory, the literal
sense is given as an historical sense standing in its own right, like Milton's say—
Not devised in order to convey a hidden truth, but given in the focus of single
vision. (Nothing of more importance could happen in Dante criticism at present than
a general recognition of this fact)" (p. 15).

Whatever Dante's intent in inventing his allegory, the text of the *Commedia* reveals
that the poet was influenced by the truths discovered both in the Book of God's
Works, the emblematic natural world and its objects, and the Book of God's Words,
the Holy Scripture. A pilgrim on his way to Jerusalem and Rome "read" of historically
true biblical events by looking at emblematic stones, trees, pools, mountains, icons,
and other physical things supposedly placed in the Holy Land by the Divine Author;
the pilgrim's own journey was, in fact, a series of historical events centering on the
conversion of the soul in preparation for the viewing of God's image in the eternal

reasonable to expect them to figure something equally concrete and "real" here, some pattern of worldly episodes irrevocably embedded in the physical as well as spiritual experience of men living in the historical present of Dante's period. Dante, then, would be shadowing patterned occurrences more materially tangible than simply the state of souls in life, more directly and immediately known than biblical history of the past and future, though the state of souls and biblical scenes would, of course, be incorporated centrally into the typology.

In the *Commedia* the mirroring of a very tangible group pilgrimage becomes possible for the first time when Dante and Virgil join a group of souls on the desert strand before Mt. Purgatory. Unlike the dead personalities doomed forever to specific terraces of the *Inferno*, these souls have been granted the power—not exercised to best advantage—of moving forward and upward in a body over a purgatorial pathway toward Heaven; thus their collective actions can effectively shadow those of pilgrim groups upon earth. Before tracing that part of a Great Circle pilgrimage reflected in the movement of Dante and his guides through the *Inferno* and *Paradiso*, it is useful to begin in medias res by considering the twofold trails followed by a group of Christian souls in *Purgatorio* II.

With some excitement Dante and Virgil initially see the dead souls, more than one hundred in number, approaching the Exodus-like landscape of the desert shore in a boat propelled by an angel; the souls, moreover, are heard singing together about the escape of the Israelites from Egypt:

> "*In exitu Isräel de Aegypto*"
> cantavan tutti insieme ad una voce,
> con quanto di quel salmo è poscia scripto.
>
> [*Purg.* II, 46–48]

> ["In exitu Israel de Aegypto,"
> they all sang together with one voice,
> with what of that psalm is thereafter written.]

The psalm (114), the same one mentioned in Dante's letter to Can Grande, contains allusions to places along the route of the

city of Rome. In the *Commedia* the "true" journey beyond points back to the "true" historical events of pilgrimage, and these latter events gain in significance from the pilgrim's reading of the Books of God's Words and Works.

Exodus actually visited by palmers in the poet's time: the supposed locales where the Red Sea parted, where Moses struck a fountain from the rock, where the River Jordan stopped flowing before the tribes of Israel. When the band disembarks, Virgil warmly greets them calling the souls pilgrims and including himself and Dante in the reference: "noi siam peregrin come voi siete" (*Purg.* II, 63: "we are pilgrims even as you are"). And the souls, noticing that Dante is breathing, rush forward to hear the latest news as to a messenger (*Purg.* II, 70: "come a messagger"). Their enthusiasm is such that they trample on one another's feet (*Purg* II, 72: "e di calcar nessun si mostra schivo"). Quite unexpectedly, Dante's friend in life, Casella, steps from among the dead and embraces the poet with great affection. And the poet, forgetful that Casella is now a shade, speaks of his attempt to return the embrace:

> tre volte dietro a lei mani avvinsi,
> e tante mi tornai con esse al petto.
>
> [*Purg.* II, 80–81]

> [Three times behind him I clasped my hands,
> and as often returned with them to my breast.]

Blushing with wonder, Dante looks on as the shade of Casella draws back, talks of its condition, and sings of love: "Amor che ne la mente mi ragiona" (*Purg.* II, 112): "Love that in my mind discourseth to me"). Other souls gather round to enjoy the song; but ancient Cato, the guardian of Mt. Purgatory, hurries over to chide them for their spiritual laxness in being distracted from their journey. Spurred on by his reproaches, they scatter like birds toward the mountain.

Given the Exodus song of the souls and their delineation as pilgrims, one is immediately reminded that the ancient Israelites, upon leaving Egypt, also traveled to a desert shore; they too journeyed across desert wastes; they too came to a holy mountain in the wilderness. The arrival of the souls on a desert strand beyond life does appear generally to shadow, as Charles Singleton has argued, the emergence of the Israelites from the Red Sea at the outset of their wanderings, the sea waters themselves vaguely suggesting the waters of baptism.[13] Moreover, the spiritual condition of those souls in the other realm can be seen to shadow the state of

13. See John Freccero, "The River of Death," pp. 37–42.

men's souls here in this world. But is this all? Is not a more immediate and concrete earthly episode being shadowed?

The ancient Israelites did not, after all, arrive on the Sinai
peninsula by ship; they did not trample on one another's toes seeking news from a stranger; none among them sang love lyrics in
the manner of Casella. Readers should remember that Casella, before commencing his song, informs Dante that the ship to Mt.
Purgatory left from the River Tiber's mouth near Rome, and that
for three months past (*Purg.* ii, 98: "da tre mesi") all dead souls
wishing to board were permitted to do so—remarks suggesting that
the souls are Roman Catholics benefiting from blanket indulgences
promulgated for the Golden Jubilee pilgrimage of 1300. Yet living
pilgrims during the Jubilee Year also benefited from these dispensations, and it was from the port of Rome at Ostia, on the
River Tiber's mouth, that these living pilgrims in quest of special
indulgences often embarked on earthly Exodus journeys taking
them to the shores of the Red Sea, over the Sinai sands, up the
purgatorial Mountain of God, and on to the Holy City of Jerusalem. Shortly before Casella speaks, it should be noted, Virgil
calls Dante's attention to the location of Mt. Purgatory at the
antipodes directly opposite Jerusalem. When it is dawn at Mt.
Purgatory, Virgil states, it is sunset in the Holy City (*Purg.* ii, 1–
9). Readers should recall as well the manner in which the dead
souls arrive: they sing together in the boat; the angel ferrying
them makes the sign of the cross; they fling themselves upon the
land; they hurry forward in excitement and disorder. And suddenly the primary figured meaning of the action becomes clear:
the literal events occurring on a pilgrimage near the antipodes at
Mt. Purgatory point to foreshadowing events occurring on the
opposite side of the globe on a pilgrimage to Jerusalem, the center
of the earth. Reflected in the dead souls are palmers coming
joyously to shore in the Holy Land on Easter Sunday morning
1300, the landing in the poem serving as a type for the kind of
arrivals that in Dante's time had been taking place for one
thousand years.[14] Reflected too throughout the *Purgatorio* are observances actually practiced by contemporary palmers on the Stations-of-the-Exodus route between worldly Egypt and holy Jeru-

14. Detailed accounts of such pilgrim landings can be found in chapter v, pp.
135–138.

salem. One should realize that the literal, concrete events unfolding in the present there at Mt. Purgatory shadow only in an indirect and imprecise fashion the general pattern of the past biblical Exodus on earth. Rather, the events in the present there figure most concretely the movement of palmers in the present here along the stations of a pilgrimage path designed to lift them spiritually from earth to Heaven. The pilgrimage of the dead souls in the *Purgatorio* in turn shadows both the past biblical Exodus and the pilgrimages of all true Hebrews in the past and future. Thus the figure of the past biblical Exodus, however meaningful, is in this instance a figure at second hand. In the foreground is the figure of the contemporaneous pilgrimage to Jerusalem that represented in itself certain spiritual meanings to "true Hebrews" in Dante's time.

One can now look with some perspective upon the twofold action taking place in the Exodus-like landscape of strand, desert, and mountain in *Inferno* I and II. Dante in the prologue to the *Inferno* is close to despair, but he is making his first faltering attempt to convert his soul to God. Because no direct reference to "peregrin" appears in the first two cantos, commentators have rightly suggested that Dante's movements do not figure an actual pilgrimage; instead, the scene has been read as a trial Exodus pilgrimage that fails.[15]

In the prologue the poet is lost in a dark wood somewhere in the realm of the living, and his voyage beyond life begins only after he lifts his eyes to the sun and so calms the fear that has stirred in the "lago" (*Inf.* I, 20) of his heart. Dante writes that as one who

> . . . con lena affannata,
> uscito fuor del pelago a la riva,
> si volge a l'acqua perigliosa e guata,
> così l'animo mio, ch'ancor fuggiva,

15. See Singleton, " 'In Exitu Israel de Aegypto'," pp. 1–9. In discussing generally the Exodus figure in both the *Inferno* and the *Purgatorio*, Singleton writes, "If this journey to God begins in the figure of the Exodus, and then leaves that figure, to return to it after a long descent through Hell, the reason for this is clearly a matter worthy of attention. What we have here, in simplest statement, is a first attempt to climb that fails, then a long descent that returns the wayfarer to the second attempt that succeeds" (p. 9). John Freccero in "The River of Death," p. 26, asserts that "the journey without a guide, the frustrated attempt to climb the mountain in the first canto of the *Inferno* must be considered an exodus that failed, a temporary escape that was not a definitive departure from 'Egypt' but merely a disastrous sortie."

si volse a retro a rimirar lo passo
che non lasciò già mai persona viva.

[*Inf.* I, 22–27]

[. . . with panting breath
has escaped from the deep sea to the shore,
turns to the dangerous water and gazes,
    so my mind, which still was fleeing,
turned back to see the pass
that no one ever left alive.]

Though the mind passing beyond the abode of living men is said
to be *like* a person escaping from the deep sea, the reader learns in
the next line that the poet's body is now wearied and must rest before moving in a recognizably new landscape, a "piaggia diserta"
(*Inf.* I, 29). The shore is really there; the body is really tired.
Dante seems to have emerged physically from water, but the event
is blurred by the terms of the simile, perhaps because it reflects an
attempted rather than a successful journey. The poet's escape from
the sea has been interpreted as shadowing the movement of the
Israelites from the Red Sea, the immersion in water signifying
baptism. But should one remember, as Dante did in abstract statements in the *Vita Nuova*, that palmers had to begin their trips by
moving beyond the sea to the east in the direction of the rising
sun, then a more concrete and immediate type comes to mind.

What is being reflected is more than the general pattern of the
biblical Exodus. This landing on a desert shore on Good Friday
morning shadows a pilgrim's arrival on the shores of the Holy
Land. For just as personalities beyond life are attracted across the
sea to a desert strand at the antipodes, so too pilgrims in this life
are drawn over a sea to a shore on that part of the globe directly
opposite the antipodes.[16] The pilgrimage of the dead at the antipodes shadows the pilgrimage of the living at the center of the
earth. But the reflected Christian in the prologue to the *Inferno*
is not aided spiritually by a boatman who makes the sign of the
cross as are the souls in the *Purgatorio*. The Christian cannot
throw himself immediately upon the land; he must struggle la-
boriously from the sea because his spiritual state is more sinful
than that of the dead souls. The Christian next moves over the
desert to the lower slope of a beautiful mountain where suddenly

16. Dangerous arrivals of this kind are discussed in chapter v, pp. 134–136.

appear the three beasts; and it is now possible to trace in this and other incidents the general course of a figured pilgrimage from Egypt to an eternal city.

One after the other, the spotted leopard, hungry lion, and ravenous she-wolf are seen by the startled poet; and each animal becomes successively more menacing. The leopard, by simply standing on the way of ascent, causes Dante to halt; the lion seems to advance:

> Questi parea che contra me venisse
> con la test' alta e con rabbiosa fame.
>
> [*Inf.* i, 46–47]

> [He seemed to be coming against me
> with head erect, and furious hunger.]

The she-wolf definitely paces toward the poet and forces him into a downward retreat away from the symbolic light of Heaven's morning sun (*Inf.* i, 49–60). When Virgil enters and generously offers to guide his charge over a different path, Dante cries out that the she-wolf has turned him back, and the Mantuan replies that this

> . . . bestia, per la qual tu gride,
> non lascia altrui passar per la sua via,
> ma tanto lo 'mpedisce che l'uccide;
>   e ha natura sì malvagia e ria,
> che mai non empie la bramosa voglia,
> e dopo 'l pasto ha più fame che pria.
>
> [*Inf.* i, 94–99]

> [. . . beast, for which you cry out,
> lets no one pass along her way;
> but so entangles that she slays them;
>   and has a nature so perverse and vicious,
> that she never satiates her craving appetite;
> and after feeding, she is hungrier than before.]

Reserving until later a specific figural analysis of this episode, one can point out that the three beasts have long and rightly been thought to symbolize sins assailing Dante and thrusting him back from the light of God, the last sin being the most devouring and universal. What beast symbolizes what sin is by no means self-evident in the text; but most likely the beasts do represent, among other things, the three divisions of sin in the *Inferno* with the leopard suggesting Fraud; the lion, Violence; and the she-wolf, Incontinence. Yet seen in the larger figural context of the *Commedia*, the association of each beast with a special sin is not all-important; what matters is the awareness, emphasized by critics, that the ancient Israelites were also beset and led astray by sinful temptations during their flight from Egypt across a great desert, and in the fears and deviations of a poet confounded by sin are shadowed the corresponding sinful defects and wanderings of God's chosen tribe.

The Bible does not record, however, that a noble pagan guide came to the rescue of the ancient Israelites by offering to conduct them on a different path to a holy mountain; it was left for later pagans to make such offers to palmers who, wishing to avoid the tribulation and expense of forty years' wandering, were willing enough to accept the advice of trusted infidels. Nevertheless, true Hebrews in Dante's period, marching as did the Israelites over the Sinai wastes toward the rising sun, well knew that through physical or spiritual error they might be driven from the true path and led to their death upon the desert. During their dangerous crossing, it has been noted, they meditated on their sins and prayed for deliverance. And not a few must have wondered whether God would see fit to keep them on the way of light and allow them to arrive safely at the mountain of their desire.

Though Dante's confrontation with the three beasts reflects the Israelites' meeting with temptations, the event far more immediately shadows an individual Christian's experience of manifested sins on the Stations-of-the-Exodus path. And in Virgil's actions are figured those of an ideal infidel guide who is sent by Heaven to aid the distraught Christian.

At this juncture one plainly perceives that Dante has been unable to make a figured Exodus pilgrimage: the poet has struggled wearily to a desert strand mirroring a seacoast in the Holy Land; he has moved toward a beautiful mountain that would seem to reflect Mt. Sinai; but, terror-stricken by a she-wolf shadowing a sinful temptation, he has fled from the mountain to a low defile in the desert and there has met Virgil. In a comment providing further information on the strange spiritual geography of the region, the Mantuan declares that a blessed lady named Lucy,

looking down from the lofty heights of Heaven, has watched with
pity as the poet combatted death before a mysterious river. In
Virgil's account, Lucy requested Beatrice to intervene in aid of
the troubled poet:

> " 'Non odi tu la pieta del suo pianto,
> non vedi tu la morte che 'l combatte
> su la fiumana ove 'l mar non ha vanto?' "
>
> [*Inf.* II, 106–108]

> [" 'Do you not hear the misery of his plaint?
> Do you not see the death which combats him
> upon the river over which the sea has no boast?' "]

Beatrice is then said to have come down from Heaven to ask
Virgil's assistance in saving Dante (*Inf.* II, 109–117).

Now in the first two cantos Dante has not observed any river,
and most commentators have assumed that Lucy on high must
have gazed upon the River Acheron, the first of four infernal
streams later to be seen by the poet during his descent through
Hell. The difficulty with this reading is that the River Acheron lies
at some distance from Dante's position on the low desert: the river
is beyond the gate of Hell, beyond a wide and dismal plain, beyond troops of sinners tortured by the stings of wasps and hornets.
It has therefore been suggested that Lucy, with illuminated vision,
has in fact looked upon another river, a holy rather than an infernal stream that flows outside the Gate of Hell through the
desert rift in which Dante stands in canto II. But the spiritual
blindness of the poet would prevent him from seeing these blessed
waters.

While the mysterious river discerned by Lucy can sustain various meanings, John Freccero has convincingly pointed out that, in
terms of the prologue's Exodus pattern, its waters shadow those
of the River Jordan. Baptism in the stream, Freccero maintains by
citing patristic writings, was a traditional figure for the death of
pride and the gaining of new life through humility; a descent from
egotism into the holy waters was necessary before an ascent
toward God. Though in patristic commentary baptism in the Red
Sea is said to wash away original sin, later baptism in the River
Jordan is supposed to serve the higher spiritual function of opening the gates of Heaven. Thus, it is the Red Sea, according to

Freccero, that can have no spiritual "boast" over the River Jordan.[17]

In the prologue Dante, stained by sin, can neither climb a beautiful mountain nor, from the viewpoint of Lucy, cross a mysterious river on the reflected Exodus route; the poet must first make a prolonged detour through Hell before he can progress again *in figura* from Egypt toward Jerusalem and then on to an eternal city. Yet as has been noted, the ultimate figured goal of the journey is not left in doubt. It is at this stage in Dante's otherworldly adventure that the poet learns he is to travel in the footsteps of Aeneas and St. Paul who went to "the holy place, / where the Successor of the greatest Peter sits" (*Inf.* II, 23–24: "lo loco santo, / u' siede il successor del maggior Piero"). And as if to dispel any doubts about the matter, Dante here proclaims his determination to go initially to the underworld and then to "the Gate of St. Peter" (*Inf.* I, 134: "la porta di san Pietro").

After the opening two cantos of the *Inferno*, the narrative is sharply broken off, the scene instantly shifted. No longer are Dante and Virgil in a figured Exodus landscape; in canto III they stand before the gate to the underworld.

Because Dante's fearful descent through the terraced funnel of Hell is undertaken to gain rational understanding rather than grace, nowhere in the *Inferno* is it suggested that the poet is a pilgrim. And neither Virgil nor any of the damned qualify for that role. In Hell Dante is exposed to corrupt landscapes that figure, as Erich Auerbach has disclosed, a distorted image of this world;[18] and around the poet are ranged numerous reflected examples of a debased earthly society. Dante cannot acquire in this region the spiritual illumination that would transform this part of his journey into a Christian pilgrimage. When allusions to pilgrims occur in the *Inferno*, the damned actors in each case can only imitate true pilgrims in a false and external fashion.

In the eighth circle naked panderers and seducers, scourged from behind by demons, lift high their smarting legs and dash onward around a ledge, some going one way, some the other; and these two harried columns of the damned are compared in simile to Romers who, during the year of Jubilee (*Inf.* XVIII, 29: "l'anno del

17. "The River of Death," pp. 34–42.
18. *Dante, Poet of the Secular World* (Chicago, 1961), pp. 122–130.

giubileo"), press in opposite directions across the bridge of Castel St. Angelo, one group headed toward St. Peter's Basilica, and the other toward one of the hills of Rome. After speaking of the movements in two directions of the panderers and seducers, Dante draws the analogy in the following words:

> come i Roman per l'essercito molto,
> l'anno del giubileo, su per lo ponte
> hanno a passar la gente modo colto,
>   che da l'un lato tutti hanno la fronte
> verso 'l castello e vanno a Santo Pietro,
> da l'altra sponda vanno verso 'l monte.
>
> [*Inf.* XVIII, 28–33]

> [thus the Romans, because of the great throng,
> in the year of Jubilee, upon the bridge
> have taken means to pass the people over;
>   so that, on the one side, all have their faces
> towards the Castle, and go to St. Peter's;
> at the other ledge, they go towards the Mount.]

Though the damned are said to be like the Romers, those inhabitants of Hell under the lash of demons surely lack the outward composure and inner harmony of true pilgrims. Moreover, the analogous Romers would here seem to be the objects of Dante's subtle ridicule. Ideal pilgrims would not press in throngs against one another and so require special "traffic control" measures for their passage; they might be expected to have sufficient self-discipline to form unaided into columns and move forward in procession possibly singing hymns and reciting prayers. The Romers' outward actions by implication reveal their inner spiritual confusion, and Dante may well be cleverly suggesting that these living persons, engaging in a corrupt imitation of pilgrimage, are in fact also among the damned.

Later in the eighth circle the pagan Ulysses, recounting his voyage over the same course sailed by dead souls to Mt. Purgatory, movingly speaks of how he and his shipmates drowned within sight of that high eminence. After passing beyond the normal human confines of the Gates of Hercules, Ulysses explains, he and his crew voyaged westward into regions forbidden to living men, and there they had "experience / of the unpeopled world behind the sun" (*Inf.* XXVI, 116–117: "l'esperïenza, / di retro al sol, del

mondo sanza gente"). They saw dimly rising before them the outline of God's purgatorial mountain; but according to Ulysses, it
pleased the Creator that at the very moment of their apparent
triumph they should be swept to their deaths in a whirlpool. This
voyage was no true pilgrimage, as the hero now realizes. It was a
"foolish flight" (*Inf.* xxvi, 125: "folle volo") entered into out of
pride and therefore ending in disaster.

It was surely to be expected that early commentators would
associate the underworld's imprisoned souls and their gloomy environment with the heretics and infidels living in the "cursed"
land of worldly Egypt. Patristic commentary repeatedly cited
Egypt as the traditional figure for Hell, Pharaoh for the Devil.
And it should now be quite obvious that by Dante's time pilgrims
for centuries had been castigating Egypt, and particularly the
Soldan's or Pharaoh's capital of Babylon, as a noisy, dangerous
place filled with shouting heretics damned by the Almighty.

The identification of Egypt with the *Inferno* was taken up by
the earliest commentators on the *Commedia*. Dante's son, Pietro,
remarking upon the ancient Israelites who died in the desert of
Exodus, writes that "others died in Egypt, and these are those
stubbornly wicked people who remain until death in slavery to
Pharaoh, that is, in servitude to sin . . . and about these the
author spoke, as above, in the book of the *Inferno*." [19] Benvenuto
da Imola in his commentary on the *Commedia* notes that "Egypt,
a land full of horrors, labors, and serpents, is symbolically a land
full of sins and dangers, the ruler of which is the devil, who is
called the prince of this world, as was clearly shown in the final
canto of the *Inferno*." [20] Similar reflections relating Egypt and the
Inferno would doubtless have occurred to many readers of Dante's
period.

Certain allusions in the *Inferno* sustain a specific figural link
between Hell and an Egypt dominated by a heretical Moslem culture. In first glimpsing the city of Dis, Dante sees on the skyline

19. *Pietri Alligherii Dentis Ipsius Genitoris Comoediam Commentarium*, p. 540;
translated by Dunstan J. Tucker in " 'In Exitu Israel de Aegypto'," *The American
Benedictine Review* (March–June, 1960), p. 54.

20. *Benvenuti de Rambaldis de Imola Comentum Super Dantis Alligherii Comoediam*, 3 : 63; translated by Dunstan J. Tucker in " 'In Exitu Israel de Aegypto'," p.
55. Jean Daniélou in *From Shadows to Reality* (London, 1960) presents numerous
examples of medieval figural commentary linking Egypt and Hell, pp. 175–201.

the minarets of a Moslem metropolis. The poet says to his
Mantuan guide:

> . . . "Maestro, già le sue meschite
> là entro certe ne la valle cerno,
> vermiglie come se di foco uscite
>   fossero".

[Inf. VIII, 70–73]

> [. . . "Master, already I discern its minarets
> distinctly there within the valley,
> red is if they had come
>   out of the fire."]

Like pilgrims at the Egyptian capital of Babylon, a city controlled
by a Moslem counterpart for the Devil, Dante and Virgil enter
into Dis only after much trepidation and difficulty. Outside the
city on the rim of the abyss, the poet and his guide had previously
observed the Moslem leader Saladin among a group of noble but
unbaptised pagans (Inf. IV, 129); and far below the walls of Dis
they come upon schismatics among whom are Mohammet and his
brother Ali, both cleft partly in half (Inf. XXVIII, 31–33). Within
the city proper are found certain souls led into error by the doc-
trines of the Arab theologian Averroes (Inf. X, 22–136).

The Moslem culture associated with the Hell of worldly Egypt
also probably contributed to Dante's presentation of the architecture, punishments, and even characters of the Inferno. As already
has been observed, Isra and Miraj legends and works such as Al-
Futuha-al-makkiza have been shown by Asín Palacios and others
to be replete with infernal horrors similar to those found in Dante's
underworld. The Moslem Hell like Dante's is a vast funnel pointed
downward below Jerusalem, and it is laced with various terraces,
each inhabited by a special category of sinner. In this Moslem underworld of the infidels, adulterers are hurled upwards and downwards in a hurricane of fire; usurers swim in a bloody lake; the
authors of schisms are knifed by demons; gluttons and thieves,
tortured by serpents; and the worst sinners, punished in a realm of
ice.[21] In a very general sense, however, Egypt as a figure for Hell
can be regarded as mirroring the entire corrupt earthly world and

21. See Miguel Asín Palacios' Islam and the Divine Comedy, pp. 68 ff., and
E. Blochet's Les sources orientales de la Divine comédia.

all men who, in Pietro di Dante's words, live "in servitude to sin."

Dante's climb down through this brutalized social environment is increasingly unpleasant and difficult; the poet as he progresses is surrounded by scenes of ever-greater ugliness and violence. Dante is sharply addressed by Charon at the River Acheron (*Inf.* III, 83–93); on the River Styx the wrathful Filippo Argenti rises alongside the boat in which Dante sails and tries to overturn it (VIII); furies and demons deny the poet entrance for a time to the city of Dis (*Inf.* VIII, 115–130); other demons later threaten and chase the poet in Malebolge (XXI–XXIII). With a connecting bridge in this last region broken, Dante must scramble downward into the "bolgia" of the hypocrites (XXIII). On the frozen floor of Cocytus at the bottom of Hell, the poet, walking amid heads imprisoned in ice, strikes his foot sharply against the face of Bocca degli Abbati (*Inf.* XXXII, 76–81). When the poet reaches the grotesque form of Satan, a three-headed giant incarcerated chest-deep in the frozen wastes, Dante clings to Virgil's back. The Mantuan in turn grasps the monster's shaggy hair and by this means descends the final, terrible "scale" of Hell (*Inf.* XXXIV, 82); then the pair mount through a crevice in the rocks to a purgatorial island at the antipodes. Dante in the isolation of the timeless *Inferno* enjoys no ease of movement like that which comes in the *Purgatorio* when the soul, rising toward God in a realm of time, is converted along with other souls from sin to grace.

In the second canticle the poet returns to a desert shore below the craggy heights of Mt. Purgatory, and there Dante's meeting with newly arrived souls, who sing an Exodus psalm, is just one among numerous incidents suggesting that a figured Egypt-to-Jerusalem pilgrimage is commencing. Later in ascending the mountain Dante will join socially with one group of spirits after the other; Statius will even accompany the poet through the upper terraces of Purgatory into Eden. The fact that Dante can establish a harmonious social relationship with the souls is in itself significant; for in the *Purgatorio* as in collective pilgrimage upon earth, man in fellowship and song, repentance and hope, is able to confess and be forgiven his sins while progressing up the steep path to salvation. The poet has indeed become a true pilgrim.

Though criticism has perceptively seized upon a variety of

events making up the extended Egypt-to-Jerusalem pilgrimage figure in the *Purgatorio*, one must admit that, when critics relate the journey beyond exclusively to past biblical episodes, some of the associations drawn seem at times rather tenuous. The following readings of the figured biblical Exodus pattern in the second canticle serve to illustrate the kind of interpretations that have been advanced.

Prior to the landing of pilgrims on the strand before Mt. Purgatory, Dante and his guide, on instruction from the mountain's venerable guardian Cato, move downhill over the desert to the edge of the sea where Virgil girds the poet with a rush plucked from the shore (*Purg.* I, 130–136). These actions have been said to reintroduce the reflected Exodus journey abandoned by Dante in the prologue to the *Inferno*, for on the scene once more is a strand that has already been found to reflect the one affording safety to the Israelites after their escape from worldly Egypt. There are waters mirroring those of the Red Sea, a barrier between evil and holy places that came to be known as the Sea of Rushes. And it has been urged that Dante, in descending to the shore and being girded with a rush, is *in figura* descending to humility before starting out again on a shadowed Exodus pathway across a desert and up a holy mountain.[22]

When the musician Casella sings of love following his arrival by ship on holy ground, the accompanying pilgrim souls together with Dante are observed to forget the object of their sojourn and to tarry in delight (*Purg.* II, 76–133). Criticism has adjudged the poet and the souls as beset by temptation just as were the Israelites during their flight from Egypt, the temptation posed by Casella's song in turn corresponding to the ones that assailed Dante in the symbolic forms of the three beasts in *Inferno* I. But in the *Purgatorio* Dante does not partially succumb to vice and retreat from the right path; Cato is there below Mt. Purgatory to insure that the way to spiritual liberty is kept open, and the poet is compelled by the guardian to give up mundane pleasure.

In a small valley before the gate of Purgatory proper, Dante at sunset comes upon a "noble army" (*Purg.* VIII, 22: "essercito

22. Singleton, " 'In Exitu Israel de Aegypto'," p. 12. See also Robert Hollander's claim that Cato is the type of Moses in *Allegory in Dante's Commedia* (Princeton, 1969), pp. 124–129.

gentile") of negligent Christian princes. All in this army, pas-
sively waiting beneath a blessed mountain, sing "Salve Regina"
and then "Te lucis ante" in the hope that the Virgin will protect
them from an evil "Adversary" whose approach is anticipated at
nightfall (*Purg.* vii, 82–84; viii, 13–18). In the light of the Exodus figure in the *Purgatorio*, the army has been found to reflect
Hebrew forces arrayed below Mt. Sinai before a meeting with
the enemy.

The army of princes, though negligent, is seen to assume an
attitude of humility with all heads turned toward Heaven and all
lips united in supplication of the Virgin. This humble stance is
prudently adopted, for Mary soon grants the longed-for help: two
armed angels come down from the bosom of God's Mother to take
up positions as guards or sentinels on the flanks of the encamp-
ment. In the gathering dusk the Adversary soon appears in the
form of a serpent, but Mary's angelic sentinels quickly drive off
this evil beast (*Purg.* viii, 22–108). As took place when Dante and
other pilgrim souls were tempted by Casella's song, functionaries
of Heaven have intervened to assist Christians, who figure the
Israelites, to overcome sin and so to prepare for spiritual ascent
(Singleton, "Exitu Israel," pp. 14–15).

Finally, Dante, having joined the "essercito" of souls before
Purgatory's gate, looks up after dark to see three glimmering stars
in the southern hemisphere near the pole. In that same celestial
position on the morning of the poet's emergence from Hell, Dante
had earlier noticed four stars, not three (*Purg.* i, 22–24). He is
now told by Virgil that the four lights have replaced the three, the
one group of stars presiding over the purgatorial landscape by day
and the other by night (*Purg.* viii, 88–93). These two curious
groups of stars, it has been held, figure the two great physical
signs that guided the Twelve Tribes over the Sinai sands: the pillar
of cloud by day and the pillar of fire by night (Singleton, "Exitu
Israel," pp. 14–15).

One perhaps hesitates before accepting such readings, noting
the critical caution with which they are posited. Yet the overall
outline of the figured Exodus is certainly there in the text lending
force and weight to the specific interpretation of isolated events.
But why do these isolated events mirror the Exodus in a rather
vague fashion? Why is there such a gulf separating the details of

the original biblical episode from the figured acting out of the episode in the world beyond?

Again it must be stressed that the original biblical Exodus is not the earthly event being directly imitated; again one notes how that ancient journey is being obscurely shadowed in a far more graphic, tangible, and immediate earthly action. For when the souls in the *Purgatorio* are closely observed, one sees directly figured in them, not the Hebrews of the biblical Exodus, but somewhat distracted, nonbiblical pilgrims who wander forward, under strange desert stars, gossiping, lingering, embracing, singing, asking the news, seeking out fellow countrymen, chatting with pagan guides and guardians, encamping under lofty peaks, witnessing supposed miracles, and at last climbing a mountain of God. Before taking up in the last chapter the particulars of the pilgrims' reflected earthly journey, a few general statements can be made about the incidents just discussed.

Reading the narrative of the *Purgatorio* as a figure for a contemporaneous pilgrimage on earth, one becomes aware that old Cato, like Virgil, shadows a noble pagan of the sort that actually kept Christians on the true Stations-of-the-Exodus path and saved them from physical and spiritual death. Casella, who appears from his sinful manner to have been admitted to Purgatory only because he gained special Jubilee year dispensations, plainly represents an indulged, friendly, artistic palmer who is a bit out of place amid very spiritual surroundings. Though his actions suggest secular temptation, they carry also a rather pragmatic and faintly amusing moral: good Christian artists on pilgrimage between the Red Sea and Mt. Sinai had best not stand about in the desert singing love lyrics. The fearful princes encamped beneath the mountain of God are deficient in a very special sense: unlike the crusaders of *Paradiso* xiv–xv, who gathered together armies and marched over pilgrimage routes to liberate the Holy City, these negligent rulers—Emperor Rudolf I, Philip (III) the Bold of France, Peter III of Aragon, Charles II of Naples, and others— never seriously took up arms to open, and to keep safe from attack, pathways leading to Jerusalem. Now in a demonstration of God's "contrapasso" Justice, the princes after death are placed on the Jerusalem route, formed into an army, and forced to confront a terrible enemy. The pagan Cato, the artist Casella, the negligent rulers—these souls act out their parts beneath a reflected and transformed image of that largely unknown desert sky spanning the center of the earth near Jerusalem, a most holy sky in which stars miraculously blaze forth to signify the birth of Christ or to mark the location of Mt. Sinai.[23]

Near the valley of the princes, Dante at twilight is reminded of new pilgrims setting out on their travels. It is the hour, the poet writes,

> . . . che lo novo peregrin d'amore
> punge, se ode squilla di lontano
> che paia il giorno pianger che si more.
>
> [*Purg.* VIII, 4–6]

> [. . . that pierces the new pilgrim with love,
> if from afar he hears the chimes
> which seem to mourn for the dying day.]

The valley is thus singled out as the starting point for earnest pilgrimage because, once beyond this place and past the nearby gate of Purgatory proper, souls are no longer subject to distracting temptations and to attempted attacks by evil forces. The very next morning Dante kneels before an angelic porter at Purgatory's gate and then marches on to the first of seven terraces, there to begin a more intensified and directed Exodus journey. On a ledge occupied by the Proud, the poet soon hears supplications for spiritually uplifting help from Heaven, but not for aid that will merely repel an evil adversary like the serpent. The Proud on their figured pilgrimage call out for "cotidiana manna" such as that granted to the Israelites on the "aspro diserto" (*Purg.* XI, 13–14). Somewhat further on, among a band of the Envious, Dante listens as the lady Sapia, wife of Viviano dei Saracini, proclaims the souls citizens

---

23. In *The Book of the Wanderings of Brother Felix Fabri*, trans. Aubrey Stewart (London, 1893), vol. 2, part 2, Fabri maintains that he and his group were guided across the desert by a holy star glimmering above Mt. Sinai. "We . . . directed our steps towards St. Catherine's Star," he writes, "and went towards the south without any road . . ." (p. 507). A similar holy star was reported to have appeared at certain times above the Church of the Holy Sepulchre in Jerusalem. Antoninus Martyr in *Of the Holy Places Visited*, trans. Aubrey Stewart (London, 1887) mentions having seen the star: "When the holy cross is brought forth from its chamber to the atrium of the church to be adored, at the same hour a star appears in heaven and comes above the place where the cross is placed. . . . When the cross is shut up, the star appears no more" (p. 17).

in a true city beyond life. But she quickly realizes that Dante is interested only in those souls that before death lived as pilgrims in Italy.

> "O frate mio, ciascuna è cittadina
> d'una vera città; ma tu vuo' dire
> che vivesse in Italia peregrina."
>
> [*Purg.* XIII, 94–96]

> ["Oh brother mine, each one is a citizen
> of a true city; but you would say
> that lived a pilgrim in Italy."]

Sinful Christians converting their souls on the higher ledges of Mt. Purgatory display ever-increasing haste as they rush to obtain the full blessings of this true city, the goal of Exodus travel. The Gluttonous, for example, hurry by each other in a way compared to the "peregrin" passing one another on the road:

> Sì come i peregrin pensosi fanno,
> giugnendo per cammin gente non nota,
> che si volgono ad essa e non restanno,
>   così di retro a noi, più tosto mota,
> venendo e trapassando, ci ammirava
> d'anime turba tacita e devota.
>
> [*Purg.* XXIII, 16–21]

> [Even as musing pilgrims do,
> who overtaking strangers on the way,
> turn round to them without stopping,
>   so behind us, moving more quickly,
> coming and passing by, a throng of spirits,
> silent and devout, gazed wondering upon us.]

These are the people, Dante remarks, who "perdè Jerusalemme" through their appetites (*Purg.* XXIII, 29), for he thinks of them in terms of the Jewess Mary who, in that city, killed and devoured her child during the siege of Titus.

Just below the Earthly Paradise on the uppermost ledge of the purgatorial mountain, the Lustful hastily kiss one another and dash forward crying out the names of cities whose supposed locations, only a few miles from Jerusalem, were regularly pointed out to earthly Christians on the last stages of the Exodus pilgrimage. "Soddoma e Gomorra" chant the Lustful in their shame and degradation (*Purg.* XXVI, 40).

Quite early in the *Purgatorio*, Dante makes an announcement that leaves no doubt about regions in which this twofold action occurs. The equator, Dante says, passes equidistant between the hot lands frequented by the Hebrews and the site of Mt. Purgatory island (*Purg.* IV, 76–84). In the poet's words, the equator

". . . quinci si parte
verso settentrïon, quando li Ebrei
vedevan lui verso la calda parte."

[*Purg.* IV, 82–84]

[". . . departs here
towards the North, as far as the Hebrews
used to see it towards the hot climes."]

And one already knows from Virgil's comments in *Purgatorio* II, that the locale of the Hebrews' Exodus near the middle of the earth is opposite Mt. Purgatory at the antipodes. Thus in the poem geography reinforces typology.

Dante's sins are purged one by one as he climbs God's holy mountain, and the ascent of the poet concludes once he reaches the Jerusalem of the Earthly Paradise on the summit. Because an analysis of this figured setting and the incidents taking place in it will be made later, one now has only to note that Dante in Eden at last encounters his lady Beatrice and, with her close at hand, sees visions of the Church Militant. Beatrice admonishes the poet to carry within him pictures of all that he has observed

. . . per quello
che si reca il bordon di palma cinto.

[*Purg.* XXXIII, 77–78]

[. . . for the reason
that the pilgrim's staff is brought back wreathed with palm.]

The poet is now likened to those pilgrims who, after having arrived at the Holy City from Egypt, return home bearing staffs wrapped with palms.

In *Paradiso* I, Beatrice performs the initial action that launches the poet on a final voyage to "la porta di San Pietro": she lifts her eyes to the sun. "Never did eagle look so fixedly thereon" (*Par.* I, 48: "aguglia sì non li s'affise unquanco"), writes the poet, for God's light is the element which invariably draws the fixed gaze of both Beatrice and the eagle of Rome. Following the example of his lady, Dante in the second action of the *Paradiso* looks upward, his eyebeams racing above "like as a pilgrim whose will is to return" (*Par.* I, 51: "pur come pelegrin che tornar vuole"). Dante's use of the term "pelegrin" at this point is noteworthy; the word emphasizes once again that it will be as a pilgrim that the poet journeys back to his spiritual home.

The pervasive imagery of water and light used to depict a pilgrimage of return is apparent even in this opening canto of the *Paradiso*. The third action that is performed, the movement of Dante's eyes from the sun to Beatrice, results in the poet's claiming that his interior state is like that of Glaucus who, according to Ovid, leaped into the sea after eating a herb that had revived a fish.

> Nel suo aspetto tal dentro mi fei,
> qual si fé Glauco nel gustar de l'erba
> che 'l fé consorto in mar de li altri dèi.
>
> [*Par.* I, 67–69]

> [Gazing on her so I became within,
> as was Glaucus, tasting of the grass
> that made him a sea-fellow of the other gods.]

Dante, like Glaucus taking a plunge into water, now sets forth on his voyage through the nine revolving spheres to the timeless Empyrean. As the mind of the poet is lifted to the spheres and he hears their music, he observes that the sun illuminates so vast an expanse of Heaven "that rain nor river ever / made a lake so wide distended" (*Par.* I, 80–81: "che pioggia o fiume / lago non fece alcun tanto disteso"). God's light, then, is said to be more efficacious than rain or river; it reveals to the traveler visible realms more spacious than any lake upon earth. In explaining the order of these realms to Dante, Beatrice calls them "the great sea of being" (*Par.* I, 113: "lo gran mar de l'essere"). All things incline by instinct, says Beatrice, to appropriate places located at varying degrees of proximity from God who is their goal (*Par.* I, 103–107).

> onde si muovono a diversi porti
> per lo gran mar de l'essere, e ciascuna
> con istinto a lei dato che la porti.
>
> [*Par.* I, 112–114]

[Thus they move to diverse ports
over the great sea of being, and each one
with a given instinct to bear it on.]

This "istinto" is said to knit the earth together, to lift fire toward
the moon, to move the hearts of mortal creatures, and to carry
creatures of intellect and love toward their end (*Par.* I, 115–120).

Having been compared to a pilgrim returning home and to a
person leaping into the sea, Dante, in accord with Beatrice's
comments, can also be viewed as a man of intellect and love moving across a sea of being toward a suitable port. Eventually he will
arrive at Heaven's white rose in which Beatrice will be seen gazing
upon God. And in Dante's voyage toward Beatrice and what she
terms "nostra città" (*Par.* XXX, 130) of the eternal rose, one discerns the reflected voyage of an earthly pilgrim toward the eternal
city of Rome.

Dante, in the following cantos of the *Paradiso,* turns his eyes
upon one celestial body after another while soaring through space
just as a Christian pilgrim on earth, returning from the Holy Land
to Rome, stares deep into the sky and waters while sailing silently
over the sea. Sometimes vapors and cloudlike substances obscure
the vision of the pilgrims in the two worlds, but the sense of water
and light is always present. The moon itself is like a dense, shimmering cloud; it receives Dante and Beatrice "as water doth receive
a ray of light" (*Par.* II, 35–36: "com' acqua recepe / raggio di
luce"); the souls in the moon appear as persons reflected in water
(*Par.* III, 11–12). The light of souls near the planet Venus is seen
through a chill cloud (*Par.* VIII, 19–24). In the sun the sounds of
blessed spirits are said to be like the vibrations of a ship (*Par.* XIV,
1–3). Flaming lights within Mars perform movements in a cloud
(*Par.* XVIII, 34–37). The sound of flowing water is heard in the
same planet following the singing of souls (*Par.* XX, 19–21). And
when the voice of St. John pauses in the Stellar Heaven, the silence
is compared to that following the withdrawal of oars from water
(*Par.* XXV, 130–135); here Dante is said to lift his head to Beatrice
as spray presses upward against a wind (*Par.* XXVI, 85–90). And
in following the course of Dante's twofold voyage through the vast
sea of being, numerous other examples of related light and water
imagery can be found.

Nearing the outside limits of the physical universe in the sphere of the fixed stars, the poet, before soaring into the Primum Mobile which lacks clear physical "place" (*Par.* xxvii, 109–111), looks back upon the Book of God's Works below. This last glimpse of the earth from celestial space is indeed significant, for it comes at a moment when Dante grows conscious through rumination and conversation of exactly where he has been and exactly where he has yet to go. In the *Vita Nuova* he had written of a twofold earthly and otherworldly sojourn that inspired an initial conception of the long pilgrimage in the *Commedia;* and now as he prepares to leave the physical Book of God's Works, he takes note of his position. Dante becomes aware of the Primum Mobile far above, a sphere having its

> . . . interna riva
> tanto distante, che la sua parvenza,
> là dov' io era, ancor non appariva.
>
> [*Par.* xxiii, 115–117]

> [. . . inner shore
> so distant that from
> there where I was, it had not yet appeared to me.]

This is the "riva" or shore bordering the heavenly realm in which Dante will see the eternal city of the rose. And the poet next stares below upon a twofold pilgrimage route that had only been vaguely suggested at the termination of the *Vita Nuova.* Like many another traveler in every age, the poet reviews his possible intinerary before he sets out and his actual itinerary after he arrives.

As Dante looks down upon what he terms the "aiuola" or threshing floor of earth (*Par.* xxvii, 86), he first gazes westward beyond Cadiz in Spain toward "the mad way / which Ulysses took" (*Par.* xxvii, 82–83: "il varco / folle d'Ulisse"). The way taken by Ulysses was mad, as has been shown, because this proud man while alive sailed beyond the human limits of the Pillars of Hercules and drowned off the coast of Mt. Purgatory at the antipodes. The poet next looks eastward "on this side, hard by the shore / where Europa made herself a sweet burden" (*Par.* xxvii, 83–84: "di qua presso il lito / nel qual si fece Europa dolce carco"), nearly to the eastern Mediterranean coast of Phoenicia, that coast from which Jupiter, manifesting himself as a bull, carried off the lady Europa on his shoulders. Given this exalted view, the poet's approximate position in the physical universe can be quickly located. On medieval Sallust and Beatus type T-O *mappaemundi* with detailed geographical projections, the eternal city of Rome is drawn midway between the Pillars of Hercules to the west and the Holy City of Jerusalem, drawn always close to the line of the Phoenician coast, to the east. The poet in the fixed stars, then, is high above Rome, the position in which traditional Dante commentary has also placed him.[24] Since the Roman church's first bishop, St. Peter, is the first and last person encountered by Dante in the stars, and since St. Peter condemns the corruption of the Roman papacy just before the poet looks below, one realizes that Dante is very appropriately located over the "seat" of those popes castigated by the Saint.

In gazing west along the sea course followed by Ulysses to the isle of Mt. Purgatory, Dante is tracing with his eyes the first segment of the pilgrimage route also sailed by the souls in *Purgatorio* II, who left from the "marina" or seashore at the River Tiber's mouth near Rome. By traveling over the general course outlined by Ulysses in *Inferno* XXVI, these souls, like the pagan hero, would have had to voyage close to the shores of Spain and Morocco (*Inf.* XXVI, 103–104), through the "narrow pass, where Hercules / assigned his landmarks" (*Inf.* XXVI, 107–108: "foce stretta / dov' Ercule segnò li suoi riguardi"), and across the ocean of the southern hemisphere to the antipodes. Continuing their pilgrimage beyond life, souls such as these climb Mt. Purgatory in order to expiate their sins; and when their purgatorial punishment is complete, they fly upward to Heaven as the lower part of Mt. Purgatory quakes and souls on the mountain sing "Glorïa in excelsis Deo" (*Purg.* XX, 136). Virgil on the fifth terrace of the mountain says,

> Tremaci quando alcuna animo monda
> sentesi, sì che surga o che si mova
> per salir sù; e tal grido seconda.
>
> [*Purg.* XXI, 58–60]

24. Edward Moore in *Studies in Dante: Third Series* (Oxford, 1919), pp. 62–71, sums up persuasive arguments to show that Dante is over the city of Rome. William Warren Vernon also presents arguments for this view in *Readings on the Paradiso of Dante*, rev. ed. (London, 1909), 2 : 349–351.

[It quakes here when some soul feels herself
cleansed, so that she may rise up, or set forth,
to mount on high, and such a shout follows her.]

Dante in his pilgrimage beyond has passed over the greater part
of the otherworldly pathway, although there is no reference in the
Commedia to his sailing from the Tiber's mouth to Mt. Purgatory.
In *Inferno* I, the poet simply moves from a wood in life over "the
pass that no one ever left alive" (*Inf.* I, 26–27); and like a man
emerging from dangerous waters, he arrives on the "piaggia
diserta" (*Inf.* I, 29) near an unidentified mountain (*Inf.* II, 120).

When amid the stars Dante turns his gaze toward the Phoenician
coast to the east, the poet's line of vision extends over the general
course taken by the pilgrim ships that for centuries carried Christians, after their visit to Jerusalem, from Phoenicia toward Rome.
And in voyaging from the Jerusalem of Eden through "lo gran mar
de l'essere" (*Par.* I, 113) to a place among the fixed stars high
above the city of Rome, Dante fulfills in the world beyond the
earthly journey of a Christian who moves from the Holy City to a
"riva" near the gates of St. Peter below.

It is among the fixed stars, one will recall, that the first stage of
Dante's reflected earthly pilgrimage is also mentioned; Beatrice
here announces to St. James that the poet has made the trip from
Egypt to Jerusalem (*Par.* xxv, 52–57). Though this blessed lady
speaks as well of the pilgrimage route leading to the shrine of St.
James in Spain, it is significant that she makes no mention of the
poet's having taken this particular path. Other pilgrims, she makes
clear, go to Galicia. Cries Beatrice upon initially seeing St. James,

> . . . "Mira, mira: ecco il barone
> per cui là giù si vicita Galizia".

> [*Par.* xxv, 17–18]

> [. . . "Look! look! behold the Saint
> for whose sake, down below, they seek Galicia".]

On the other hand, both St. Peter and St. James, who hover as
flames over Rome, appear to be associated like Dante with earthly
visits to Jerusalem. The poet addresses St. Peter as one who "didst
overcome more youthful feet drawing / anigh the sepulchre"
(*Par.* xxiv, 125–126: "vincesti / ver' lo sepulcro piu giovani

piedi"). And St. James declares that the virtue of Hope followed him "even to the palm and issuing from the field" (*Par.* xxv, 84: "infin la palma e a l'uscir del campo"). Obviously, St. James alludes to the palm of triumph won because he died a martyr in the Holy Land. Yet because the virtue of Hope is said to have drawn Dante from Egypt to Jerusalem so that he can see (*Par.* xxv, 52–57), it is possible that St. James is being identified with early pilgrims who carried a palm of triumph to that often embattled Holy City. From other passages in the *Paradiso,* one can even determine where on this earth Dante had been before passing into the other world and into a twofold pilgrimage, and where among the living the poet hopes to go after his twofold journey is over. St. Peter in the fixed stars asserts that the poet "shall return below once more" (*Par.* xxvii, 65: "ancor giù tornerai"), and Dante expresses his desire to go eventually back to Florence, that sheephold in which he was baptised into the faith. Dante's intention is that

> con altra voce omai, con altro vello
> ritornerò poeta, e in sul fonte
> del mio battesmo prenderò 'l capello.
>
> [*Par.* xxv, 7–9]

> [with changed voice now, and with changed fleece
> I shall return, a poet, and at the font
> of my baptism I shall assume the chaplet.]

The poet in Heaven speaks of himself as a person

> . . . che al divino da l'umano,
> a l'eterno dal tempo era venuto,
> e di Fiorenza in popol giusto e sano.
>
> [*Par.* xxxi, 37–39]

> [. . . who to the divine from the human,
> to the eternal from time had passed,
> and from Florence to a people just and sane.]

Whether the just and sane society into which Dante passes exists on earth or among the redeemed in Heaven—and the second possibility seems most likely—there can be no doubt that the poet had been in his native city at some time before his movement from the human world to the divine, from time to the eternal.

From Florence to Egypt, Jerusalem, Rome, and possibly back to

Florence—this is the poet's complete Great Circle itinerary, the Egypt-Jerusalem-Rome portion of the tour taking place during the Golden Jubilee pilgrimage year of 1300 and so meriting extraordinary indulgences. The first and last stages of the trip, the voyage from Florence and the possible return to that city, represent a journey in life set before and after the time period in which the central twofold pilgrimage beyond occurs in the *Commedia*.

Following his miraculous ascent from sphere to sphere, Dante, from his position in the fixed stars, has been noted to observe the distant shore of the Primum Mobile just prior to testifying to his complete acceptance of Christ and the theological virtues; and during his examination on these virtues, the shore is for a time forgotten. Only after the questioning concludes does the poet speak of his being placed by the consciousness of God upon the "riva" or shore of right love (*Par.* xxvi, 63). Immediately thereafter, Beatrice and the redeemed burst into song chanting, "Santo, santo, santo!" (*Par.* xxvi, 69); in the next canto the poet soars upward to the Primum Mobile and toward the rose of Heaven.

The conclusion of Dante's voyage in the *Commedia* is strikingly similar to that of the sigh in the *Vita Nuova;* the sigh travels beyond the sphere to Beatrice, while in the world below, pilgrims with Rome as their goal move into Beatrice's unnamed earthly city. In the *Commedia* Beatrice is now associated with an eternal city both in this world and in Heaven; Dante moves beyond the sphere to Beatrice's city of the rose and sees within it his lady staring at God. Reflected in these actions is the Christian pilgrim entering into and looking upon Rome. And if in the *Vita Nuova* the pilgrims on earth sought as the end of their Rome pilgrimage the viewing of the Veronica, the reader finds that Dante compares one of his last acts in the *Paradiso* to this holy experience.

The poet's vision of the rose takes place in stages. As Dante stares at it for the first time, he sees the ranked figures within all looking at the threefold light of a single star nearby, the visible manifestation of Three Persons in One God (*Par.* xxxi, 25–30). He then confesses himself as stupefied by the sight as were northern barbarians looking upon the mighty works of Rome when the "Lateran transcended mortal things" (*Par.* xxxi, 35–36: "Laterano / a le cose mortali andò di sopra"). Since the Lateran was named after a Roman family and served as the palace of the early Roman emperors, the simile primarily associates Dante's surprise with that of uncouth residents of the empire seeing the imperial city possibly before the time of Christ. But since the Lateran was also later the palace of the popes and the alleged mother church of Christianity, it has been suggested that the barbarians' astonishment might appropriately mirror that of rude and uneducated Christians confronted by the eternal city.[25] In any case, the simile is introduced directly after the description of the blessed in the rose gazing upon the star of God. And in the Lateran visitors to Rome in Dante's time gazed in a similar fashion upon an especially revered iconographic image of God that was said not to be made by mortal hands.[26] The icon, possibly dating from the fourth century, was displayed in the poet's period in that Lateran Church rebuilt by Pope Sergius III after A.D. 896; the relic still survives and is venerated in a chapel building near the present-day Lateran. Like the rose in Heaven, the Lateran transcends mortal things because it can be understood to be the home of God's eternal city and church. And if an image of the Creator can be seen by figures in the rose, so can God's image also be seen by pilgrims in the Lateran.

After Dante's first sight of the rose, Beatrice vanishes from the poet's side. She reappears in the rose, smiles down on the poet, and turns her eyes toward God—the posture in which she was last described in the *Vita Nuova*. Replacing the lady alongside Dante is St. Bernard, the cleric who by tradition had seen mystical visions of the Creator. St. Bernard's face is spiritually illuminated by the experience of vision, and Dante compares his own viewing of the face to that of a person seeing "our Veronica" (*Par.* XXXI, 104: "Veronica nostra"). Inspired by the saint's visage, Dante looks back again to the rose where he observes the blessed ordered about the Virgin Mary. To the Virgin's right sits St. Peter, who had examined the poet on the subject of faith in the realm of the fixed stars. Peter is described as

25. N. Zingarelli in *Dante e Roma*, pp. 21–23, discusses the Lateran in relation to the pilgrimage tradition. He suggests that the corruption of Rome in Dante's time would have caused the poet to write of how the Lateran once towered above mortal things.

26. See Thurston, *The Holy Year of Jubilee*, pp. 172–178; and Johannes Baptist v. Toth, *Die Kathedrale des Papstes* (Freiburg, Roma, and Wien, 1966), pp. 199–215.

> . . . quel padre vetusto
> di Santa Chiesa a cui Cristo le chiavi
> raccomandò di questo fior venusto.
>
> [*Par.* xxxii, 124–126]

> [. . . that ancient Father of Holy Church
> to whom Christ entrusted the keys
> to this lovely flower.]

As Dante watches, the Virgin Mary moves her eyes toward God, and the poet, imitating her action, sees at last the Beatific Vision.

The *Commedia* understandably contains no reflected pilgrimage analogues on earth exactly comparable to that vision, yet actions in this world do approximate actions above taking place just before the final viewing of God. In the foreground of the realm beyond, Dante observes the radiant face of St. Bernard appearing as the Veronica. And in the background St. Peter sits within the eternal city of the rose. He holds keys to a flower that encompasses all the blessed and contains honored thrones for Beatrice and Mary (*Par.* xxxii, 124–126). So too the pilgrim in Rome sees the Veil of Veronica exposed at St. Peter's, the church dedicated to the apostle who was given the spiritual keys of Heaven and Hell. The church lies within an eternal city, and in a spiritual sense the church encompasses all the blessed including Beatrice and Mary. For Beatrice's city beyond the sphere is the Rome of the eternal rose; her city below the sphere, the place to which Dante journeys in the *Purgatorio,* is the Jerusalem of the Earthly Paradise.

Viewed in perspective, Dante's attempted and actual pilgrimage to grace and vision takes place in the first two cantos of the *Inferno* and throughout the *Purgatorio* and *Paradiso.* The literal sense of the pilgrimage there beyond reveals Dante, in the prologue to the *Inferno,* moving into a region beyond life and attempting unsuccessfully to climb from a desert shore up a mountain. In the *Purgatorio* the poet ascends a mountain identified as Mt. Purgatory at the antipodes; and in the *Paradiso* he soars from Mt. Purgatory's summit beyond the sphere to Beatrice and God.

A single Christian pilgrim, in the foreshadowing pilgrimage here, is turned back at the beginning of the *Inferno* in his attempted movement over the Sinai deserts and mountains on the Exodus route from Egypt to Jerusalem. After descending to the

Egypt of this world in the *Inferno*, the Christian in the **Purgatorio** succeeds in climbing uphill over the globe to Jerusalem, located at the center of the earth on Mt. Sion opposite Mt. Purgatory.
In the *Paradiso* the pilgrim sails from Jerusalem to Rome and
there gazes upon the Veronica at St. Peter's.

The *Commedia*, then, points back to this world, but not as has
been claimed to a world that is essentially secular. The pilgrimage
pathway revealed here below is the most blessed that living men
can tread, for it passes through the holiest lands, cites, and places
in the entire iconographic Book of God's Works. And the goal of
the journey for the persevering pilgrim is a glimpse in this life of
God's Divine Visage.

3

Three Typological Modes of Dante's *Commedia:* Biblical Imitation, Internal Recurrence, and Worldly Imitation

By avowing that the allegorical technique employed by the early Church Fathers in their exegesis of the biblical Exodus should also be employed in reading the *Commedia,* Dante Alighieri, expounding his allegorical views in epistle x to Can Grande della Scala, provided later commentators with a precise, theoretical statement on the proper critical approach to his poem. Dante's explicit comments on how to read the *Commedia* are well worth considering once more:

> Ad evidentiam itaque dicendorum, sciendum est quod istius operis non est simplex sensus, immo dici potest polysemos, hoc est plurium sensuum; nam primus sensus est qui habetur per literam, alius est qui habetur per significata per literam. Et primus dicitur literalis, secundus vero allegoricus, sive moralis, sive anagogicus. Qui modus tractandi, ut melius pateat, potest considerari in his versibus, "In exitu Israel de Aegypto, domus Iacob de populo barbaro, facta est Iudaea sanctificatio eius, Israel potestas eius." [1]

> [To elucidate, then, what we have to say, be it known that the sense of this work is not simple, but on the contrary it may be termed polysemous, that is to say, "of more senses than one"; for it is one sense that we get through the letter, and another which we get through the thing the letter signifies; and the first is called the literal, but the second allegorical or mystic. And this mode of treatment, for its better manifestation, may be considered in this verse: "When Israel came out of Egypt, and the house of Jacob from a people of strange speech, Judaea became his sanctification, Israel his power."]

The *Commedia,* Dante explains, is to be treated in the same fashion as an episode in Holy Scripture. And for the poet and his contemporaries, the events recorded *in verbis* in the Bible, the eternal Word of God, simply had to signify *in facto* true historical

---

1. *Le Opere di Dante Alighieri,* ed. E. Moore, rev. Paget Toynbee, 4th ed. (Oxford, 1924), pp. 415–416.

events. If the Bible said that "Israel came out of Egypt," then early readers and commentators had no other recourse than to accept on faith that the Israelites really did leave Egypt to begin their forty-year wandering on the Sinai deserts. The literal sense of the Bible pointed to the true event, and figured relations or spiritual senses could only be derived from what was regarded as the indisputable historical fact of that event.

When in following Dante's advice the *Commedia* is approached as this kind of "allegory of the theologians," then the literal sense of the poem, like that of Scripture, must be read as though it signified true historical episodes. The reader, through a willing suspension of disbelief, is asked to regard the sojourn of a single, living poet through Hell, Purgatory, and Heaven as something that actually happened. "The fiction of the *Divine Comedy*," writes Charles Singleton in support of such an interpretation, "is that it is not fiction." [2]

2. "The Irreducible Dove," *Comparative Literature* 9 (1957) : 129. In a very important reading of the *Commedia*, Singleton in *Dante Studies 1: Elements of Structure* (Cambridge, Mass., 1965), pp. 1–17, 84–98, maintains that the *Commedia* is an "allegory of the theologians" with a literal sense which in context should be considered true; he further develops his position in *Dante Studies 2: Journey to Beatrice* (Cambridge, Mass., 1958); " 'In Exitu Israel de Aegypto'," *Seventy-Eighth Annual Report of the Dante Society* (Boston, 1960), pp. 1–24; and " 'Sulla fiumana ove'l mar non ha vanto' (*Inferno* ii, 108)," *Romanic Review* (Dec., 1948), 269–277. The view that the poem is composed as "an allegory of the theologians" is also taken by two other recent commentators whose interests are theological and who read the *Commedia* in the light of traditional biblical exegesis; see John Chydenius, "The Typological Problem in Dante" in *Societas Scientiarum Fannica: Commentationes Humanarum Litterarum* 25 (Helsingfors, 1958) : 1–159; and A. C. Charity, *Events and their Afterlife: The Dialectics of Christian Typology in the Bible and Dante* (Cambridge, England, 1966). Affirming the central significance of the literal sense of the *Commedia*, A. Camilli in "Le figurazioni allegoriche," *Studi Danteschi* 37 (1949) : 197–215, insists that there is no continuously sustained revelation of hidden ideas in the poem. He advises strict adherence to the literal sense, as signifying historical events, and to possible symbolic meanings arising from the literal sense, except in certain instances when abstract allegory seems the only possible explanation of passages. Luigi Pietrobono likewise suggests that in the *Commedia* Dante rejects the traditional medieval allegorism and didacticism to create symbols having wide poetic import: see "Allegoria o arte?" *Giornale Dantesco* 36 (1936) : 85–102. Helmut Hatzfeld in "Modern Literary Scholarship as Reflected in Dante Criticism," in *American Critical Essays on the Divine Comedy* (New York, 1967), states that recent criticism "raises the question whether the literal, eschatological sense of the *Commedia*," which Hatzfeld believes points to true events, "is still open to embellishment by further senses—either the allegorical, moral, and anagogical senses which Dante had in mind." After summing up conflicting views on the issue, Hatzfeld concludes that

Before entering into a detailed theoretical discussion of Dante's allegory, it should be observed that the new reading of Great Circle pilgrimage typology in the *Commedia*, when considered against statements in epistle x, affords solid grounds for believing that the author of the letter should be taken at his word. Serious scholars agree that medieval typology, that allegorical mode used by theologians to discover how in the Bible one historical event foreshadows and is fulfilled in another historical event, depends for its existence upon a literal sense that signifies historical persons, things, and episodes.[3] Thus the words of Scripture point to

Singleton "solves the problem by not overstressing the metaphorical senses, by restricting them to the action rather than to the characters, and by not clinging to them pedantically" (pp. 202–203). An extended and very effective defense of the *Commedia* as an "allegory of the theologians" is available in Robert Hollander's *Allegory in Dante's Commedia* (Princeton, 1969); it should be noted, however, that Hollander argues that the various senses of allegory can be found throughout Dante's poem (pp. 50 f.).

A brief but interesting reading of Dante's poem, which relates typology to medieval conceptions of visionary experience, can be found in Joseph Anthony Mazzeo's "Dante and the Pauline Modes of Vision," *Harvard Theological Review* (Oct., 1957), where the author maintains that Dante in the world beyond life at times shadows earthly persons such as St. Paul and Moses (pp. 297–301). The visionary aspect of the poem, together with comments on medieval allegory and typology, is taken up also by Giorgio Padoan, "La Mirabile Visione di Dante e L'Epistola a Cangrande," *Dante e Roma: Atti Del Convegno di Studi* (Firenze, 1965), pp. 283–314; Romano Guardini, *Über das Wesen des Kunstwerks* (Stuttgart, 1949), pp. 16 f.; and M. Grace Monahan, "Dante's Perception of the Soul's Purgation," *Ursuline Tradition and Progress* 4 (1944) : 23–40.

3. As H. A. Wolfson reveals in *The Philosophy of the Church Fathers* (Cambridge, Mass., 1956), 1 : chap. 2, 22 f., a large number of early Church Fathers in the Near East followed St. Augustine in giving historical, concrete readings to Scripture, and these interpretations depended in large measure upon the figural relation of biblical events. Typological readings of this kind are discussed at length by Fr. Jean Daniélou, *From Shadows to Reality*, trans. W. Hibberd (London, 1960); and Beryl Smalley, *The Study of the Bible in the Middle Ages*, 2nd ed. (Oxford, 1952). An essential and extremely detailed study of medieval figurism and allegory has been compiled by Fr. Henri de Lubac, *Exégèse médiévale, les quatre sens de l'Écriture*, 4 vols. (Paris, 1959–64). An important earlier work, containing a "Table des commentaires bibliques" which lists passages from the Bible interpreted by medieval commentators, has been written by C. Spicq, *Esquisse d'une histoire de l'exégèse latine au moyen âge* (Paris, 1944). Helpful studies of the historical background of medieval allegory can be found in Jean Pépin, *Mythe et Allégorie: Les Origines Grecques et Les Contestations Judéo-Chrétiennes* (Aubier, 1958), and in E. R. Curtius, *European Literature and the Latin Middle Ages* (New York, 1963). For a brief but illuminating statement on medieval figurism, see Erich Auerbach, "Figura," *Archivum Romanicum* 22 (1938) : 436–489, an essay slightly altered and reprinted from *Neue Dantestudien* (Istanbul, 1944). The distinction between figurism and the medieval "allegory of the poets" is

the historical Exodus, the *type;* and the historical Exodus in turn signifies happenings in future biblical history, happenings which represent the *antitype.* If on the other hand the literal sense is a fiction which derives its existence from underlying abstract ideas, that kind of work called an "allegory of the poets" by Dante in the *Convivio,* then the literal sense will, of course, signify the hidden abstract ideas, but it will not, according to medieval criteria, prefigure other historical episodes. Only historical events referred to by the words of a true literal sense can foreshadow through figural association other historical events. And only when the *Commedia* is approached as an "allegory of the theologians" with a literal sense signifying episodes that are assumed to be true can the reader have theoretical assurance, according to medieval notions, that typological relationships are operative in the poem: the words of the poem signify true events in a pilgrimage through the other world, and those events unfolding beyond life in turn shadow an historical Great Circle pilgrimage in this world.

In a poem as long and subtle as the *Commedia,* absolute consistency in the presentation of detail is too much to be expected; still, the definition of a general critical stance toward Dante's allegory—the poem as artifact concealing ideas, or the poem as historical truth signifying ideas, values, and figured relations—is a prerequisite of sophisticated criticism and has far-reaching implications.

Past commentators unfamiliar with the poem's Great Circle

very forcefully made by Erich Auerbach in "Typological Symbolism in Medieval Literature," in *American Critical Essays on the Divine Comedy,* ed. Robert J. Clements (New York, 1967), reprinted from *Yale French Studies* (Sept., 1952): "May I draw the attention of my readers to the important difference which obtains between figurism and other similar forms of thinking such as allegorism or symbolism. In these patterns, at least one of the two elements combined is a pure sign, but in figural relation both the signifying and the signified facts are real and concrete historical events. In an allegory of love or in a religious symbol at least one of the terms does not belong to human history; it is an abstraction or sign. But in the sacrifice of Isaac considered as a figure of the sacrifice of Christ, it is essential, and has been stressed with great vigor, at least in the occidental tradition, that neither the prefiguring nor the prefigured event lose their literal and historical reality by their figurative meaning and interrelation. This is a very important point" (pp. 107–108).

See also E. R. Rust, *The Christian Understanding of History* (London, 1947); and Robert M. Grant, *A Short History of the Interpretation of the Bible,* rev. ed., (New York, 1963).

pilgrimage typology in general have, it seems to me, wrongly approached the *Commedia* as an "allegory of the poets" with a fictive literal sense which veils abstract ideas. Criticism in past years accordingly has developed along two lines: the supposed outward, fictive fable comprising the work's literal sense has been regarded with delight or perturbation as exotic, grotesque, or artistically appropriate— depending upon the commentator's sensibility and the norms of evaluation. The description of Aristotle and Plato before their castle in the *Inferno* may in context be considered quaint, and that of the Gluttons embedded in mire, gruesome; nevertheless, the critic always proceeds in the belief that the outward narrative points to fictitious events devised by a mortal poet to hide various abstract ideas. Effort is then usually centered upon the quest for the concealed abstract truth of the poem, and here the critic can indulge in a certain amount of labeling: in the first canto of the *Inferno*, the dark wood can represent Error, and Virgil, Reason; later Beatrice can represent Theology, and so on throughout the poem. As the labeling continues, the abstractions can be seen to arrange themselves into a gigantic, pyramidal hierarchy with Pure Being at the summit; and the commentator, if he has the capacity, can then dedicate himself to the task of relating and explaining the total ideology of this fascinating philosophical-theological construct.

This generally has been the approach adopted by early commentators on the poem, by writers such as Goethe, Coleridge, and Horace Walpole, by modern readers of popular anthologies, and even by a number of recent scholars including Theophil Spoerri and Fr. P. Mandonnet.[4] Consequently, there has been gathered to-

4. Quotations from commentators who wrote on the *Commedia* in Dante's period and for several centuries afterward have been brought together in the appendix of Robert Hollander's *Allegory in Dante's Commedia*.

A bibliography of important nineteenth-century Dante criticism is available in Karl Vossler's *Medieval Culture: An Introduction to Dante and His Times* (New York, 1958), 2 : 428–429. Although almost all nineteenth-century critics regarded the literal sense of the *Commedia* as a fiction, it should be added that some Victorian commentators so enjoyed drawing maps and charts of the other world, estimating the height, weight, and cubic content of Mt. Purgatory, and plotting to the hour the probable time when almost every major event beyond life occurred, that a true, historical, literal sense might be said to have materialized from their scrupulous calculations. See the nineteenth-century maps, astronomical drawings, dimensional measurements, and time charts collected in Giovanni Agnelli's *Topo-Cronografia del Viaggio Dantesco* (Milano, 1891) ; and see also the diagrams by nineteenth-century

gether over the years an enormous store of lengthy footnotes providing complementary, alternate, or conflicting abstract meanings for most of the important persons, events, objects, and places in the poem. Readers of unflagging determination can proceed directly through the whole of Dante's supposed fable with one eye on the author's text and the other on the scholars' notes, but for less willful mortals interest in either the alleged fiction or the ideas often wanes far short of Beatific Vision. Hell is the domain of the general reader; Paradise the preserve of the expert. Aware of the great weight of abstract meaning that traditional commentators have insisted is borne by Dante's alleged airy fable, one can evince at least a measure of sympathy for T. S. Eliot's unscholarly admonition to new readers of the *Commedia:* first enjoy the imagery; save the meaning until later.[5]

But should one accede to the comments in the letter to Can Grande and interpret the *Commedia* as an "allegory of the theologians," the approach advocated here, then the poem is instantly transformed into a very different kind of work. Gone is the fabulous artifact of past centuries, and in its place stands a compo-

---

scholars in Edoardo Coli's *Il Paradiso Terrestre Dantesco* (Firenze, 1897), figures 20–25.

Theophil Spoerri holds in *Einführung in die göttliche Komödie* (Zurich, 1946) that all senses in the *Commedia* are fictions except the moral which alone is said to be "true." Fr. P. Mandonnet finds numerous ideological meanings "veiled" by the supposedly fictional literal sense of the poem in *Dante le Théologien: Introduction à l'intelligence de la vie, des oeuvres, et de l'art de Dante Alighieri* (Paris, 1935); but Fr. Mandonnet's arguments and conclusions have been comprehensively and, it is not an exaggeration to say, remorselessly attacked by Étienne Gilson who, in *Dante the Philosopher*, trans. David Moore (New York, 1949), avows that at times the literal sense points to historical events.

The traditional view that the literal sense of the *Commedia* is a poetic fiction has been advanced by F. Flamini, *I Significati reconditi della Commedia di Dante e il suo fine supremo* (Livorno, 1903), 1 : 58; (1904) 2 : 1–25. A more recent adherent of this view is Francis Ferguson, *Dante's Drama of the Mind* (Princeton, 1953), pp. 3, 22–29. Allen Gilbert in *Dante and His Comedy* (London, 1963) also avers that the poem is "a work of fiction," and he adds that "fact and fiction may interpenetrate each other. But fiction is the master" (p. 6). For a recent discussion of the supposed iconographic qualities of the angels and certain character-types in the *Purgatorio*, see Enrico De' Negri, "Tema e Iconografia del 'Purgatorio'," *Romanic Review* (April, 1958), pp. 81–104. A useful summary of relatively up-to-date Dante criticism, including readings of the literal sense of the *Commedia* as a fiction, appear in Aldo Vallone's *La Critica Dantesca Contemporanea* (Pisa, 1953).

5. Eliot's comments can be found in "Dante," in *Selected Essays* (London, 1966), p. 242.

sition with a literal sense grounded firmly in reality and history. Images of men and women, thought to be iconographic fictions, suddenly come alive as existing persons with actual identities; many objects and places in the other world now take on a startling new reality. That this realm beyond death is the creation of a poet's imaginative vision cannot be denied. Yet through a willing suspension of disbelief, made possible by this different approach to the poem, one now regards all or most of the beings in the other world—persons, objects, events, landscapes—as having genuine existence within the context of the work. The concentrated search for an inner core of meaning, the supposed truth of the poem, gives way to an awareness of shifting relationships among "real" persons, objects, and landscapes. Often beings in the narrative may be seen to represent only themselves; at other times they may suggest one or more of the traditional spiritual senses of allegory. But as persons and things considered as existing in their own right, they serve most effectively to suggest figural associations and a wide range of symbolic values; and like prisms reflecting rays of multicolored light, they radiate, as the literal narrative unfolds, ever-changing patterns of figural and symbolic meaning.

Certain modern scholars including Bruno Nardi, Luigi Pietrobono, and Colin Hardie have vehemently opposed the view that the work's literal sense signifies historical events.[6] They have maintained that a mortal man would not presume to create a "secular" work with a true literal sense, that only God's Scriptures can be composed of words which signify historical episodes, and that, therefore, Dante would not have written all or at least crucial parts of epistle x.

There is really little need to press far into the inferno of conflicting opinion on the authenticity of the letter. It should simply

6. Bruno Nardi first reviews scholarship on the subject and then attacks the authenticity of the letter in *Il punto sull'Epistola a Cangrande* (Florence, 1960); Colin Hardie in "The Epistle to Cangrande Again," *Deutsches Dante Jahrbuch* 38 (1960) : 51–74, speculates that the letter was probably composed by an "unknown struggling *grammaticus*" after Dante's death (pp. 55–56). In earlier studies the authenticity of the letter was called into question by Luigi Pietrobono, "L'Epistola a Can Grande," in *Nuovi saggi danteschi* (Torino, 1954), pp. 199–244; and by Francesco d'Ovidio, "L'epistola a Cangrande," in *Studii sulla Divina Commedia* (Palermo, 1901), pp. 448–485. Quite recently Allan Gilbert has opposed the view that Dante wrote the epistle in "Did Dante Dedicate the *Paradiso* to Can Grande della Scala?" *Italica* 43 (1966) : 100–124.

be noted that doubts about Dante's authorship have never been proved from external historical evidence. They have been predicated largely on the assumption that Dante must have been using "poetical" allegory of a kind made famous by Prudentius, Martianus Capella, medieval exegetes of classical literature, and later by Spenser and Bunyan; and then this assumption is buttressed by citations of supposed inconsistencies in the letter's internal content. Yet claims for and against the epistle can be tested in a most obvious and crucial way: through a very close application of the allegorical statements in the letter to the *Commedia* itself. If the statements in the epistle are taken seriously, and if one consequently assumes that Dante did imitate God's way of writing by devising an artistic typology of his own, then it seems to me that the internal content of the letter is so applicable to the *Commedia*, and merges so well with comments by Dante in the *Convivio*, that its authenticity is to a large degree established. Even should it be granted that all or parts of the epistle were not composed by the poet, the letter would still serve as an extraordinarily illuminating guide to the typological makeup and structure of the *Commedia*.

Recently Francesco Mazzoni, John Chydenius, A. C. Charity, Charles Singleton, and others have maintained quite convincingly, in the exacting manner of modern critics, that the letter is authentic and that it does most helpfully reveal figural elements in the *Commedia*.[7] But their combined studies have never progressed

7. Mazzoni in "L'Epistola a Cangrande," *Rendiconti dell' Accademia Nazionale dei Lincei* 10, fasc. 3–4 (1955) : 157–198, presents an extremely cogent and careful argument for authenticity taking into account previous scholarship. Using medieval theologians' interpretations of the Bible as background for his views, Chydenius defends Dante's authorship of the epistle in *The Typological Problem in Dante*, pp. 1–159; the same approach is adopted and a similar defense is made in Charity's excellent *Events and their Afterlife*, pp. 11–50, 199–207. Singleton, although he does not delve into historical background materials, offers a detailed theoretical argument for authenticity in the appendix of *Dante Studies I: Elements of Structure*, pp. 84–98. Hollander also provides arguments for the poet's authorship in *Allegory in Dante's Commedia*, pp. 24–53. The early debate on the subject is reviewed by Edward Moore, who concludes that epistle x was written by Dante, in *Studies in Dante: Third Series: Miscellaneous Essays* (Oxford, 1903), pp. 284–369. Helen Dunbar in *Symbolism in Medieval Thought* (New York, 1961), pp. xi–xiii notes that, even if Dante did not write the letter, the ideology which it contains would have been in accord with his thought. For an introduction to the letter and a reproduction of its complete contents, see Nancy Howe, "Dante's Letter to Can Grande," in *Essays on Dante*, ed. Mark Musa (Bloomington, Ind., 1965), pp. 32–47.

In works cited elsewhere (chap. 2, n. 2) and in the respective works cited above, beyond employing the letter to show how *two* biblical events, the Exodus and the Redemption, are figured in the *Commedia,* and how persons and things in this world are shadowed *in figura* in the poem's other world.

A new perspective on the typological structure of the *Commedia* can be gained, it seems to me, from an analysis of how the letter alludes to *three* biblical events or types which foreshadow imitative actions performed by Dante in the poem's other world and by Christian men in this world. These three episodes or types, written in the Book of God's Words and alluded to by Dante in his letter, are the same key events acted out by Christians making a Great Circle pilgrimage through the Book of God's Works. They are the same three events mirrored centrally in the *Commedia.* Moreover, two of these three biblical episodes are used by Dante in his explanation of allegory in the *Convivio.* Thus if one major thesis of this study is correct, it will be seen from a cumulative, interrelated argument that Dante based his artistic typology in large measure upon a figural imitation of these three events as he found them inscribed in both the Books of God's Words and Works; and a consistent, interwoven pattern of key types will be disclosed relating epistle x, the *Convivio,* the *Commedia,* the Bible, and the World.

Such an analysis will show, in addition, that Dante's account of the other world draws its literal truth, not from the independent wisdom of the author or from analogical similarities with the Bible and the world, but from its figural association with episodes signified in both the Books of God's Words and Works; for there is, as A. C. Charity has rightly stated, a degree of "historical de-

---

Fr. Dunstan Tucker, John Freccero, Charles Singleton, Robert Hollander, and A. C. Charity have all used the letter to suggest an Exodus motif in the *Commedia;* Singleton and others, turning to the epistle and also to the poem, have also placed stress upon the Redemption motif in the *Commedia,* as has Thomas M. Greene in "Dramas of Selfhood in the Comedy," in *From Time to Eternity: Essays on Dante's Divine Comedy,* ed. Thomas G. Bergin (New Haven and London, 1967), pp. 103–136. Speaking of what he calls Dante's "retrospective vision" of earth implied by passages about the *Commedia* in the letter, Greene, noting allusions in the letter to the Exodus, writes, "Now it has generally been assumed that Dante did not choose this scriptural passage as his example arbitrarily but rather meant to suggest that redemption was also the theme of his own work. If we accept this assumption, as I think we should, we are left with two subjects—one, the dynamic, involving a process, redemption, and the other, the static subject, the state of souls after death" (p. 117). Despite his use of the word "static" to refer to the state of souls after death, Greene reveals in his essay how the actions of dead souls disclose character traits and moral values.

pendency and continuity between the events which typology relates." [8] Dante and the souls beyond life act out, fulfill, and so embody *in figura* those absolutely true earthly episodes that the Divine Author himself has caused to be written. And for a poet holding Dante's typological views, there could be no doubt of the basic figural veracity of a work so conceived.

To discover the important scriptural types and the various figural modes alluded to by Dante in his letter, it is essential to recall once more very briefly the poet's much discussed conception of biblical allegory. Dante in his letter follows St. Thomas Aquinas in the *Summa Theologica* in enumerating the four traditional senses of medieval scriptural allegory: the literal (historical), the allegorical (typological), the moral (tropological), and the mystical (anagogical).[9] The first sense, the literal or historical, requires no further explanation; and the second sense, the allegorical or typological, will for the moment be passed over. The third sense, the moral or tropological, as traditionally employed draws an ethical maxim from the episodes signified by the literal sense, and this moral sense is circumscribed in its meaning by the specific historical events from which it issues. The fourth sense, the mystical or anagogical, according to traditional usage derives a meaning from the signified historical events which relates them to eternal glory, that is, to the timeless afterlife.

In the writings of Dante and St. Thomas on scriptural exegesis, the term "allegory" has two meanings: it is employed in a general way to denote all three spiritual senses which arise from the single, historical sense of Scripture; but it is also used in a different manner to denote the second of the four senses, the typological or figural. And here some clarification may be necessary. From remarks

8. Charity, *Events and their Afterlife*, p. 199.

9. See the *Summa Theologica*, vol. 1, part 1, article 10, responses 1–3. A discussion of St. Thomas Aquinas' allegorical conceptions can be found in William G. Madsen's *From Shadowy Types to Truth* (New Haven and London, 1968), pp. 22–53. For recent, comprenhesive studies of the four senses of medieval biblical allegory and their use by Dante, see Chydenius, *The Typological Problem in Dante*; Charity, *Events and their Afterlife*; and Hollander, *Allegory in Dante's Commedia*. A briefer discussion of Dante's allegory can be found in Olaf Graf's *Die Divina Comedia als Zeugnis des Glaubens Dante Und die Liturgie* (Freiburg, Basel, and Wien, 1965), pp. 105–161. Fr. Jean Daniélou in *Sacrementum Futuri: Études sur les origines de la typologie biblique* (Paris, 1950) presents the historical background to traditional medieval allegory with emphasis upon typology.

already made about this second sense, it has been suggested, but not emphasized, that typology reveals how biblical events point through figural relations in two directions.

First, the historical episodes signified by the words of Scripture have been seen to prefigure other important events in the established, public chronology of biblical history. For as is well known, the Church Fathers divided the whole of meaningful Christian history into typological epochs among which were the Fall of Adam and Eve from Eden, the Exodus of the chosen people from the Promised Land, the Redemption of man through Christ, the Second Coming of Christ and the Last Judgment, and the soul's eternal bliss in the heavenly kingdom of God. But a wide time gap separated such preordained events. To bind together these and other holy episodes scattered through the eons of past and future time, the Church Fathers, using the Bible as their primary source work, spun an ingenious web of typological relations and so linked *in figura* the successive epochs of history.

Second, typology was utilized to disclose how a biblical event prefigured actions that could be performed in the lives of Christian men. Figurism of this kind, which is in fact no more than the typological unfolding of Christian history in the present rather than in the past and future, has for reasons of lucidity been called "applied typology" by A. C. Charity. Past and future biblical episodes, in the words of Charity, "relate to the 'now' of decision" for man in this immediate epoch of Christian history.[10] They confront man with an existential choice; and man must decide to imitate the prefigured episodes to gain spiritual fulfillment from them. The failure of many critics fully to perceive that figurism points to man in the present, as well as to scriptural episodes in the past and future, has been responsible, in my opinion, for the restricted way in which Dante's letter has been interpreted.

10. Charity studies "applied typology" and its uses by early Church Fathers in *Events and their Afterlife*, pp. 179–207. He takes issue with a number of modern commentators for whom, he believes, typology is a "wooden, mechanical game of contrivance which may or may not have some validity in so far as it shows that there is a correspondence between historical realities at different stages in sacred history. . . . Lamp, Phythian-Adams, Hebert, Daniélou, de Lubac, almost all the contemporary defenders of 'typology,' ignore its critical character as the 'word' of God's act—more exactly, of his new act—which faces the present with an existential decision and a call to existence" (p. 58).

Given this awareness of biblical typology, it is now possible to demonstrate how Dante, following the example, among others, of Latin hymnologists in the Carolingian period and of anonymous authors of medieval mystery plays, applied the theologians' techniques to purposes other than scriptural explication and developed an original artistic typology. This unique artistic typology, it has been noted, extends far beyond the confines of biblical scenes, the events and persons beyond life figuring the entire range of holy and secular human history in this world.[11] Mirrored images of pagan, Roman, contemporaneous, and future earthly history are, however, set within the dominating pattern of Judaic-Christian biblical episodes, the whole constituting the poet's shadowed vision of universal Christian history as disclosed primarily through the Books of God's Words and Works. But to give dramatic unity to the shadowed diversity of human history in the *Commedia*, to embrace the staggering variety of earthly life within some general sequence of events, it has been shown that Dante had recourse to the typology of a Great Circle pilgrimage; and the various modes of the poet's figurism, as referred to both directly and indirectly in letter x, can rather arbitrarily be disentangled and explained un-

11. This comprehensive view of Dante's figurism underscores the numerous studies of Auerbach and his followers. The main thesis of Auerbach's work on Dante can in some measure be illustrated by quoting excerpts from "Typological Symbolism in Medieval Literature" in *American Critical Essays on the Divine Comedy*. After discussing the medieval figural tradition, Auerbach comments, "Dante's mind was deeply rooted in this tradition, and I believe that not only many particular passages in the *Commedia* can be explained in this manner, but that the whole conception of the great poem has to be considered from this angle. . . . Dante is not the first to subject all the material of human history to the figural conception; Biblical history, Jewish and Christian, came to be seen as universal human history, and all pagan historical material had to be inserted and adapted to this framework" (*Critical Essays*, p. 108). Auerbach observes, however, that Dante was unique in creating characters that preserved their strength and individual shape beyond the grave. "Earlier poets," the critic writes, "never used figurism in such a universal and audacious manner; they confined figurative treatment in most cases to the poetical illustration of sacred history; figurative interpretation of other events or of life in general was mostly unconscious" (p. 110).

See also Auerbach's *Mimesis: The Representation of Reality in Western Literature*, trans. Willard Trask (New York, 1957), pp. 151–177, 191–203; and *Dante: Poet of the Secular World*, trans. Ralph Manheim (Chicago, 1961). Joseph Anthony Mazzeo comments on Dante's use of a "private" typology, developed from traditional typological techniques, in "Dante and Epicurus: The Making of a Type," *Medieval Cultural Tradition in Dante's Commedia* (Ithaca, 1960), pp. 174–204.

der three main headings: the typologies of biblical imitation, internal recurrence, and worldly imitation.

In creating an artistic typology of biblical imitation, Dante discerned that, if living Christians could be joined *in figura* to biblical episodes by somehow imitating them, then the depicted persons or souls in a poem could also act out and so benefit from these episodes. Objects and landscapes beyond, moreover, might also fulfill earthly models mentioned in biblical accounts. This kind of typology calls the reader's associative powers into play; a pattern of biblical action must be uncovered, a figural relation noticed between scriptural history "outside" the poem and the real action within.

This mode of artistic typology can be detected from Dante's remarks in epistle x on the spiritual senses of biblical allegory:

> Nam si ad literam solam inspiciamus, significatur nobis exitus filiorum Israel de Aegypto, tempore Moysi; si ad allegoriam, nobis significatur nostra redemptio facta per Christum; si ad moralem sensum, significatur nobis conversio animae de luctu et miseria peccati ad statum gratiae: si ad anagogicum, significatur exitus animae sanctae ab huius corruptionis servitute ad aeternae gloriae libertatem. Et quamquam isti sensus mystici variis appellentur nominibus, generaliter omnes dici possunt allegorici, quum sint a literali sive historiali diversi. Nam allegoria dicitur ab alleon graece, quod in latinum dicitur alienum, sive diversum.

> [For if we inspect the letter alone, the departure of the children of Israel from Egypt in the time of Moses is presented to us; if the allegory, our redemption wrought by Christ; if the moral sense, the conversion of the soul from the grief and misery of sin to the state of grace is presented to us; if the anagogical, the departure of the holy soul from the slavery of this corruption to the liberty of eternal glory is presented to us. And although these mystic senses have each their special denominations, they may all in general be called allegorical, since they differ from the literal and historical. Now allegory is so called from "alleon" in Greek, which means in Latin "alieum" or "diversum."]

This passage indicates that the spiritual senses of the historical Exodus do in fact apply to all living persons. They point directly at "us" and at Dante and at every man. The allegorical sense presents "our Redemption"; the moral, "the conversion of the soul";

and the angogical, "the departure of the holy soul from the slavery and corruption of this world to the liberty of eternal glory." And it is of "our" soul and the souls of all men that the poet is speaking.

If the states of the soul disclosed by the spiritual senses are arranged according to their hierarchical importance, there takes shape another of those "spiritual ladders to salvation" so common to medieval literature. On the first step of the ladder, the soul is converted from sin to grace; on the second, the soul next "receives Christ" through enjoyment of the spiritual benefits of the Redemption; and on the third, the soul, having been freed from the corruption of this world, enters into the spiritual realm of eternal glory.

Of these three steps necessary for "our" soul's movement upward to eternal glory, the first step, the moral conversion of the soul from sin to grace, is very immediately figured in the historical event of the Exodus itself. In the patterned, literal movement of the Israelites from a worldly land to a Holy City there is manifest an *exemplum* of right conduct that can serve as a guide to "us" and to Dante in pilgrimages through life. By acting now in imitation of the Exodus, the moral sense of the event is embodied in "us" spiritually, and there is established at the same time a figural relation between the foreshadowing type, the biblical episode, and its fulfilled antitype, "our" conduct.

Spiritual fulfillment *in figura* deriving from behavior modeled after the Exodus, however, is obviously limited by the dispensation of the Old Law to the soul's conversion. The Exodus itself can signify the moral and anagogical senses of allegory; it can also prefigure through the typological sense both New Testament episodes and "our" future moral conduct. But when a figural relation links the literal actions of a man to an historical biblical occurrence like the Exodus, the degree of the man's spiritual benefit normally cannot be expected to exceed that intrinsic to the original event. Thus "our" actions patterned after the Exodus prefigure but do not fulfill the promise of the New Testament Redemption of man by Christ. To attain complete spiritual fulfillment in this life, mortal man, every time he falls into sin, must act out and fulfill in sequence several gradated spiritual occurrences that carry him step by step upward to eternal glory.

The second necessary spiritual step that "we" must take, according to the figural content of the letter, is imitation of Christ's Redemption, a New Testament event prefigured by the Exodus. Having attained the conversion of the soul by acting out an Old Law episode, "we" must receive Christ and his grace under the New. But before taking a third step, "we" must discover yet another biblical event, one foreshadowed by the Exodus and implied in the letter, which like the Exodus signifies through its anagogical sense the promise of the soul's movement from "this corruption to the liberty of eternal glory," a movement that might be expected to terminate in Beautific Vision.

One may perhaps remember, as Dante did when he wrote the *Commedia*, that an important biblical episode traditionally thought to point to the soul's future ascent to Beatific Vision is the New Testament Transfiguration of Christ before the Apostles Peter, John, and James on Mt. Tabor. And the time-honored prefiguring type for the Transfiguration resides in certain actions performed by Moses during the historical Exodus. That Old Testament leader, leaving the corruption of this world behind, ascended a holy mountain of God, received the most important commandments of the Old Law, and through the world's darkness, gazed upon the image of the Creator. Origin in his *Homilies on Exodus* provides a typical statement on how the vision of Moses on Mt. Sinai prefigures and then is fulfilled in the New Testament Transfiguration of Christ:

> There was nothing glorious in the Law, save only Moses countenance, whereas the whole of the Gospel is radiant. Hear what the Gospel says: "Jesus taketh unto him Peter, James, and John and bringeth them up into a high mountain, and he transfigured before them. And behold there appeared to them Moses and Elias, appearing in majesty and speaking with him." It is not said that Moses' countenance was glorified, but his whole body as he spoke with Jesus. The promise which was made to him on Sinai was thus fulfilled.[12]

The anagogical sense of Moses' ascent of Mt. Sinai and vision of God during the Exodus was a subject of lively interest among the early Church Fathers. Speaking of the matter in *Questions and Answers on Exodus*, Philo Judaeus presents the common view:

12. See *Homélies sur l'Exode*, trans. P. Fortier, intro. and notes H. de Lubac (Paris, 1947), section XII, subsection 3. This passage is echoed by Clement of Alexandria in *Stromata* II, vol. 2, pp. 115–116. The English translation by W. Hibbard is in Fr. Jean Daniélou's *From Shadows to Reality* (London, 1960).

What is the meaning of the words, "Come up to Me to the mountain and be there."

This signifies that a holy soul is divinized by ascending not to the air or to the ether or to heaven which is higher than all but to a region above the heavens. And beyond the world there is no place but God.[13]

The invitation extended to Moses to climb mountain heights and to see the Almighty, as Philo states, should be understood in terms of the soul's journey to eternal glory. Passing beyond air, ether, and the physical heavens, the soul enters the immaterial realm of the Creator and is there "divinized." Now the vision on the mountain-top for Moses individually, as for the "holy soul" of man in general, was said by Philo to signify exceptional illumination in a kingdom beyond time and place. Speaking of the Old Testament leader in *The Posterity and Exile of Cain,* Philo comments,

But so unceasingly does he himself yearn to see God and to be seen by Him, that he implores Him to reveal clearly His own nature which is so hard to divine, hoping thus to obtain at length a view free from all falsehood. . . . So see him enter into thick darkness where God was, that is, into conceptions regarding the Existent Being that belongs to the unapproachable region where there are no material forms. For the Cause of all is not in the thick darkness, nor locally in any place at all, but high above both place and time.[14]

St. Gregory of Nyssa in his *Life of Moses* denies that man's reason can comprehend the Creator, but in general the saint advances the well-known anagogical interpretation of the Old Testament leader's ascent:

What is the meaning of Moses entering into darkness and seeing God? In the measure that man's spirit sees forward in the way of perfection and gets nearer to God, the better does he realize that the divine nature is invisible. Leaving aside all appearances, both of the senses and the spirit, he goes ever more forward into the invisible and incomprehensible. It is in this that the true knowledge of him whom he seeks consists. He who is sought surpasses all knowledge, being enshrined in the unknowingness as in darkness.[15]

In Moses' entering into the darkness and looking upon the Almighty is presented man's spirit as it finally approaches God and learns

13. *Questions and Answers on Exodus,* trans. Ralph Marcus (London and Cambridge, Mass., 1953), vol. 2, part 40, extract xxiv. 12 a, pp. 82–83.

14. *Philo,* trans. F. H. Colson and G. H. Whitaker (London and New York, 1939), vol. 2, sections 12–13, pp. 334–335.

15. *Life of Moses,* trans. Fr. Jean Daniélou, in *From Shadows to Reality,* p. 225.

that the Divine Nature is invisible and incomprehensible. And it is surely not difficult to understand why for the Church Fathers the Exodus vision signified a patterned type foreshadowing a greater vision still to come. Under the aegis of the Old Law, Moses, and Elijah too, spoke with God upon holy Mt. Sinai; and then under the New Law, these same men appeared from the dead to talk again with God and to see him radiantly transfigured on Mt. Tabor.

From the typological suggestions of the letter, the Transfiguration emerges as that third biblical event that "we" and Dante and all Christian men must reenact in taking the last step to bliss. After converting the soul by imitating the Exodus, and after receiving Christ by imitating the Redemption, "we" must act out the drama of Mt. Tabor and so rise spiritually to the highest level of visionary experience.

Should further support for the figural implications of the letter he desired, one need only observe the three biblical episodes, upon which the steps to glory are founded, that centrally occupied the thoughts of Dante when he described the allegories of the poets and theologians in his prose writings. The Transfiguration is used in the *Convivio* to illustrate one of the spiritual senses common to all allegory. After discussing in that tract the fictive literal sense employed by poets, Dante calls attention to allegory's spiritual meanings, supplying only one spiritual sense for the events on Mt. Tabor.

What is particularly arresting here is the thrust of the poet's associations:

> Il terzo senso si chiama *morale;* e questo è quello che li lettori deono intentamente andare appostando per le scritture, a utilità di loro e di loro discenti: siccome appostare si può nel Vangelio, quando Cristo salio lo monte per trasfigurarsi, che delli dodici Apostoli, ne menò secro li tre: in che moralmente si può intendere, che alle secretssime cose noi dovemo avere poca compagnia.[16]

> [The third sense is called moral; and this sense is that for which teachers ought as they go through writings intently to watch for their own profit and that of their hearers; as in the Gospel when Christ ascended the Mount to be transfigured, we may be watchful of His

16. The Italian text of *Il Convivio* is from *Le Opere di Dante Alighieri*, ed. E. Moore, 4th ed., p. 252. The English trans. is that of William Walrond Jackson in *Dante's Convivio* (Oxford, 1909), pp. 73–74. The passages quoted are from *Il Convivio* II, cap. 1, ll. 42–65.

taking with Himself the three Apostles out of the twelve; thereby
morally it may be understood that for the most secret affairs we
ought to have few companions.]

Immediately thereafter, Dante mentions the Exodus to illustrate
the anagogic sense:

> Lo quarto senso si chiama *anagogico,* cioè sovra senso: e quest' è,
> quando spiritualmente si spone una scrittura, la quale, ancora [sia
> vera] eziandio nel senso litterale, per le cose significate significa
> delle superne cose dell' eternale gloria: siccome veder si può in quel
> canto el Profeta, che dice che nell' uscita del popolo d' Israele d' Egitto
> la Guidea è fatta santa e libera.

> [The fourth sense is called anagogic, that is, above the senses; and
> this occurs when a writing is spiritually expounded, which even in
> the literal sense by the things signified likewise gives intimation of
> higher matters belonging to eternal glory; as can be seen in that
> song of the prophet which says that, when the people of Israel went
> up out of Egypt, Judea was made holy and free.]

Though one might wish that Dante had stated all three spiritual
senses which arise from each event, he has at least revealed the
general trend of his thought. In the *Convivio* the poet comments
upon the Transfiguration and the Exodus in the developing chain
of his allegorical speculations; then in the letter he openly refers
to the Exodus and the Redemption and, by explaining the spiritual
senses of the Exodus, gives the reader the means of deducing quite
commonplace figural views: that events taking place during the
Exodus foreshadow both the Redemption and the Transfiguration.

But most important of all, by insisting that the Exodus manifests
that mode of treatment to be accorded the *Commedia,* Dante directs
attention to that scriptural event whose figural modes provide a
new perspective on the typological structure of the great poem, a
structure developed in part through application of an artistic
typology of biblical imitation. The text of the *Commedia* will be
seen to confirm that the patterned Exodus in the poem's prologue
and second canticle indeed foreshadows a Redemption figure in
the last cantos of the *Purgatorio;* Dante's trip from the Egypt of
this world to the Jerusalem of the Earthly Paradise culminates in
the poet's figured reception of the redeeming person of Christ. And
the early Exodus motif in the poem foreshadows as well a dramatic
acting out of the Transfiguration in the *Paradiso;* in the last stages

1. The world (1285) by Richard of Haldingham showing Jerusalem at the geographic middle of the land mass (small central oval), the Earthly Paradise at the furthest point east (larger oval at the top), and the Mediterranean Sea extending through the central and western regions of the earth (large darkened areas toward the bottom). The map is believed to have been used by world pilgrims as a guide to Jerusalem.

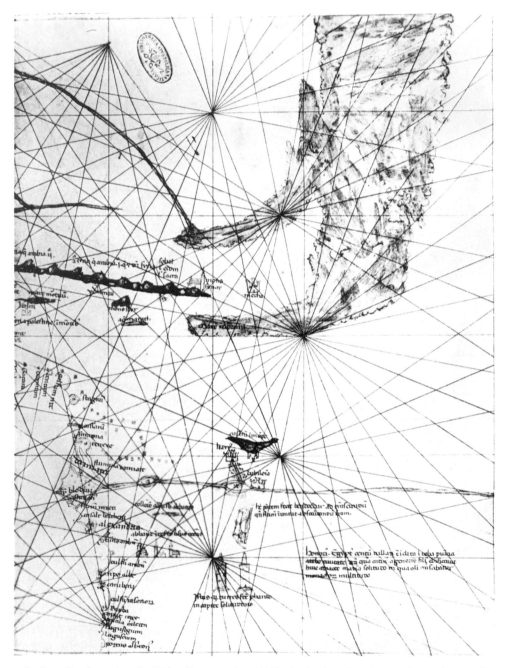

2. A medieval sea chart by Pietro Vesconte (ca. 1320) of a kind used to direct pilgrim ships to the shores of Egypt. A church (left of center), drawn between the arms of the Red Sea and the Gulf of Aqaba, marks Mount Sinai. Loxodromes or rhumb lines, showing the direction of prevailing winds, pass on either side of Damina (Damietta) on the Egyptian coast and then extend toward Mount Sinai. From the Vatican Library collection.

3. The first stages of a long pilgrimage beginning in England. Christians traveled from London through Canterbury to Dover. From Matthew of Paris's *Itinerary*, thirteenth century.

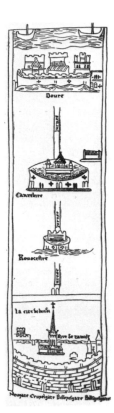

4. A semicircular line (lower left) on the Hereford *mappaemundi* (1285) discloses the supposed pathway of the Exodus over the Red Sea and past the triangular drawing of Moses on Mount Sinai. The Nile River in Egypt is rendered as a vertical line on the right.

5a. Ancient Stations-of-the-Exodus sand tracks, linking Elim and Gebel Musa (Mount Sinai), still serve modern travelers who are now transported in automobiles through the Wilderness of Sin.

5b. Camels are used by travelers—and monks—to cover stretches of the pathway joining the stations on the Gebel Musa "ring".

6. Palmers and their guides passing the Graineries of Joseph (the pyramids) and the Colossus (the Sphinx) outside Babylon (Cairo), in a drawing printed in George Sandys's *A Relation of a Journey* (1610).

7a., b. The palms and waters of Ain Musa or biblical Marah, identified by Fetellus (ca. 1130) and Anonymous Pilgrim VI (ca. 1140) as the fifth Station of the Exodus, rest on a flat, sandy desert one and a half miles east of the Red Sea. Medieval palmers were told that here Moses turned bitter waters sweet by casting a tree into the spring.

8. Wádi Feirán, the eleventh Station of the Exodus and the supposed site of biblical Rhaphidin, viewed from the ruins of a medieval church on the hill of al-Meharrat. St. Silvia in the fourth century was the first pilgrim to record stopping at this famous station, a place celebrated in the Middle Ages for its anchorite monks.

9. The great boulder at Massah (or Meribah), on the Exodus route between Wádi Feirán and St. Catherine's Monastery, was revered by medieval pilgrims. Water is said to have flowed from the rock after Moses struck it with his rod (*Exodus* 17:5–7).

10. The medieval Monastery of St. Mary, later renamed after St. Catherine, rests at the foot of Gebel Musa and is listed in early pilgrim guidebooks as the twelfth Station of the Exodus. Visible are the Charnel House in the monastery garden, the forward walls constructed by the Emperor Constantine, the steeple and roof of the Church of the Transfiguration, and the back wall and residence built by engineers in Napoleon's army. The vague line of a pathway can be seen leading from behind the monastery to the Mount Sinai "ring."

11. Bedouin and their camels rest in early morning shadows at the mouth of Wádi el Lejá, the rock-strewn rift separating Mount Sinai and Mount St. Catherine. St. Silvia journeyed into the Wádi and there began her ascent of Mount Sinai.

12. Gebel Musa or Mount Sinai, a figural source for Dante's Mount Purgatory, appears in a French pilgrim book along with Gebel St. Catherine as ringed with terraces which slope from the summits to the ground. The drawing is found in the *Journal des Voyages de Monsieur de Monconys, Conseiller du Roy en ses conseils d'Estat et Privé et Lieutenant Criminel au Siège Présidial de Lyon* (Paris, 1695), vol. 1.

13. The Mountain of God with its terraces photographed from the pathway used by medieval pilgrims on Gebel St. Catherine. The terraces are outlined with particular sharpness in the late afternoon sunlight. Beginning in the tenth century, when pilgrims climbed Gebel St. Catherine as a regular part of their "round," they passed from three to four hours in the afternoon facing this view of Mount Sinai during their descent.

14. From Domenico di Michelino's representation of Dante before the Mount of Purgatory. The fresco (ca. 1465) hangs in the Duomo, Florence.

15. A late lithograph (ca. 1778), after an historical icon of Mount Sinai, revealing the monastery, the Burning Bush, the mountain pathways, the Gates of Confession and St. Stephen, the hermitages with saints, and Moses receiving the Commandments.

16. A diagram of some of the stations on the Gebel Musa "ring" in Jacopo di Verona's *Liber Peregrinationis* (1335). Shown (from bottom to top) are the towered Monastery of St. Catherine, the Church of St. Mary of the Apparition (with checkered wall and a door), the plain of Elijah (church with crosses on roof), the pathway of purgation (curving lines with dots), buildings marking the mountain's summit and the supposed place where Moses received the Law, and the garden of repentance between Gebel Musa and Gebel St. Catherine (semicircular figure on right).

17. An icon at St. Catherine's Monastery illustrating Bishop of Sinai John Climacus' seventh-century devotional work, *The Ladder of Divine Ascent*. Many medieval icons and illuminated manuscripts at the monastery depict the ladder.

18. The Gate of Confession and some of the approximately 3,400 stone steps that alternate with paths on the route up Mount Sinai.

19. Sandro Botticelli's illustration (ca. 1490) depicting Dante and Virgil, together with dead souls, at the base of Mount Purgatory.

20. The remains of the Porter of the Gate, St. Stephen, who in the sixth century sat at one of Mount Sinai's gates hearing the confessions of pilgrims and permitting them to pass. The skeleton of St. Stephen, clothed in the "megaloschemos" or "angel robe" of the highest monastic rank, now rests just within the entrance to the Charnel House at St. Catherine's Monastery.

21. A bush at the Monastery of St. Catherine that is said by the monks to be grown from the original Burning Bush. St. Silvia (ca. 385) is the first pilgrim to have reported seeing at the monastery "a bramble bush in which the Lord appeared to Moses."

22. The sixth-century mosaic of Christ's Transfiguration in the apse of the Church of the Transfiguration at Mount Sinai. Medieval palmers, after purging their souls of sin on the Mount Sinai "ring," received communion beneath this mosaic before continuing on their pilgrimage to Jerusalem.

23. The author at the foot of the Mount of Olives with the eastern wall of Jerusalem in the distance. Medieval Palm Sunday processions, figured in *Purgatorio* XXIX and XXX, moved through the Golden Gate (background center) to the traditional site of the Temple (the Dome of the Rock, background left of center). The medieval ceremony of opening the sealed Golden Gate for the procession is believed to be the source for the opening of the sealed Golden Door of St. Peter's basilica on Holy Jubilee pilgrimage years.

24. A map of important Exodus land-marks included with sailing directions written by Leonardo or Goro Dati in *La Sfera* (1422). Among the sites shown are the Red Sea (dark area on far right), Mount Sinai (church on the right), the city of Sodom and the Dead Sea (grey area below the church), the River Jordan flowing into the Dead Sea, and the walled, circular city of Jerusalem.

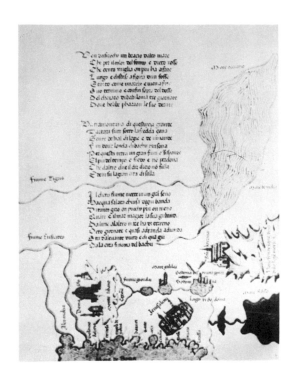

25. A drawing and list of main sites in Jerusalem from George Sandys's *A Relation of a Journey.*

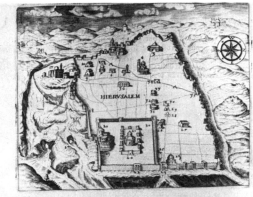

The Temple of Chrijts Sepulcher, &c.

MONT CALVARIÆ

26. A view of Calvary in the Church of the Holy Sepulchre, showing the traditional place of the Crucifixion (A), the Roman Catholic Chapel (B), and the Chapel of Adam with tombs (E and F) beneath the Crucifixion site. The illustration, which reveals how the sites were situated within the church in Dante's time, is reproduced from George Sandys's *A Relation of a Journey*.

27. Stone marking the "middle of the world" in the Church of the Holy Sepulchre, Jerusalem. In the fourteenth century the Florentine pilgrim Giorgio Gucci, while visiting the Church, was shown "a round stone, with a hole in the middle." The pilgrim was told that here "Christ placed his foot and said: 'This is the center of the world.' " In *Purgatorio* II, Dante, in accord with medieval geographical views, writes of Jerusalem's central position on earth.

28. A bronze of St. Peter, possibly dating from as early as the fifth century, was venerated through the years in St. Peter's basilica, where it still remains. The right foot of the statue has been worn smooth by the kisses of the pilgrims.

29. A fresco by Giotto of Pope Boniface VIII proclaiming the Roman Church's first Holy Year Jubilee pilgrimage in 1300. The fresco was completed at the time and now hangs in St. John Lateran.

30. The Papal Altar with an ancient icon of Christ, as photographed in the Sancta Sanctorum Chapel at St. John Lateran. During the Golden Jubilee pilgrimage of 1300, Christians were granted extraordinary indulgences for venerating the icon, a work said to be made by other than human hands.

of pilgrimage, Dante, with soul converted and redeemed, has a visionary experience figuring the one on Mt. Tabor.

Dante's second mode of artistic figurism, called here for convenience the typology of internal recurrence, has been remarked upon at length by commentators and can be very easily discerned from the letter's references to foreshadowed and fulfilled biblical episodes. Dante perceived that, if the Book of God's Words is indeed linked together in an ascending hierarchy of virtue by various figures, then the persons and things in the cantos and canticles of a poem depicting spiritual ascent might be similarly joined. The most casual reading of the *Commedia* will bring to light a seemingly endless array of such internal figural correspondences. The foreshadowing dark wood in *Inferno* I reappears, delightfully altered and spiritually transfigured, in the fulfilled divine wood of Eden; the mysterious cord encircling Dante's waist in Hell has its counterpart in the reed girdle worn by the poet on Mt. Purgatory; the noble philosophers and poets of limbo appear to prepare the reader for the negligent princes outside Purgatory's gate; the fiery-eyed Charon, for the liberated Cato; Virgil for Beatrice; and Beatrice for St. Bernard. Then too there are the recurring events: Dante's downward movement near a mountain in *Inferno* II foreshadows the poet's very slight descent to a shore in the *Purgatorio*; the sighting by Dante of the debased city of Dis points toward his vision of the heavenly city of the rose; his coming to a stream in the Earthly Paradise prefigures his arrival before a heavenly river of light.

In hypnotic succession basic typological patterns recur again and again, yet always in elaborated and transformed contexts as the poet mounts upward from one stage of spiritual illumination to another. Only when memory, intellect, and imagination take a sudden leap, uniting the event in the present to its prefigured occurrence in the past, only then do the contrasting contexts in which the event is framed release a flood of revelatory associations. With sudden insight the reader grasps the full meaning of what is taking place during yet another stage in Dante's sojourn to God.

Because the poet's typology of internal recurrence binds together past, present, and future figures contained entirely within the fabric of the *Commedia,* and because it is not grounded in true, historical biblical events in the actual world at large, this internal

typology is only *like* scriptural figurism and carries no overt suggestion of either the historicity or the fictive quality of the poem's
literal sense. The reader becomes aware that one internal type
foreshadows another, but because these types are only *similar to*
the general figural patterns inscribed by God in his two books, the
figures remain internal creations that, in their literal sense, might
or might not be fictions.

   In inventing a third artistic figural mode, the typology of
worldly imitation, Dante related *in figura* events signified by the
literal sense of the *Commedia* to historical events in this life. The
reader is referred beyond the poem to the true, iconographic
"words" found in this mortal world, "words" in the form of
people, animals, buildings, landscapes, cities, and even secular and
religious institutions such as the Roman Empire and Church. In
epistle x to Can Grande this worldly typology is suggested by
Dante's statement on the subject of the *Commedia:*

>   Est ergo subiectum totius operis, literaliter
>   tantum accepti, status animarum post mortem
>   simpliciter sumptus. Nam de illo et circa
>   illum totius operis versatur processus. Si
>   vero accipiatur opus allegorice, subiectum
>   est homo, prout merendo et demerendo per
>   arbitrii libertatem iustitiae praemiandi et
>   puniendi obnoxius est.
>
>   [The subject of the whole work, then, taken in
>   the literal sense only is "the state of souls
>   after death" without qualification, for the
>   whole progress of the work hinges on it and
>   about it. Whereas if the work be taken
>   allegorically, the subject is "man as by good
>   or ill deserts, in the excercise of the freedom
>   of his choice, he becomes liable to rewarding
>   or punishing justice."]

   The literal sense of the *Commedia,* then, points to the "state of
souls after death"; the allegorical sense (in this context meaning
the typological sense), to man exercising his choice, man becoming
liable to reward or punishment. Because in the fulfilled realm after
death choice is no longer possible and reward or punishment im-
posed, the typological sense can only refer back to persons in this
world who through their moral choices are meriting either salva-

tion or damnation. Commentators have sometimes been confused by Dante's statement, yet one can well understand why the poet presented the traditional typological sense as pointing back to this world. Like the souls in the realm beyond, Dante simply had no choice. Excepting the temporal region of Purgatory where souls are placed only for limited periods, it is apparent that in the other world there is no time; everything is complete; nothing more can be added to existence. There every soul is actualized according to its highest potentiality for moral degradation or perfection. Still, the other world is not a static altar piece gleaming with colorful but motionless iconographic images. The strongly individualized souls beyond life, though judged by God and rendered incapable of further moral action, are seen to gesture, speak, and move in ways characteristic of mortals in this actual world. As the poet passes among these souls, they are animated in such a fashion that they do fulfill, through the power of Dante's art, the final promise of prefiguring actions performed in this life. In other words, a figural relation is forged between the earthly event and the fulfilled otherworldly event.

Early readers conversant with the Italian "vulgar tongue" were in effect being invited to reflect upon familiar individuals and places on earth presumably known to the relatively small, cultivated society of medieval Europe. Today one learns only with the aid of historical scholarship the earthly nature of many forgotten persons and locales. The wrath of Filippo Argenti in Hell, one discovers, is the final manifestation of the less powerful anger of the living man as he was described by Giovanni Villani.[17] The heretical Farinata rising from his tomb in the city of Dis is found to be even more forceful in his heresy than when walking the streets of his native city; the fulfilled St. Francis and St. Benedict in the sphere of the sun, more intense in their holiness than during their life upon earth. Though the vagaries of critical fashion occasionally dictate that the *Commedia* can only be appreciated in isolation from historical studies, this view surely leads to the slighting of Dante's typology of worldly imitation; lost would be many of the aesthetic pleasures dependent upon a comparison of the mortal and the eternal state of souls.

17. Examples of the sarcasm and wrath of Argenti in life are given in *Villani's Chronicle,* trans. Philip H. Wicksteed (London, 1906).

Some modern commentators, it should be observed, claim that *only* persons and things in this world are reflected in the poem's regions beyond life. John Chydenius and Bernard Stambler, for example, lacking an awareness of the historical pilgrimage tradition and so finding no parallels upon earth for Dante's entire movement through the eternal realm, have contended that the otherworldly journey of the living poet is definitely a fiction inserted into a narrative that otherwise shadows varying degrees of "factual" or historical truth.[18] But from the historical materials concerned with pilgrimage, from the analysis of Dante's writings, and from the explanation of the poet's typological techniques, one should by now have a very cogent realization of how and why Dante's journey beyond life mirrors that of a Christian's in this world. And from the letter to Can Grande, one is given assistance in finding in the *Commedia* the primary and most immediate earthly events acted out by that Christian.

Now a believing man upon earth can walk in the Paschal Candle procession during Holy Week and so, Roman liturgy suggests, renew again the meaning of the Exodus; participation at holy mass joins the Christian spiritually to Christ's death and Redemption; Christ himself can be received through confession and communion. Prayer, fasting, and long vigils before candlelit images of Christ and the Apostles can spiritually relate the Christian to New Testa-

18. In writing of Dante's tour through the other world, Chydenius in *The Typological Problem in Dante* states that "taken as a whole, this journey is a literary fiction, which cannot as such have typical signification"; yet Chydenius, considering other elements in the narrative of the poem, thinks that its literal sense points to historical events because Dante "in the *Divine Comedy* . . . passed over to the allegory of the theologians, that is to say, typical interpretation. In this, Dante diverges from the prevalent opinion that Scripture alone could contain typical signification" (pp. 49–50). According to Bernard Stambler in *Dante's Other World* (New York, 1957), "the *journey* of the poem is contrived; it is a fiction in the sense of something made or put together rather than being something pre-existent or supplied, as history or an actual journey would be." Stambler, quoting from and in part agreeing with Singleton, distinguishes this "made up" journey from the rest of Dante's unique allegory which, he thinks, has a literal sense that, though presumed to be fictional, nevertheless is said to point to "things believed to be essentially as therein presented—a belief based on all the faith, hope and intelligence of the poet" (pp. 67, 69). Allan Gilbert in *Dante and his Comedy* indicates, as has been noted, that "fact and fiction may interpenetrate" in Dante's poem, but he favors considering the work a fiction partly because, in his view, the poet's journey cannot be "real": "The feigned quality of the visit to the other world should ever be in the reader's mind. . . . Dante the traveller is never exactly the historical Dante who lived in Florence . . ." (p. 6).

ment events and to the eternal glory of Heaven. And in Dante's poem such forms of figural imitation are variously shadowed. But most forcefully and tangibly reflected in the *Commedia* is a Christian on a long pilgrimage who confesses his sins on Mt. Sinai and, in converting his soul on the Exodus journey, ascends to the place where Moses saw God. This Christian next receives Christ in Jerusalem, and there enjoys the fruits of the Redemption; and, on a journey to the eternal city of Rome, this same Christian is spiritually exalted through the veneration of sacred images associated with Christ's Transfiguration.

4

Invention from the Book of God's Words

Midway between God's single flame at the loftiest point in the universe and Satan's grotesque hulk in the bottom-most pit of Hell, Dante Alighieri stands in Eden on Mt. Purgatory's summit and watches enraptured as a Heavenly procession, glowing with the bright luminosity of the night-time moon, wends its way downward to earth from the eastern sky.

The garden in which the poet enjoys this celestial vision is an ideal place on earth: green boughs stir in a gentle and continuous breeze; flowers and luxuriant grasses abound; a crystalline stream flows at the poet's feet; the air about the poet shimmers as though ablaze. And strange indeed is the radiant procession of elders, beasts, virgins, and holy objects that descends to this ideal green world.

First, seven golden trees—or so they appear—are seen in the distance gliding forward; but upon closer approach, the trees are discerned to be seven giant candlesticks. From each of the golden forms trail rainbow-hued bands of light that hover like wavering banners over the rest of the procession.

Marching two by two behind the candlesticks come twenty-four elders in vestments of unearthly white; and following them, four exotic beasts surrounding a chariot, each having six wings studded with eyes that look both forward and back.

At the middle of the parade, a two-headed, winged beast identified by Dante as a Gryphon pulls forward the triumphal chariot. Seven virgins accompanying the chariot dance beside its two wheels, four virgins on the left side and three on the right; and seven old men, their heads wreathed with roses and other flowers, walk at the rear of this remarkable vehicle.

Here in the members of the procession are symbolized the Holy Bible, a book unforgettably placed at the core of the *Commedia* and affecting through its descent a convergence of the temporal and the eternal, of the changing spiritual history of man and the unchanging truths of God. For the candlesticks have long been recognized as symbolizing the seven gifts of the Holy Spirit; the twenty-four elders, the books of the Old Testament; the four beasts around the chariot, the four Gospels; and the elders behind the chariot, the books of the Bible comprising the Acts of the Apostles, the Epistles, and Revelation. And if epistle x implies that one can anticipate finding in the poem a figured depiction of Christ's appearance and Redemption of man, there at the center of the parade—and at a central geographical point between Heaven above and Hell below —Dante sees a chariot representing the Roman Church drawn by a Gryphon rightly interpreted as symbolizing Christ. The Redeemer, then, is symbolically coming with Bible and Church to a perfected place in the world where stands Dante, the Christian man. And very special "words" of God, pointed to by epistle x, are there in the poem marching symbolically before the watchful gaze of Dante and the readers. In the form of elders, books that include the story of the Exodus move in front of the beast representing Christ; around and following the symbolized Redeemer are procession members representing books that include accounts of the Redemption and Transfiguration.

By studying in the *Commedia* those figural components of structure underscored in the letter to Can Grande, the reader can observe how the Exodus typology in the prologue to the *Inferno* blends, through a system of foreshadowing and fulfilled episodes, into figured biblical events of higher spiritual significance, namely, the Redemption and the Transfiguration.

Into the pattern of Exodus action in *Inferno* ii, there intrudes a distinctly foreign element, a story told by Virgil of Beatrice's descent from Heaven to Hell (ll. 52–120). Far above in the Heavens, says the Mantuan to Dante, the blessed Lucy, at the request of the Virgin Mary, sought out Beatrice and pleaded with Dante's lady to intercede below in the despairing poet's behalf. Beatrice then came down from Heaven's light into the saturnine abode of wise pagans located in Hell's vestibule, and there she asked for Virgil's intervention, her bright eyes filled with tears.

The descent of Beatrice into the *Inferno*, taking place though it does within the context of an Exodus figure, nonetheless establishes a foreshadowing pattern of redemptive action that will find its fulfillment in Dante's personal redemption through Beatrice and Christ on the heights of Mt. Purgatory. In the course of redeeming the poet on that mountain, Beatrice, performing actions reflecting those of the Son, will descend from Heaven, directly minister to her sinful ward, and provide the spiritual means by which Dante can mount toward God. But all this can be fully acted out only after the poet has converted his soul through successful imitation of the Exodus, and in the prologue to the *Inferno*, the time is not yet right for Dante's spiritual regeneration.

Within the time sequence of the poem, Dante's trial Exodus pilgrimage is thwarted on Good Friday, the day on which Christ was crucified and was said to have descended into Hell. It was a day associated with grief and spiritual irresolution, for limited man could not be certain of Redemption until the Son manifested his Godhood by triumphing over death on Easter Sunday. Beatrice's own sorrowful movement down into Hell has been convincingly interpreted as figuring Christ's; [1] it comes at a moment in the pattern of spiritual history when the blessed lady cannot personally confront the sin-blackened Dante in a manner that will lead to his Redemption. Beatrice must await the poet's conversion through future Exodus pilgrimage up Mt. Purgatory, and she must await as well the day of Christ's Resurrection. In the meantime, she appeals to an enlightened pagan in the hope that Virgil's sure abilities as a guide will help to foster Dante's conversion.

After clambering downward with Virgil through Hell, Dante climbs to the spacious realm of Mt. Purgatory island on Easter Sunday, the day of Christ's Resurrection and thus a time most propitious for spiritual ascent. Hope wells in the soul of the poet as he toils upward, on this and two succeeding days, in a successful Exodus peregrination that requires no further elaboration. One by one angels of God come forward to erase seven "P's" for seven *peccata*, outward signs of sin, scored on the poet's forehead. And on the topmost stair of the mountain, Virgil, before taking his leave, crowns and mitres his charge as a sign of Dante's self-possession and spiritual conversion (*Purg.* XXVII, 139–142). In a regenerate Eden on Mt. Purgatory's summit, neither the mundane institutions of Church or Empire are necessary to the pilgrim; Dante has become his own bishop and his own emperor. He has

1. The descent and resurrection theme in *Inferno* I and II is outlined by John Freccero, "Dante's Firm Foot," *Harvard Theological Journal* 53 (1959) : 245–281. See also Charles S. Singleton, *Dante Studies I: Elements of Structure* (Cambridge, Mass., 1954), pp. 53–59; and the same author's *Essay on the Vita Nuova* (Cambridge, Mass., 1958), pp. 20–24.

arrived in the loftiest spiritual and physical position that he has yet attained; and, as another geographical reference here makes plain, he stands in a garden raised from the earth opposite Jerusalem (*Purg.* XXVII, 1–6). For Dante must gently remind the reader once more that the Earthly Paradise mirrors God's Holy City among the living. In accord with the figure of Redemption to be developed, the poet speaks of Jerusalem as that place where the "Creator shed His blood" (*Purg.* XXVII, 2: "fattor lo sangue sparse").

When Dante finally walks amid the verdure and gentle breezes of Eden, Beatrice fulfills the promise of her previous descent and returns to assume again the figural role of the Redeemer. But on this occasion she does not sink low into the gloom of limbo; she does not weep; she does not need the help of a pagan, however noble or talented. Easter Sunday has passed; Christ has arisen; and Dante's soul has been converted. Beatrice accordingly arrives in triumph, amid holy song and a rain of flowers, the last member of the heavenly procession to appear. And Dante, assisted by a maiden called Matelda symbolizing the Active Life, advances to meet personally his intercessor at the green summit of the world.

The advent of Beatrice in the Earthly Paradise is a striking incident: the poet, after following Matelda along the banks of a crystalline stream that turns toward the east, prepares for his lady's approach by gazing, at the moment of dawn, toward that point where the sun has risen (*Purg.* XXIX, 7–12). Immediately one recalls how, in the account of St. Jerome, the pilgrim Paula stood in the Holy Land facing east and "as the sun rose, remembered the Son of righteousness"; how Constantine constructed the main basilica of the New Jerusalem with "three gates facing the rising sun" so as to receive the morning light of Christ; how the Temple of Solomon was commonly believed to have been similarly oriented to catch the sun's first rays.[2] Although Dante in Eden will not completely understand what he is about to witness, later

2. Paula's experience is narrated by St. Jerome in *The Pilgrimage of Holy Paula*, trans. Aubrey Stewart, notes C. W. Wilson (London, 1887), p. 12. The orientation of Constantine's basilica in the New Jerusalem is mentioned in Eusebius's *Life of Constantine*, trans. John H. Bernard, notes T. Hayter Lewis (London, 1896), pp. 7–8. The anonymous author of *The City of Jerusalem*, trans. and notes C. R. Conder (London, 1896), pp. 13–14, speaks of the location of steps and pavement at the eastern entrance to the Temple.

in the *Paradiso*, when Jesus descends toward the poet in the form of a blazing orb, Dante will know Christ as the sun (*Par.* XXIII, 29).

Christ is coming to Jerusalem, so the figured narrative informs the reader. And as dazzling light flashes and the heavenly procession glides into view, the poet hears the hosts of Heaven sing "Hosanna" (*Purg.* XXIX, 51). This is the chant—recorded in the Gospels of Matthew, Mark, and John—cried out by the throngs as Christ came down the Mt. of Olives, climbed the western slope of Mt. Sion, and entered the Harem or Temple area of Jerusalem through a passageway that medieval writers identified as the Golden Gate.[3] Soon thereafter the pageant of candlesticks, elders, beasts, and virgins that accompanies the Gryphon-drawn chariot abruptly halts. The elders turning to the car chant, 'Come to me from Lebanon, my spouse' (*Purg.* XXX, 11: '*Veni, sponsa, de Libano*'), and so suggest the marriage of Christ to his Church. The other marchers are said to repeat the words like saints on the day of Judgment:

> Quali i beati al novissimo bando
> surgeran presti ognun di sua caverna,
> la rivestita voce alleluiando,
>   cotali, in su la divina basterna,
> si levar cento, *ad vocem tanti senis,*
> ministri e messaggier di vita etterna.
>
> [*Purg.* XXX, 13–19]

> [As the blessed at the last trumpet call
> will rise quickly each one from his grave,
> with regained voice and singing Halleluiah,
>   so, above the divine chariot
> rose up a hundred *ad vocem tanti senis,*
> ministers and messengers of life eternal.]

By analogy the drama in Eden is being related to incidents that medieval tradition averred would occur at Jerusalem; it was thought that the Last Judgment, like Christ's entry into the Holy City, would take place in the tiny Hebron Valley joining the Mt. of Olives to Jerusalem's Temple Mount. The members of the procession, however, do not actually sing the "Halleluiahs" of the delivered saints; the marchers chant only *as* those saints, and the words uttered are different from those to be heard at the Last

---

3. See medieval references to this entry in chapter v, pp. 172–173.

Judgment. While the analogical shadings of the passage suggest the future Second Coming and Last Judgment of Christ, the primary figured action still centers upon Christ's movement into Jerusalem.[4] The very next chant of the marchers makes this point clear.

"Blessed is He that comes" (*Purg.* xxx, 19: '*Benedictus qui venis!*'), cries the procession as a cue for the arrival of Dante's blessed lady; the voices echo words—quoted in all four Gospels —that were shouted when Christ went into His Holy City. And as flowers are thrown by angelic hands, the veiled form of Beatrice at last appears within the chariot. She is said to come like the morning sun burning through mists (*Purg.* xxx, 22–27).

By imitating church sacramental ritual, the poet, a type for the Christian pilgrim, secures his spiritual Redemption while standing before Beatrice, a type for Christ. When Dante's lady demands that the poet make a sincere "confession" (*Purg.* xxxi, 6) and do "penance" (*Purg.* xxx, 145, "pentimento"), her words do not go unheeded. Dante openly laments his unfaithfulness; he is overwhelmed by a flood of tears and sighs; and he swoons on the bank of the River Lethe (*Purg.* xxxi, 85–89). Upon regaining consciousness, Dante finds that Matelda is leading him through and submerging him in the healing river of forgetfulness, a stream whose waters purge from the soul all memory of past sin. On the opposite bank he is met by the four virgins who were first seen dancing on the left side of Beatrice's chariot; at this dramatic moment they embrace the poet, draw him into their dance, and move with him toward his blessed lady (*Purg.* xxxi, 103–114). Compelled by the four handmaidens to stare at Beatrice, Dante at last "receives" Jesus by seeing, mirrored like the sun in his lady's shimmering eyes, the re-

---

4. It can also be said that Beatrice in *Purg.* xxx and xxxi "judges" Dante for his sins after her second descent to earth, her first descent having been recounted by Virgil in *Inf.* ii. Nevertheless, no close perusal of the text can fail to disclose that Dante does not receive his "last judgment" from Beatrice in *Purg.* xxx and xxxi, for the poet continues to grow in virtue as he ascends throughout the *Paradiso*; his spiritual place in the other world is by no means eternally "fixed" by Beatrice's action, as it would be if the Last Judgment were the primary figure of the episode. Beatrice in fact admonishes Dante so that he may repent, be forgiven his sins, and be redeemed. And on the day of final judgment, it will be too late to repent, too late to ask forgiveness, too late to be redeemed. Although the Last Judgment may be vaguely suggested by Beatrice's actions, the figure of the Redemption through Christ remains the central biblical type for the events acted out in Eden.

fulgent twofold form of the Gryphon symbolizing Christ, that Redeemer who has two natures in one Divine person:

> Come in lo specchio il sol, non altrimenti
> la doppia fiera dentro vi raggiava,
> or con altri, or con altri reggimenti.
>
> [*Purg.* XXXI, 121–123]

> [As the sun in a mirror, not otherwise
> did the twofold beast shine within them,
> now with the attributes of one, now of the other nature.]

So that there can be no mistake about what is happening, the
poet, in an emphatic aside to the reader, explains that his soul
partakes of a most desired food as he gazes at the Gryphon glimmering in Beatrice's eyes; and this food is enjoyed, the poet continues, at a time when the three virgins to the right of Beatrice
dance forward:

> Pensa, lettor, s'io mi maravigliava,
> quando vedea la cosa in sé star queta,
> e ne l'idolo suo si trasmutava.
>   Mentre che piena di stupore e lieta
> l'anima mia gustava di quel cibo
> che, saziando di sé, di sé asseta,
>   sé dimostrando di più alto tribo
> ne li atti, l'altre tre si fero avanti,
> danzando al loro angelico caribo.
>
> [*Purg.* XXXI, 124–132]

> [Think, reader, if I marveled within myself
> when I saw the object remain motionless,
> and yet change in its image.
>   While my soul, filled with wonder and joy,
> was tasting of that food
> which, satisfying of itself, causes thirst of itself,
>   the other three, showing themselves to be
> of the chief order in their bearing,
> drew forward, dancing to their angelic roundelay.]

Though Dante writes of the drama in the Earthly Paradise using
allegorical and symbolic as well as typological allusions, the pattern of the narrative reveals with considerable clarity what is
being acted out, particularly when read in the context of the poem's
total pilgrimage figure. In the Holy City of Jerusalem, a shadowed

Christian pilgrim has watched the advance of a pageant whose stately movement, bannerlike lights, and holy songs have suggested to critics a procession of Church clerics bearing with them Christ in the form of the Host.[5] The pilgrim has confessed his sins, done penance, and been cleansed by holy water. Fortified spiritually by four cardinal virtues, the pilgrim is next redeemed by Christ through reception of the Host, a "food which, satisfying of itself, causes thirst of itself." And this action brings the three theological virtues near to the pilgrim's soul.

In the fulfilled and perfected otherworld, however, Dante has a great advantage over the reflected pilgrim in the finite world of the living. Beyond death in Eden the poet in the act of being redeemed can be purged of all memory of past sin, whereas the mortal pilgrim in Jerusalem, though absolved of personal sin through Christ, must travel on through life carrying sad memories of evil.

Once Dante has retraced in ritual his past sins and his present Redemption, the figured, symbolic, and allegorical drama on Mt. Purgatory's peak expands to embrace the corruption and Redemption of both mankind in general and of mankind's major earthly institutions, the Church and Empire. Under the auspices of Beatrice, Dante watches as strange persons, animals, and objects act out historical events in the garden. The eagle of a corrupt Empire swoops down and attacks the chariot of the Church; but during a second descent, the eagle, by gently dropping plumes upon the holy car, displays that under the Emperor Constantine it too received Christ and "donated" to the support of his Church (*Purg.* xxxii, 124–126). The chariot has of itself remarkable powers of renewal. Next besieged and damaged by the dragon of schism, the car with bottom wrenched out miraculously covers itself with the eagle's plumage (*Purg.* xxxii, 130–141). When somewhat later the seven virgins of virtue see a foul harlot, symbolizing the papal court, sitting upon the blessed chariot, they weep and recite the opening words of Psalm 79 that tells of the defiling of Jerusalem's Temple: '*Deus, venerunt gentes*' (*Purg.* xxxiii, 1). But to remind the reader that Jesus overcomes such evil through his death, Dante writes that

5. See Lizette Andrews Fisher, *The Mystic Vision in the Grail Legend and in the Divine Comedy* (New York, 1917), pp. 102–116; and Bernard Stambler, *Dante's Other World* (New York, 1957), pp. 27 f.

Beatrice listens to the virgin's lament in the manner of Mary before the Cross at Golgotha:

> e Bëatrice, sospirosa e pia,
> quelle ascoltava sì fatta, che poco
> più a la croce si cambiò Maria.
>
> [*Purg.* XXXIII, 4–6]

> [and Beatrice, sighing and compassionate,
> was listening to them so altered,
> that Mary was changed little more at the Cross.]

For always underlying the theme of corruption and renewal in Eden is the figure of Christ's Redemption of man in Jerusalem, a figure that gives richness and depth to the symbolic and allegorical events unfolding before Dante.

Just as Beatrice's descent into the *Inferno* functions within the Exodus figure as a foreshadowing of a second and higher plane of figured action centered upon the Redemption, so too, once this second stage is reached in the Earthly Paradise, other "insets" placed within the fulfilled Redemption figure foreshadow yet a third spiritual plane, that mirroring the Transfiguration. The text must be carefully examined on this point because, in the regular chronology of scriptural history, Christ's Transfiguration on Mt. Tabor occurs prior to the Redemption on the Cross. Nevertheless, there is no mistaking Dante's artistic intent. In associating the Transfiguration with the highest form of vision, the poet, utilizing the typology of internal recurrence for his own aesthetic ends, introduces this figured event last.

One episode in Eden foreshadowing the Transfiguration involves Dante's observation of a despoiled tree that towers almost completely barren of leaves and flowers in the garden. Dante, looking at the tree, first hears holy voices whispering "Adamo" (*Purg.* XXXII, 37), a suggestion that from these naked boughs once grew the forbidden fruit tasted by the father of mankind during the Fall. Yet the tree is said to have a crown or "coma" of foliage (*Purg.* XXXII, 40) which in context would associate it with the crown of Empire. As Dante watches, the Gryphon performs a most significant gesture by binding the pole protruding from the chariot to this most venerable tree, thus apparently forming a Cross that would symbolically link the car of the Church to the tree of Empire and of Good and Evil. This interpretation seems most likely, for medieval writers asserted that the tree of Good and Evil supplied the wood for the Cross on which Christ died.[6] Dante next sees this miraculous tree renew itself by flowering (*Purg.* XXXII, 38–60). Then the poet, growing drowsy and falling asleep, experiences an awakening so meaningful that it is compared to that of Peter, John, and James at Christ's Transfiguration:

> Quali a veder de' fioretti del melo
> che del suo pome li angeli fa ghiotti
> e perpetüe nozze fa nel cielo,
>   Pietro e Giovanni e Iacopo condotti
> e vinti, ritornaro a la parola
> da la qual furon maggior sonni rotti,
>   e videro scemata loro scuola
> così di Moïsè come d'Elia,
> e al maestro suo cangiata stola;
>   tal torna' io, e vidi quella pia
> sovra me starsi che conducitrice
> fu de' miei passi lungo 'l fiume pria.
>
>   [*Purg.* XXXII, 73–84]

> [As to behold some flowerets of the apple tree,
> which makes the angels greedy for its fruit,
> and makes a perpetual marriage-feast in heaven,
>   Peter and John and James were conveyed,
> and being overcome, recovered at the word
> by which greater slumbers had been broken,
>   and saw their band diminished
> by Moses, as well as by Elias,
> and their Master's raiment changed,
>   even so I came to myself, and saw that pitying one
> bending over me, who before was guide
> to my steps along the stream.]

Now it is Christ who in the *Song of Solomon* (chapter 2, verse 3) is called an apple tree; and it is Christ, the tree, who renewed himself, not only in Jerusalem through the Redemption, but also on Mt. Tabor through the Transfiguration. By watching the blossoming of a tree in the figured setting of the Holy City, Dante has witnessed a fulfilled type for the Redemption; and by claiming that he is like Peter, John, and James looking upon the flowering apple tree of

6. This view is expressed, for example, by the anonymous author of *The City of Jerusalem* (ca. 1220), trans. and notes C. R. Conder (London, 1896), p. 22.

Christ, Dante associates his own experience with the event that the Redemption foreshadows, that is, the Transfiguration.

Other types in Eden also point, though somewhat indirectly, to the great occurrence on Mt. Tabor. It will be remembered that, when Dante gazed into Beatrice's eyes, the three virgins of theological virtue placed themselves between the poet and his lady, but they neither reached nor touched Dante. To enjoy a more fulfilling vision of the Creator than that granted in Eden, Dante, it is plain, must in the *Paradiso* encounter and completely embrace perfected figures of Faith, Hope, and Charity; and the three virgins foreshadow types obviously linked to the events on Mt. Tabor.

Among the fixed stars in the *Paradiso* are the three apostles whose appearance was prefigured in the *Purgatorio* by Dante's memory of the Transfiguration, the three who were said to be closest to Christ and who actually saw his renewal on Mt. Tabor. These apostles—Peter, James, and John—in the form of fiery lights, sweep down into the path of Dante's flight and place themselves between the poet and the glory of Heaven. Questioning Dante on the subjects of Faith, Hope, and Charity, the apostles respectively reveal themselves as the fulfilled types of these theological virtues. And the light that is John, in joining the gyrations of the other two lights, is distinctly compared to a virgin entering into a harmonious dance:

> E come surge e va ed entra in ballo
> vergine lieta, sol per fare onore
> a la novizia, non per alcun fallo,
>   così vid' io lo schiarato splendore
> venire a' due che si volgieno a nota
> qual conveniesi al loro ardente amore.
>
> [*Par.* xxv, 103–108]

> [And as a joyous virgin rises and goes her way and enters
> the dance (only to honor the bride,
> and not for any wrong motive),
>   so did I see the illumined splendor
> join the other two, who were wheeling round
> in such a guise as befitted their burning love.]

According to the Gospels of Matthew 17 : 1–21, Mark 9 : 2–29, and Luke 9 : 28–43, Peter, James, and John on a mountain saw Christ transfigured while conversing with Moses and Elijah. From on high the apostles heard the voice of God proclaiming Jesus as the Son. On the command of Jesus, they lifted up their eyes to him; and the Son of God demanded secrecy of them, telling them to speak to no one of this vision in the near future. In considering this holy incident upon a mountain, Dante finds in the historical event of Christ's Transfiguration the moral meaning previously quoted in the *Convivio:* "for the most secret affairs we ought to have few companions."

During the initial stages of his figural acting out of episodes on Mt. Tabor, Dante in the *Paradiso* engages in dialogue: he proves by his statements to Christ's closest followers that he has indeed been spiritually transfigured in preparation for mystical vision. Faith, the poet avers, is the substance of things hoped for, the evidence of things not seen (*Par.* xxiv, 64–66); Hope, Dante says, is the expectation of future glory and the product of divine grace (*Par.* xxv, 67–69).

As the examination progresses, Dante's soul and mind are turned to the past. The poet names for St. Peter certain holy men, some of Old Testament fame, from whom the faith is derived. Truth is said to proceed

> per Moïsè, per profeti e per salmi,
> per l'Evangelio e per voi che scriveste
> poi che l'ardente Spirto vi fé almi.
>
> [*Par.* xxiv, 136–138]

> [through Moses, through the Prophets and through the Psalms,
> through the Gospel and through you who wrote
> when the glowing Spirit had made you fosterers.]

And the poet, thinking of how the Old Law was given, later says to St. James that Love has been learned from the voice that spoke to Moses on Mt. Sinai:

> Sternel la voce del verace autore,
> che dice a Moïsè, di sé parlando:
> "Io ti farò vedere ogne valore".
>
> [*Par.* xxvi, 40–42]

> [It is brought down to me by the voice of that veracious author
> who said to Moses, speaking of himself:
> "I will make you see all worth".]

Yet if the Exodus occupies the thoughts of Dante, so does Christ's Redemption of man on the Cross. Speaking on the subject of Hope, the poet recalls Christ and "the death that he sustained

that I might live" (*Par.* xxvi, 59: "la morte ch'el sostenne perch'
io viva"). And Beatrice, when introducing John, notes this apostle's very special relationship to Christ at the time of the Crucifixion; for she says, "this was he chosen from upon the Cross for
the great office" (*Par.* xxv, 113–114: "questi fue / di su la croce
al grande officio eletto"). Furthermore, she asserts that James represented Hope on those occasions—one of which was clearly the
Crucifixion—when Christ spiritually illumined the three apostles.
In the words of Beatrice to James,

> "Inclita vita per cui la larghezza
> de la nostra basilica si scrisse,
>   fa risonar la spene in questa altezza:
> tu sai, che tante fiate la figuri,
> quante Iesù ai tre fé più carezza".

[*Par.* xxv, 29–33]

> ["Illustrious life, by whom the generosity
> of our court was chronicled,
>   make hope sound forth in this height;
> you know that you figured it all those times
> when Jesus gave most light to the three".]

One can easily understand, of course, why Dante mentions the
Exodus, why Beatrice makes veiled and open allusions to the
presence of the three apostles at the Crucifixion. In both the text
of the *Commedia* and the letter to Can Grande, these two events
have been seen to foreshadow the figural episode now being imitated, an episode representing the third occasion on which God
had spoken with and given spiritual light to his chosen servants
upon a mountain.

In acting out this third episode, the Transfiguration, Dante lifts
up his brow to the light of St. Peter (*Par.* xxiv, 53–54: "io levai
la fronte / in quella luce onde spirava questo"). Then the poet's
eyes are uplifted to the mountains toward the flame of St. James
(*Par* .xxv, 38–39: "io levài li occhi a' monti / che li 'ncurvaron
pria col troppo pondo"). And Dante, with but few companions
about him, learns that he is to be granted holy audiences in the
utmost secrecy. St. James announces to the poet,

> ". . . vuol che tu t'affronti
> lo nostro Imperadore, anzi la morte,
> ne l'aula più secreta co' suoi conti".

[*Par.* xxv, 40–42]

> [". . . our Emperor wills
> that before your death you be confronted
> with his Saints in his most secret hall".]

So dazzling is the flame of John, the third apostle to appear, that Dante cannot closely follow all of its movements. Flashing down from on high, the flame joins the other two apostles and wheels dancing with them in a brilliant circle of fire. Then the light that is John approaches the poet, but Dante, attempting to look upon this apostle, is blinded like one gazing upon "the sun eclipsed a little" (*Par.* xxv, 119: "eclissar lo sole un poco"). When his sight is restored following John's examination, the poet, as one awakening happily from slumber, turns his eyes upon light emanating from Beatrice in a manner reminiscent of his first vision of the lady in the Earthly Paradise:

> così de li occhi miei ogni quisquilia
> fugò Beatrice col raggio d'i suoi,
> che rifulgea da più di mille milia.
>
> [*Par.* xxvi, 76–78]

> [so Beatrice dissipated every mote
> from my eyes with the ray of her own
> that shone for more than a thousand miles.]

How revealing is this example of the poet's typology of internal recurrence! In the Earthly Paradise Dante had watched Beatrice appear as the rising sun of Christ, and his soul had tasted a most desired food upon seeing in her eyes the glittering shape of the Gryphon. Among the fixed stars before taking his theological examination, he had seen Christ, surrounded by the heavenly hosts, approaching from afar in the form of the sun; and after the poet's mind had failed, Dante had been ordered by Beatrice to look upon her smile:

> "Apri li occhi e riguarda qual son io;
> tu hai vedute cose, che possente
> se' fatto a sostener lo riso mio".
>
> [*Par.* xxiii, 46–48]

> ["Open your eyes and look on what I am:
> you have seen things which have made you
> able to sustain my smile".]

Now once again a holy soul appears as the sun; the poet loses his sight, but quickly regaining it, seeks out with his eyes a ray of light coming from his lady.

There is variety here as well as sameness. Each incident is cleverly contrived to convey its own tonalities and meanings, each captures the reader's interest with fresh and unexpected detail. Yet contrasts in the repeated motifs demonstrate Dante's increasing holiness. In Eden the new, morning sun, to which Beatrice is compared, is shrouded in mists and bearable to the onlooker's eye. The sun that descends in the fixed stars, before the poet's examination, comes from the distant constellation Gemini and remains well away from Dante and the other foreground actors on the scene. But here is the apostle of Love moving into the immediate vicinity of the poet like the sun blazing at full strength and eclipsed only "un poco." And this fiery light, appearing as an image of Christ, shines before Dante just after a dance by the three apostles who saw the Son transfigured and who symbolize the theological virtues. John is being disclosed *in figura* in the role of the Son on Mt. Tabor; Dante, in the role of a Christian seeking to lift his eyes to the light of Christ on a mountain. Though the poet has at last attained the spiritual powers necessary to endure the close approach of this most powerful of holy lights, his sudden blindness prevents him from raising his eyes for a third time to enjoy even a partial vision of God. The reason is obvious: Dante at this point has rationally demonstrated his acceptance of Faith and Hope; he has yet to prove that he has embraced the all-important virtue of Charity. But his mind does not fail him as it did when Christ descended as the sun from Gemini, and the poet now shows through rational discourse that he at least partly comprehends the third of the theological virtues. Charity, the poet tells John, is the good that represents the Alpha and Omega of all Scripture (*Par.* XXVI, 16–18).

Having proved that his soul has been renewed, Dante exalted by the theological virtues, will now be raised with the help of Beatrice and later St. Bernard, to the highest Heaven of the eternal Empyrean, and there he will completely fulfill the promise of the Transfiguration. He will first look upon the face of St. Bernard, a face corresponding to the image of Christ on the Veronica. And before the Rose of Heaven with St. Bernard at his side and Beatrice visible within God's city of the rose, he will for the third time lift up his eyes beyond all previous light as to a mountain, his movements reflecting those of the apostles on Mt. Tabor:

Io levai li occhi; e come da mattina
la parte orïental de l'orizzonte
soverchia quella dove 'l sol declina,

  così, quasi di valle andando a monte
con li occhi, vidi parte ne lo stremo
vincer di lume tutta l'altra fronte.

[*Par.* XXXI, 118–123]

[I lifted my eyes, and as at morn
the oriental part of the horizon
outshines that where the sun goes down,

  so, as from the valley rising to the mountain,
I saw with my eyes a part of the edge
surpass all the remaining ridge in light.]

The vision of an image of God denied the poet before John will now be realized, for Dante will not lower his eyes from holy illumination. He will focus them upon the glowing souls in the Rose, raise them higher to the light of the Virgin Mary, and finally, following the direction of the Virgin's gaze, lift them higher still to a single flame that will eventually appear, transfigured by Dante's powers of vision, as three colored lights circling a human form (*Par.* XXXIII, 90–138).

5

Through Shadowy Realms of the Living

I am not of this people, nor this age,
And yet my harpings will unfold a tale
Which shall preserve these times when not a page
Of their perturbed annals could attract
An eye. . . . [The voice of Dante in *The Prophecy of Dante,* by George Gordon, Lord Byron]

Leaving a dark wood midway in his journey through life, Dante Alighieri, at the outset of the *Commedia,* crosses a "passo" that no one ever left alive, and comes to rest on a desert strand glowing in diffused morning sunlight.

This passage of the poet from the world of the living to that of the dead, and the resulting start of a double journey, is managed with such surface simplicity that the step through the looking glass of mortality goes almost unnoticed. And after it has been taken, one might not immediately be aware that an actual and a reflected journey have begun, or that the unfolding landscape of the world beyond—a sea, a grand desert, a mountain—serves to place the literal and shadowed action in two identifiable regions on the globe's surface. In accord with the poem's depiction of repeated but varied figural patterns, expanded understanding comes when the figured action and landscape of the prologue reappear in the *Purgatorio,* when a pilgrimage beyond life at the antipodes is seen to figure a pilgrimage in life near the earth's middle at Jerusalem. With this insight one becomes fully cognizant that even in the prologue, by means of the typology of worldly imitation, two figurally related narratives are being presented: attention is being centered upon action taking place both in an environment beyond life and on the Exodus pathway near Jerusalem in this life. This double narrative continues throughout all three canticles.

With the complete outline of the dual Great Circle journey disclosed, and with Dante's figural techniques readily apprehended, the reader is at last in a position to look intently upon the poem's literal sense, the otherworldly pilgrimage, and to see shadowed in that tour, as in a glass darkly, previously unnoticed stations on the earthly Great Circle route. This close perusal of the poem's shadowed meaning, the worldly pilgrimage, is best accomplished at the expense of certain contemporary attitudes. Many modern readers, unaccustomed to thinking of the Bible as historically true or of medieval holy sites as historically authentic, may be understandably troubled by a religious outlook that placed so much importance upon a supposedly blessed collection of rocks, trees, relics, and places on earth. Modern sensibility is not attuned to such literal-mindedness; and readers today cannot be expected to be especially responsive to the world conceived of and experienced as an iconographic book. Yet it is notable that the delicate symbolic shadings admired in the *Commedia* arise from the historicity of the poem's literal sense, and this historicity has been seen to be grounded in Dante's purposeful figural reflections of those very same objects, relics, and places that may trouble modern taste. The subtle symbolism of the *Commedia* has had over the centuries no lack of commentators; it is the typological basis for this symbolism that is most in need of elucidation. If Dante's worldly typology is to be properly examined, one is forced to overcome modern bias and to accept a medieval literal-mindedness that makes possible the perception in the poem of specific earthly objects.

Another difficulty is soon encountered in any modern examination of Dante's worldly typology. The poet, setting the action of his work in the Golden Jubilee year of 1300, could assume on the part of his educated contemporaries a knowledge of the most important stations on the Exodus and Rome routes. Dante doubtless believed that those most blessed pathways and the iconographic Holy Lands through which they passed would remain for the instruction of man until the end of the world. But because of radical shifts in cultural views and resulting differences in the common knowledge of educated men, it is too much to expect modern readers to identify figured objects and landscapes with which they are unfamiliar. Today the particulars of the reflected Great Circle journey, and most especially those forgotten stations linking Egypt to Jerusalem, can best be identified through historical scholarship and the experience of traveling over the ancient paths. Then one can see mirrored in the glass of the poem's literal sense a surprising number of recognizable places and things in this mortal world.

Dangerous Waters

When in *Inferno* I Dante's mind looks back over that mysterious "passo," the poet is likened, it has been noted, to a man who has just escaped from a deep sea and who turns to stare at dangerous waters (*Inf.* I, 22–27). Dante before making the crossing has been extremely fearful; God's light has only partially quelled the terror in his heart, and the poet's trepidation before landing on a desert shore is doubtless well founded.

To understand the degree to which the sea of *Inferno* I shadows dangerous earthly waters beyond which pilgrims had to pass in order to reach holy land, one has only to consult pilgrim writings. "A journey by sea is subject to many hardships," writes Felix Fabri on the hazards of pilgrimage sea voyages in a fifteenth-century account. "The sea itself is very injurious to those who are unaccustomed to it," he continues, "and very dangerous on many accounts; for it strikes terror into the soul. . . . And the most terrible danger is that it is the wise who are most afraid of it, while fools hold it cheap." [1] Christian travelers in Dante's time no doubt would have agreed. However, as preparations were under way to follow the sun's light eastward from Venice to that land beyond the sea, Florentine pilgrim Leonardo di Niccolò Frescobaldi, at a gathering with other Christians from Florence, placed himself in the hands of God and so was comforted. Frescobaldi in his fourteenth-century narrative tells of how he and his group were urged by certain Venetians not to make the dangerous voyage to Alexandria. "You Florentines," a Venetian named Remigi Soranzi is reported to have said, "are not used to the tempests of the sea as we and others of the maritime are. . . . And so all of us, none dissenting, say and advise that you put not out to sea, and you tempt not God. And the others ratified his remarks." Frescobaldi, nonetheless, was not to be dissuaded. "I replied that I tempted not God," he writes, "nay, I placed myself in His mercy: that to Him it was a light thing, not to make the infirm whole, but to make the dead live; and that I was disposed to see first the gates of the

---

1. *The Book of the Wanderings of Brother Felix Fabri*, trans. Aubrey Stewart (London, 1896), vol. 1, part 1, p. 121.

Sepulchre rather than those of Florence, and that if God permitted that the sea should be my grave, I was content." [2]

Off the coast from Lussino not far from Venice, Frescobaldi was sadly to comprehend just how dangerous waters could be. He explains that the boat on which he and his companions were sailing "met a little tempest. But since the ship was new and large it appeared to make fun of the sea. But an unarmed galley, laden with pilgrims, . . . since it was old, opened and about two hundred, all poor people, perished, and to pay little they had boarded such a bad vessel, as it so often happens, that worse arrangements are for the poor; but according to our holy Faith these have had a greater reward than we, because I believe they are at the feet of Christ" (*Visit*, p. 36).

Though God permitted most pilgrims to arrive safely off the coast of the Holy Land, he sometimes took the lives of a few almost at the moment they were about to come to shore. In the early twelfth century the pilgrim Saewulf personally saw twenty-three pilgrim ships sink during a storm off the shore from Joppa. According to Saewulf, "more than a thousand persons of either sex perished on that day." [3] Saewulf himself was saved from such a death by what he claims was the intercession of God. "On the very same day that we anchored someone said to me, God prompting him, as I believe: 'Sir, go on shore to-day, lest perhaps to-night, or early in the morning, a storm may come on and you may not be able to land.' When I heard this, I was at once seized with a desire to go ashore. I hired a boat, and with all my belongings landed. While I was landing, the sea became troubled, the tossing increased, and a violent tempest arose, but by the gracious favor of God I arrived unharmed."

On the next day Saewulf was to stand looking back over dangerous waters. "Early in the morning, as we came out from the church," he writes, "we heard the noise of the sea, the cries of the people, and all were running together, and wondering at such things as they had never heard before. When we got there, we saw

2. See Leonardo Frescobaldi, Giorgio Gucci, and Simone Sigoli, *Visit to the Holy Places*, trans. Frs. Theophilus Bellorini and Eugene Hoade, preface and notes Fr. Bellarmino Bagatti (Jerusalem, 1948), p. 34.

3. *Pilgrimage of Saewolf to Jerusalem and the Holy Land*, trans. Bishop of Clifton (London, 1896), p. 8.

the storm running mountains high, and beheld the bodies of men and women without number drowned and miserably lying on the beach" (*Pilgrimage of Saewulf*, p. 6).

Common to these writings is a profound sense that what happens to pilgrims has a cause and a meaning; chance is surely not responsible for either the disasters or the happy episodes of the voyages. It is God who sees Saewulf safely to shore, God who calls poor people to him at an unexpected time, God who is to watch over Frescobaldi on the waters. Though the Creator might move in mysterious ways, the pilgrims unquestionably believed that his will and their own interior spiritual states were to be discerned in the incidents of the journey. Thus, in *Inferno* I, when a prospective pilgrim displays great fear while being attracted to the east toward the reflected light of the rising sun, early readers could be expected to assume that this Christian is stained by sin and therefore striken with terror at the prospect of holy pilgrimage. Yet if the attempted journey is to proceed, the Christian must abandon secular activities and "pass over" eastward to a blessed land beyond the sea. The traveler in the prologue, however, negotiates the "passo" with difficulty. In landing on a shore like a person escaping from dangerous waters, this Christian is comparable to a pilgrim who seeks holy land but who is punished by God through the agency of a stormy sea. Early readers of the *Commedia* would realize that God has not ordained that the Christian easily and immediately begin a true pilgrimage, for the prospective pilgrim in the prologue to the *Inferno* can barely reach the shore.

Evil and Holy Landings

Dante arrives on that strand beyond life wearied in body and so spent that he is said to be like a man panting for breath (*Inf.* I, 22–28). The type for the earthly event shadowed in the landing beyond life is suggested by Saewulf's graphic description of the plight of pilgrims struggling against high seas off the coast of Joppa. As pilgrim ships broke apart, Saewulf observed from the beach that some Christians "stupefied with terror were drowned; some, as they were clinging, were decapitated by the timbers on their own ship. This may seem incredible to many, yet I saw it. Some, washed off from the decks of their ships, were carried out again to the deep. Some, who knew how to swim, voluntarily committed themselves to the waves, and thus many perished. Very few, who had confidence in their own strength, arrived safe on shore" (*Pilgrimage of Saewulf*, p. 7). In the shadowed typology of the poem, the reflected Christian, having seen heavenly light, is one of those with only just enough strength to reach the strand, one of those so physically and spiritually exhausted that he must rest upon landing. This Christian has only begun to be converted to God, and his complete conversion from sin to grace can come only through the arduous discipline of long pilgrimage.

In the *Commedia* other voyages to or landings on holy land have been seen to mirror this life's imperfect peregrinations. The most saintly of mortal pilgrims on earth had to sail to their destinations in frail wooden ships and expose themselves to the variables of sea, wind, and weather. Their voyage over, these good pilgrims coming to shore might sing psalms together, fling themselves elatedly upon holy soil, and remember that they stood upon land where Christ died on the Cross. Still, even the most successful of landings sometimes involved attendant dangers. "We came close to . . . rocks," writes Felix Fabri of one such arrival, "and as we passed between them through the waves which beat upon them, we were splashed with water and wetted, howbeit we escaped dashing our little bark against the reefs, which was feared, and arrived at the shore and landed. As soon as we trod the holy land beneath our feet we cast ourselves down upon our faces and kissed the sacred earth with great devotion. By merely touching the land we received plenary indulgences for the remission of sins which I have decided to mark in the sequel with this sign" (*Wanderings*, vol. 1, part 1, pp. 222–223). Two crosses are drawn on the manuscript following the last sentence.

In a fulfilled and idealized reenactment of the kind of landing described by Fabri, dead souls in *Purgatorio* II sail over a calm sea in an angelically propelled boat; they come to shore without difficulty; and they are soon sent off in the right direction by a pagan guide.

A spiritual hierarchy of evil and holy journeys, which reveal the state of the souls involved, is clearly apparent in the *Commedia*. In trying to reach the strand where the dead souls were later to disembark, Ulysses, according to his own account in *Inferno* XXVI, perished in the waves far from the coast of Mt. Purgatory island.

This pagan's unholy voyage is the fulfilled type for all blas-
phemous earthly attempts at pilgrimage. Dante's own uncertain
landing in *Inferno* I mirrors the problems encountered by very
sinful pilgrims on earth. The happy arrival of dead souls in the
company of an angel in *Purgatorio* II represents a higher, more
nearly perfected form of reflected earthly pilgrimage. Most joyful
and most remarkable of all is Dante's effortless and instantaneous
passage in the *Paradiso* through a sea of being to a holy shore, the
poet's ascent serving as the ideal otherworldly type for holy
journeys in life.

Three Beasts of the Desert

The extraordinary circumstances surrounding Dante's meeting
with a leopard, a lion, and a she-wolf in *Inferno* I are such that
one can well comprehend why the literal sense of the canto has so
often been regarded as a poetic fiction, an "allegory of the poets"
in which a series of surface, imaginative inventions depend for
their existence upon underlying, fixed ideas. In particular, the
visually powerful beast images have traditionally been interpreted as fictive veils concealing specific concepts.[4] Yet it is of

4. Étienne Gilson in *Dante and Philosophy*, trans. David Moore (New York,
Evanston, and London, 1963), observes that "although interpretations of Dante do not
always agree as to the meaning of the 'dark forest,' the Lion, the Panther, and the
She-wolf, all admit by implication that the symbolism of these things or beings is of
a simple kind. Whatever they may signify, they signify but one thing, which remains
precisely the same however varied its modes of application may be." While arguing
that the individuals in the *Commedia* have a literal, historical existence in the context of the poem, Gilson adds, in speaking of the beasts, that "their common characteristic is that they are pure fictions, or, if one prefers, simple images, to which Dante
has decided to attach once and for all a certain significance" (pp. 291–293).

T. S. Eliot in his introductory essay "Dante," in *Selected Essays* (London, 1966),
also assumes that Dante sought to express certain inner ideas through the outward
imagery of the beasts. "I do not recommend," writes Eliot, "in first reading the first
canto of the *Inferno*, worrying about the identity of the Leopard, the Lion, or the
She-Wolf. It is really better, at the start, not to know or care what they do mean.
What we should consider is not so much the meaning of the images, but the reverse
process, that which led a man having an idea to express it in images" (p. 242).

For traditional didactic interpretations of the beast images, see in particular the
notes to *Inferno* I in *La Divina Commedia di Dante Alighieri*, ed. C. H. Grandgent,
rev. ed. (Boston, 1933). The view that the literal sense of the *Commedia* is a poetic
fiction has been upheld by F. Flamini, *I significati reconditi della Commedia di Dante e
il suo fine supremo* (Livorno, 1903), vol. 1, p. 58; (1904), vol. 2, pp. 1–25. Bernard
Stambler in *Dante's Other World* (New York, 1957), pp. 54–71, somewhat modifies

considerable interest that in Dante's period leopards, lions, wolves, and other wild beasts were described as roaming the deserts along the whole of the Exodus route. In the twelfth century, for example, the Russian Abbot Daniel mentions in A.D. 1106–1107 the "many panthers and lions" to be seen in the Jordan River Valley's desert depression near the Dead Sea.[5] In A.D. 1185 the pilgrim Joannes Phocas tells of a lion in the region as does Felix Fabri as late as the fifteenth century.[6] And Niccolò of Poggibonsi records having seen in A.D. 1346–1350 "many parrots and leopards" among "numberless animals" next to a house in Cairo.[7] The Muslim Usāmah Ibn-Munquidh, in writing of the Holy Land in A.D. 1138–1147, speaks of his many personal encounters with lions and of the manner in which these beasts attack men; he also vividly explains how his party killed a wolf while on a desert hunting expedition.[8]

With wild beasts such as those referred to by Dante on the desert pathways, it would take no straining of the imagination for early readers of the *Commedia* to conceive of a shadowed Christian near the earth's middle, a counterpart for Dante in the realm beyond at the antipodes, actually confronting animals close to a purgatorial mountain on the desert of Exodus. In the opening canto of the *Inferno*, it is a leopard that first stands before the poet on the slopes of a holy mountain:

> Ed ecco. quasi al cominciar de l'erta,
> una lonza leggiera e presta molto,
> che di pel macolato era coverta.
>
> [*Inf.* i, 31–33]

> [And behold, almost at the commencement of the rise,
> a Leopard, light and very nimble,
> which was covered with spotted coat.]

---

the traditional view by admitting a degree of historical literalness while essentially maintaining that the literal sense is a fiction.

5. *The Pilgrimage of the Russian Abbott Daniel in the Holy Land*, trans. M. de Khitrowo, notes C. W. Wilson (London, 1895), p. 29.

6. The *Pilgrimage of Joannes Phocas in the Holy Land*, trans. Aubrey Stewart (London, 1896), p. 27; *The Book of the Wanderings of Brother Felix Fabri*, trans. Aubrey Stewart (London, 1893), vol. 2, part 1, pp. 26–27.

7. *A Voyage Beyond the Seas*, trans. Frs. Theophilus Bellorini and Eugene Hoade, intro. Fr. Bellarmino Bagatti (Jerusalem, 1945), p. 92.

8. *An Arab-Syrian Gentleman and Warrior in the Period of the Crusades*, trans. Philip K. Hitti (New York, 1929), pp. 136–140, 223.

And as early as the sixth century, pilgrims noted leopards as among the wild animals and strange things to be found in the deserts and valleys near Mt. Sinai, the earthly pilgrims' purgatorial mountain of God. "Between Sinai and Horeb is a valley," writes Antoninus Martyr in *Of the Holy Places Visited* (ca. 560–570), "in which at certain times dew descends from heaven which they call manna. It thickens and becomes like grains of mastic, and is collected. Jars full of it are kept upon the mountain, and they [the monks] give away small bottles of it for a blessing; and they gave us five sextarii of it. They also drink it as a relish; and they gave some of it to us, and we drank it. Upon these mountains feed lions and leopards, wild goats and mules, and wild asses together, and none of them are hunted by the lions because of the vastness of the desert." [9] In pilgrim writings the monks and hermits of Mt. Sinai were said to have spiritual aid from Heaven in controlling the wild beasts; and Sinai Abbot John Climacus writes, in his seventh-century work *The Ladder of Divine Ascent,* that St. Stephen (ca. 600), the monk who was famous for hearing the confessions of pilgrims at a stone gate on the mountain, once tamed a leopard living on nearby deserts. [10]

In the twofold narrative of the *Commedia,* the primary and reflected travelers are not harmed by the animal. But Ibn-Munquidh

9. *Places Visited,* trans. Aubrey Stewart, notes C. W. Wilson (London, 1887), pp. 30–31. In the fourteenth-century *The Book of Sir John Maundeville,* reprinted in *Early Travels In Palestine,* ed. and notes Thomas Wright (London, 1848), an author notes that at the base of Mt. Sinai "there is an abbey of monks, well built and well closed with gates for fear of wild beasts" (p. 157). This and other information about Mt. Sinai in the *Book* is confirmed by statements in the pilgrim texts and can be considered reasonably reliable; see *The Buke of John Maundeville,* ed. with French text, notes, and intro. by George F. Warner (London, 1889), pp. xv–xxii. Among the fictitious tales in the *Book* is an account of the dangerous region near the mountain of the Earthly Paradise in the southern hemisphere. "And you shall understand," writes the author, "that no man that is mortal may approach to that Paradise, for by land no man may go for wild beasts, that are in the deserts, and for the high mountains, and the great huge rocks, that no man may pass by for the dark places that are there . . ." (*Early Travels,* p. 277).

10. *The Ladder of Divine Ascent,* trans. Archimandrite Lazarus Moore, intro. M. Heppell (London, 1959), p. 121. Comments about St. Stephen can be found in Lina Eckenstein's *A History of Sinai* (London, 1921), pp. 111–112; Heinz Skrobucha's *Sinai,* trans. Geoffrey Hunt (London and Toronto, 1966), pp. 80, 98; and O. F. A. Meinardus' *Christian Egypt: Ancient and Modern* (Cairo, 1965), pp. 388, 390. Stories about the Sinai monks' control over beasts appear in Niccolò of Poggibonsi's *A Voyage Beyond the Seas,* pp. 109–110, and in *Visit to the Holy Places,* p. 115.

by contrast tells how a twelfth-century knight had a less fortunate meeting with a leopard at Hunak, one of the castles defending Ma'arrah-al-Nu'mān. The leopard attacked the knight, "broke his back and killed him." Like Christian pilgrims in the Holy Land, the Muslims in the area were quite ready to ascribe this type of event to the will of God, only from a manifestly non-Christian point of view. "The peasants of Hunak," writes Ibn-Munquidh, "used to call that leopard 'the leopard that takes part in the holy war' " (*An Arab-Syrian*, p. 140).

After Dante's forward and upward movement is blocked by the first beast, the poet becomes aware that it is the time when the morning sun and stars are in view (*Inf.* I, 37–39). Although Dante does not look directly upon these heavenly bodies as he will do later, he is given cause to hope by the hour and the season, that is, until the moment when a lion appears on the path.

> . . . che paura non mi desse
> la vista che m'apparve d'un leone.
> Questi parea che contra me venisse
> con la test' alta e con rabbiosa fame,
> sì che parea che l'aere ne tremesse.
>
> [*Inf.* I, 44–48]

> [. . . but that I feared
> a lion which appeared to me.
> He seemed coming upon me
> with head erect, and furious hunger;
> so that the air seemed afraid of him.]

An almost exact parallel for this second meeting can be found in an eighth-century pilgrim guide book, *The Hodoeporicon of Saint Willibald* (ca. 754), a work written by a nun from Willibald's dictation. In recording how the pilgrim Willibald and his party left Samaria and moved over the pilgrimage path to the Levant, the account reads: "From thence they travelled on across a wide plain full of olive-trees, and there went with them an Ethiopian with two camels and a mule. . . . And as they journeyed there met them a lion which, with open mouth, roaring and growling, sought to seize and devour them, and terrified them greatly. Then that Ethiopian said to them, 'Fear you not, but go on.' They went on immediately, and drew near to it. But the lion, by the disposition of the Almighty God enthroned on high, quickly turned another way, and left the path clear for them to pass." [11]

All the key elements are here: the hungry lion astride the path; its movement forward as if to devour the travelers; the fear experienced by the pilgrims; the ultimate influence of God upon the movements of the beast. If it were not known that the recounted meeting is from a pilgrim narrative, one might interpret the passage as a fiction introduced into a medieval morality tract to convey a moral message. But lions did roam the pilgrim paths; they did interfere with the movements of Christians. And if in the pilgrim text a lion is described in a terse, graphic account having moral overtones, that roaring animal was apparently real enough to cause Willibald and his companions considerable anxiety.

The last beast Dante meets in the prologue to the *Inferno* is

> . . . una lupa, che di tutte brame
> sembiava carca ne la sua magrezza,
> e molte genti fé già viver grame,
>   questa mi porse tanto di gravezza
> con la paura ch'uscia di sua vista,
> ch'io perdei la speranza de l'altezza.
>
> [*Inf.* i, 49–54]

> [. . . a she-wolf, that looked full of all cravings
> in her leanness; and has before now
> made many live in sorrow.
>   She brought such heaviness upon me
> with the terror of her aspect,
> that I lost the hope of ascending.]

This lean creature, a scavenger of the desert, forces Dante backward and downward toward a spiritual death resulting in part from the loss of heavenly light. And on the Sinai deserts along the pilgrim path to the mountain of God, Florentine Leonardo Frescobaldi remarked upon the wolves in the area. "There is a very great deal of partridge and francolin," he writes in a fourteenth-century account, "but nobody could catch one of these animals, save the mean wolves who feed on them and the pilgrims who die in the desert" (*Visit,* p. 57). The wolf accordingly is that mean creature associated by Frescobaldi with dead pilgrims who have failed to reach Mt. Sinai and Jerusalem. The tenacity and viciousness of wolves in the Holy Land are well attested to in the twelfth-century

11. *Hodoeporicon,* trans. Canon Brownlow (London, 1895), p. 26.

memoir of Usāmah Ibn-Munquidh. After Ibn-Munquidh and some companions had made camp in a circle one evening on the desert, "a wolf, caught in the circle, pounced upon a gazelle in the center of it, and was killed while in that position" (*An Arab-Syrian*, p. 223).

Though certain kinds of animals that once lived on the deserts of the Holy Land have today disappeared, it is enough to know that in Dante's time leopards, lions, and wolves did regularly appear before pilgrims who, in converting their souls, reenacted the biblical Exodus while traveling toward Jerusalem. But because the pilgrim texts telling of the Egypt-to-Jerusalem journey have been neglected by Dante commentators, the three beasts in the realm beyond have not generally been viewed in their proper light as fulfilled types of corresponding animals on earth.

No longer is there an absolute need for commentators to label each supposedly fictional beast image with one or more clear, fixed ideas—and then to disagree about which clear, fixed ideas Dante intended. When the three beasts of the desert are examined in context without preconceived notions about their being artifacts, they take on a fresh, three-dimensional quality that demands recognition. The animals move before the reader with far too much life, concreteness, and spontaneity to be easily confined. The spotted leopard, nimble and light, appears suddenly on the scene; the lion with head erect, furious with hunger, seems to advance; the lean she-wolf with the craving look stalks forward. Both aesthetically and in the perspective of the pilgrimage tradition, the three beasts can be regarded in the actual and shadowed senses of the poem as "real," their physical presence in turn supporting varying symbolic values.

That Place Where the Sun is Silent

Of the three beasts that bound before him, the she-wolf most afflicts Dante. This animal, the poet writes,

> che, venendomi 'ncontro, a poco a poco
> mi ripigneva là dove 'l sol tace.
>   Mentre ch'i' rovinava in basso loco,
> dinanzi a li occhi mi si fu offerto
> chi per lungo silenzio parea fioco.

[*Inf.* I, 59–63]

[which coming against me, little by little
drove me back to where the Sun is silent.
While I was rushing downwards,
there appeared before my eyes
one who seemed hoarse from long silence.]

During the poet's descent to a low place or "basso loco" (*Inf.* I, 61)
in the "gran diserto" (*Inf.* I, 64), it is Virgil, of course, who enters
and speaks in a seemingly hoarse voice:

". . . io sarò tua guida,
e trarrotti di qui per loco etterno;
    ove udirai le disperate strida,
vedrai li antichi spiriti dolenti,
ch'a la seconda morte ciascun grida".

[*Inf.* I, 113–117]

[". . . I will be your guide,
and lead you through an eternal place,
    where you shall hear the hopeless shrieks,
shall see the ancient spirits in pain,
so that each calls for a second death".]

At this point the Mantuan says that Lucy has been watching
Dante from Heaven, and this lady is quoted as saying to Beatrice:

" 'non vedi tu la morte che 'l combatte
su la fiumana ove 'l mar non ha vanto?' ".

[*Inf.* II, 107–108]

[" 'Do you not see the death which combats him
upon the river over which the sea has no boast?' ".]

In considering the mortal Egypt-to-Jerusalem pilgrimage shadowed in the poem, one has little trouble locating from these
passages a reflected earthly area on the actual Exodus route. A
low and wild (*Inf.* I, 93: "selvaggio") place in a great desert; a
place where the sun is silent, where the light of God cannot be
plainly seen; a place from which a Christian and a pagan with
Heaven's permission might descend into Hell; a place which, when
looked upon from above, appears as the site of a combat between a
Christian and Death upon a river over which the sea has no boast
—where on the Exodus pathway might this place be?
    In attempting an answer, modern scholarly maps and charts
of Dante's poetic world picture are of no use, for they are not

marked to show sacred sites on the Exodus route. However, Abraham Ortelius, in introducing a late edition of *Theatrum Orbis Terrarum*, provides an explanation, certainly valid in Dante's period, of how Christians learned of the Exodus by studying early maps. "For how much we are holpen," Ortelius writes, "when as in the Holy Scripture, we read of the journey of the Israelites, which they made from Egypt, through the Red Sea, and that same huge Wildernesse into the Land of Promise, when as looking upon the Mappe of Palestina, we doe almost as well see it as if we were there, I thinke any student in Divinite or that History hath oft made traill." The places so studied, he continues, "will the longer be kept in memory." [12]

One notes on typical and very famous medieval *mappaemundi*—those of Isidor (A.D. 775) and Henry of Mainz (A.D. 1110), the Hereford map (A.D. 1285) and the Epsdorf map (A.D. 1290)—consistent "speaking-picture" markings of the Exodus path, markings that are useful in understanding Dante's allusion to a low desert region. Babylon, Old Cairo, is always drawn on the Nile River. To the north of the city, a tiny strip of land across the Red Sea reveals the spot where the Israelites were supposed to have passed over. This landbridge points to a labeled drawing of Mt. Sinai further to the north, and close to Mt. Sinai to the northwest is a dark oval labeled *Mare Mortuum* (Dead Sea). The River Jordan is drawn as a line moving south from the marked city of Jerusalem, located in the middle of the maps; the river is depicted as emptying into the *Mare Mortuum*. On the Hereford map, which G. R. Crone thinks may have been made specifically to guide world pilgrims to the Holy Land,[13] a wide line marks the route of the

12. Ortelius' remarks are quoted by George Wesley Whiting in *Milton's Literary Milieu* (New York, 1964), pp. 97–98. The quotation is from the English edition of *Theatrum Orbis Terrarum* (London, 1606).

13. See the monograph by G. R. Crone (p. 11) published with *The World Map by Richard of Haldingham in Hereford Cathedral* (London, 1954). Outlines of *mappaemundi* by Isidor and Henry of Mainz are included among the materials published with *The World Map by Richard of Haldingham*. See also the early *mappaemundi* reproduced in Leo Bagrow's *History of Cartography*, rev. and enl. R. A. Skelton, trans. D. L. Paisey, (Cambridge, Mass., 1964) ; Giovanni Agnelli's *"Itinerario del 'Purgatorio'"* in *Topo-cronografia del Viaggio Dantesco* (Milano, 1891), pp. 81–88; C. Raymond Beazley's *The Dawn of Modern Geography*, 3 vols. (Oxford, 1906) ; the *Atlas composé de Mappemondes, de Portulans, et de Cartes Hydrographiques et Historiques*, ed. Vecomte de Santarem (Paris, 1842–53) ; and *Monumenta Cartographica Vaticana*, vol. 1 (Città del Vaticano, 1944).

Exodus. The line moves straight to the northeast from Egypt, over the Red Sea, and on to Mt. Sinai; then in three loops the line moves generally westward to the side of the *Mare Mortuum* at a place close to the drawn River Jordan. Finally, the line moves around the northeastern side of the Dead Sea to the River Jordan and comes to an end angled toward Jerusalem.

To obtain a perspective approximating the heavenly view enjoyed by Lucy in the *Inferno,* an early reader had only to look upon a medieval map and to see, running through a desert basin not far from Mt. Sinai, the River Jordan over which the adjoining Dead Sea has no power or "boast." Even without a map, an educated early reader doubtless would have been as familiar with the locations of holy places near the middle of the world—Mt. Sinai, the River Jordan, and the Dead Sea—as a modern educated reader would be with the locations of key places in the middle of Europe— for example, Mt. Blanc, the Rhine River, and Lake Leman. And in recalling the geographical position of a holy river that empties into the Dead Sea at the bottom of a barren desert depression, the reader of Dante's period would be directing his attention to what in fact is the lowest place on earth.

Generations of pilgrims believed that they were being saved from spiritual death through baptism in the river's waters, and this ritual was thought to cause the waters of the adjoining sea to rush backwards. Speaking of the Dead Sea at the time of Christ's baptism in the Jordan, the Russian Abbot Daniel writes, "Formerly the Sea of Sodom came right to the place of baptism; but now it is distant from it about 4 versts. It was then that the sea, seeing the Deity naked in the midst of the waters of Jordan fled in terror, and the Jordan turned back as the propet saith, 'Why oh sea! have you fled? And you, O Jordan! why have you turned back?' " [14]

In the sixth century Antoninus Martyr claimed to have personally witnessed a miraculous movement of the Jordan's waters during the baptism of a great throng of pilgrims. "The priest descends into the river," writes Antoninus Martyr of the ceremonies on the Epiphany, "and at the hour when he begins to bless the water, at once the Jordan, with a mighty noise rolls back upon itself. The upper water stands still until the baptism is completed, but the

14. *The Pilgrimage of the Russian Abbott Daniel in the Holy Land,* trans. M. de Khitrowo, notes C. W. Wilson, (London, 1895), pp. 27–28.

lower runs off into the sea, as the Psalmist saith, 'The sea saw it and fled: Jordan was driven back.' " [15]

The pilgrims had much to say about the terrain around the river. "The appearance of the whole desert, and Jordan, and the Dead Sea of Sodom, according to my conjecture," writes Joannes Phocas about A.D. 1185, "is much like that of Achris in Illyria; . . . here the Jordan flows into the lake. Moreover, the width of the wilderness is many times as great as the plain of Achris" (*Pilgrimage*, p. 26). In explaining why the area is a desolate and vast desert, Felix Fabri states that "the Lord rained fire and brimstone upon that country, and everything was burned, even down into the bowels of the earth. . . . When the fire ceased, Jordan and the other brooks which run into the place of burning filled up both the length and breadth of the yawning pit which the fire had left when it burned up the land, and thus the salt lake was made (*Wanderings*, vol. 2, part 1, p. 167).

In this desert basin the disc of the sun is perpetually blurred, for the salty waters of the Dead Sea evaporate at an exceptional rate; and mists of varying densities, rising through the heat and glare, hover constantly over the depression throughout the year. Thus the Venerable Bede is too cautious when he associates the phenomenon with only one season: "In summer," he writes, "an immoderate amount of vapour steams up over the plains, while the unhealthy drought and dryness of the soil unite to corrupt the air and destroy the inhabitants with deplorable diseases." [16] Other pilgrims, gazing upon the mists, insisted that they saw smoke and heavy clouds rising from the depression. Describing his journey from Jericho to Jerusalem, Antoninus Martyr writes that "towards the west, we had on our left hand the ashes of Sodom and Gomorrah, over which country there always hangs a dark cloud with a sulphurous odour" (*Holy Places*, p. 13). In the same general area, Felix Fabri notes that he and his companions fixed their "gaze upon the sea itself, and wondered at the smoke thereof, for as Abraham, when he got him up to the mountains early in the morning, looked toward Sodom and Gomorrah, and toward all the land of the plain, and behold, and lo! the smoke of the country went up

15. *Of the Holy Places Visited*, trans. Aubrey Stewart, notes C. W. Wilson (London, 1887), p. 10.

16. *The Venerable Bede Concerning the Holy Places*, trans. James Rose MacPherson (London, 1895), p. 81.

as the smoke of a furnace, as is told in Genesis xix, even so we, as we looked upon the country, saw a cloud going up, not from fire, but from water, like the smoke of a furnace" (*Wanderings*, vol. 2, part 1, p. 186).

This lowest of desert regions where the sun is actually obscured was conceived to be the main entrance to Hell because placed near to the center of the earth in a cleft below Jerusalem. As the Venerable Bede correctly observes, the Dead Sea and its neighboring desert can be seen "by those looking towards it from afar, from the watch-tower of Mount Olivet" (*Holy Places*, p. 30). And Felix Fabri, writing of the Dead Sea, notes that Roman Catholic Christians "believe that the last judgment will be held in the Valley of Jehosaphat, and that the damned will be brought along a river of fire down the Valley of Gehenna to this place, where they will be plunged into the depths of hell. . . . Hence it is plain that here is a mouth of hell, according to us Christians, because we believe that hell is in the midst of the earth, and that the Holy City standeth on the mountains above it in the midst of the earth, even as Gentiles and poets have reckoned the Isle of Crete to be the middle of the world, and hell beneath the same. Wherefore the tears from the idol which was set upon Mount Ida ran down into hell" (*Wanderings*, vol. 2, part 1, pp. 168–169).

The Hell's mouth of the Christians, located below Jerusalem, was specifically associated with sins of incontinence, for at its edge once dwelled the lustful inhabitants of the cities of the plain. Though there was some disagreement about the number of the cities, pilgrim writers held the same opinion on how the cities were destroyed and how the residents were cast into the underworld. In the "accursed" sea, writes Niccolò of Poggibonsi, "were engulfed the five wretched cities, Sodoma, Gomorrah, Seboim, Soar, and Adoma . . . ; fire rained from heaven, and the earth quaked, and so sank these cities with their denizens" (*A Voyage*, p. 73). Fetellus, presenting the traditional view, observes that the Dead Sea was called "also the Sea of the Devil, because by his stimulation and instigation those four miserable cities, Sodoma, Gomorra, Seboim, Adama, were destroyed by sulphurous fire, and from a condition of profuse luxury were submerged in that lake, as they persisted in their baseness." [17]

17. *Description of Jerusalem and the Holy Land*, trans. James Rose MacPherson (London, 1892), p. 11.

Without excluding other symbolic and allegorical interpretations of the prologue to the *Inferno*, it is nevertheless possible to suggest that the action on the low desert, studied from the viewpoint of the typology of worldly imitation, fits with remarkable exactitude into the earthly Exodus pattern of the poem's shadowed sense. Here among the living the reflected Christian is seen retreating toward the lowest point on the Exodus route, the River Jordan-Dead Sea depression near Jerusalem; and directly below the Holy City, the hollow cone of Hell projects down into the center of the earth. After falling back before a beast traditionally thought to symbolize incontinence, the reflected Christian comes to rest in a wild desert where sins of incontinence are punished, where the light of God is dimmed or blotted out, where a mouth of Hell opens upon the underworld below. This is a region identified with the sins of Sodom and Gomorrah, and it should be remembered that in *Inferno* xv, Dante's teacher Brunetto Latini, for violent indulgence in the vice of sodomy, is found condemned to a smoking desert pelted with a rain of fire.

The reflected Chistian in the prologue, however, receives heavenly assistance and so averts eternal damnation. For as St. Benedict later proclaims in *Paradiso* xxii, man's spiritual regeneration is always possible through the Creator; God is said to have displayed his redemptive power by a miracle greater than that required to rescue spiritually corrupt men. The Creator, says St. Benedict, once caused the sea to flee before the waters of the River Jordan:

> "Veramente Iordan vòlto retrorso
> più fu, e 'l mar fuggir, quando Dio volse,
> mirabile a veder che qui 'l soccorso".
>
> [*Par.* xxii, 94–96]

> ["But the Jordan back returning,
> and the sea fleeing when God willed,
> are more wondrous sights than were the rescue here.]

Now Dante in *Inferno* ii, as seen by Lucy in Heaven, combats death on a river over which the sea has no boast; and in the shadowed typology of the poem, a Christian in the Dead Sea basin seeks to avoid spiritual death near the baptismal waters of the River Jordan, waters that can cause the "accursed" sea to run back. But because of his sinfulness, the Christian, who has been driven downward after failing to climb a mountain of God, is not ready to be cleansed in a river that stands as the spiritual gateway to a Holy City. In *Inferno* III, the mirrored Christian on the Exodus path is found instead at an infernal gateway that leads down into the underworld beneath Jerusalem.

The Stance of an Idol

A red and smoking rivulet flowing into a plain of sand—this stream is so frightful in its coloring that Dante shudders when he sees it in the seventh circle of Hell (*Inf.* XIV, 76–78). The poet's courteous Mantuan guide at once announces that nothing more notable has been passed since the pair entered through the "porta" to the underworld (*Inf.* XIV, 85–90). The rivulet, Virgil states, is composed of tears flowing downward from a weeping idol on the island of Crete; this was the idol mentioned also in the pilgrim narrative of Felix Fabri. Virgil adds that this unique statue, shaped like an old man, stands on the wasted island beneath deserted Mt. Ida; the figure's head is said to be of gold; its breast and arms, silver; its lower trunk, brass; its left foot, iron; and its right foot, clay. From a fissure, splitting the idol below the head, drop tears that collect in a grotto and then fall from rock to rock into the underworld. In Hell's upper circles the tears form the Rivers Acheron, Styx, and Phlegethon, and then, by means of the smoking rivulet, they rush below to water the icy regions of Cocytus in the deepest pit of Hell (*Inf.* XIV, 106–120).

An immobile statue on a remote Mediterranean island may not at first seem related to the pilgrimage figure in the *Commedia*. But if the idol's tears are said to be the most notable thing in the seven circles of Hell, fascination centers upon the possible allegorical and symbolic significance of this weeping form.

By citing relevant source passages in the *Book of Daniel*, Ovid's *Metamorphoses*, Virgil's *Aeneid*, and other works, traditional commentary has interpreted the idol as an allegorical depiction of suffering humanity, the four metals representing the four progressively worsening ages of man; the two feet, insecure temporal and secular authority; the fissure, mankind's corruption after the Golden Age; and the tears, the pain caused by sin.[18] Just as

18. See notes on the Idol of Crete passage, for eample, by C. H. Grandgent in his revised edition of *La Divina Commedia di Dante Alighieri* (Boston, 1933), pp.

Christ's blood flowed downward to redeem man, so the tears of broken, sinful humanity fall downward to create Hell's waters and to punish the unredeemed. This image of suffering mankind, moreover, is located midway in the inhabited world between Asia, Africa, and Europe on an island cited by Fabri as having been once regarded as the navel of the earth. And the idol's peculiar stance, which is described by Virgil, suggests the relative dependence of mankind upon the cultures of both East and West:

> Dentro dal monte sta dritto un gran veglio,
> che tien volte le spalle inver' Dammiata
> e Roma guarda come süo speglio.
>
> [*Inf.* XIV, 103–105]

> [Within the mountain stands erect a great Old Man,
> who keeps his shoulders turned towards Damietta,
> and looks at Rome as if it were his mirror.]

The head of mankind, then, points to Rome, the seat of Empire and Papacy; and the shoulders are turned towards the Egyptian city of Damietta, a small coastal port situated on the Nile delta some miles north of the one-time Pharaonic capital of Tanis. Thus mankind is poised between occidental and oriental civilization.

Upon first reflection, it seems curious that the idol's stance should call attention to cities so different in size and importance as Damietta and Rome. In Dante's period the large and splendid city of Babylon, the seat of the Moslem ruler who was considered a contemporary Pharaoh, was the natural oriental counterpart to the eternal city in Italy. Unlike Rome and Babylon, the old delta port of Damietta lay in partial ruin, a city devastated by the Moslems themselves after their defeat of Christian crusaders in A.D. 1250. "The older town of Damiette is uninhabited," writes the author of the *Book of Sir John Maundeville* in the fourteenth century. The Saracens, the author adds, have "beaten down the walls" and then "made another city farther from the sea, and called it New Damiette." [19] Even in 1249 when Old Damietta was captured intact by forces led by Louis IX of France, it must have

---

127, 132–133; and by H. Oelsner in *The 'Inferno' of Dante Alighieri*, trans. J. A. Carlyle and rev. H. Oelsner, commentary P. H. Wicksteed (London, 1954), pp. 156–157.

19. See the *Book of Sir John Maundeville* in Thomas Wright, *Early Travels in Palestine* (London, 1848), p. 151.

been obvious to Christians that this port city was not the center of the infidel's power. After explaining that King Louis IX once took Old Damietta, Niccolò of Poggibonsi, during a personal visit to the city, notes that the King next "went up to Babylon against the Sultan, and the Sultan came out to meet St. Louis with his army. And as God wishes, for our sins, the Sultan overthrew the Christians, and captured St. Louis and held him some time a prisoner" (*A Voyage*, p. 120). Babylon was the Sultan's capital; Babylon was the place that had to be seized to insure decisive victory.

Why, then, does an idol depicting humanity stand with head turned toward the eternal city and shoulders turned toward a newly rebuilt and relatively small port on the Nile delta? According to traditional commentary, Dante very possibly thought Damietta to be the city of Tanis and so an ancient capital of Egypt. But since Felix Fabri remembered the idol of Crete in relation to places on the earthly Holy Land pathway, one also has reason to consider the idol's stance in the light of the poem's twofold Great Circle journey. Some living pilgrims, in the manner of the dead shipboard souls in the *Purgatorio*, did either leave from or return to the port serving Rome, the city pointed to by the head of the idol; and many living Christians in voyaging south and east did go, as the author of the *Book of Sir John Maundeville* indicates, "by water to the isle of Crete" where the idol was said to stand. Many in sailing onward proceeded to that port, renowned in both pilgrim and crusading lore, indicated by the shoulders of the idol. In the words of the author of Maundeville's travels, they journeyed to the "city of Damiette, at the entrance to Egypt, whence they go to Alexandria, which is also upon the sea"; the author adds that the "city of Damiette, is one of the havens of Egypt, and at Alexandria is the other" (*Maundeville*, pp. 150–151). Then the Christians, on their way to Jerusalem, trekked through Egypt and across the eastern deserts to Mt. Sinai.

In attempting to prove that Mt. Purgatory is modeled after a mythical "grand Sion" rising from the peaks of Horeb, Mt. Sinai, and Pharan on the Sinai peninsula, Rodolfo Benini calls attention to the comparative locations of Crete and Damietta on a medieval map of the Holy Land included in Marin Sanudo's *Secrets of the True Crusaders* (A.D. 1320). As Benini rightly observes, a straight line drawn on this map from the labeled island of Crete through the labeled port of Damietta leads exactly to a sketch of a monastery and mountain captioned "Mons Sinay." The body of humanity, represented by the body of the idol, Benini reveals, points to both the pilgrimage port of Damietta and the purgatorial mountain of God, two places on the Exodus path to the Holy City.[20]

Now the entire course of the combined "land, sea, and air route" beyond life to God has been charted by observing the movements of various character types and the directions of their gazes: sinful souls that can be saved journey from the port of Rome to Mt. Purgatory, up the mountain to the Earthly Paradise, and then upward through the spheres to God. The corresponding Great Circle journey reflected in this life, however, has been left with only three-quarters of the circle outlined: the reader has learned that earthly pilgrims are depicted *in figura* landing on a desert shore, moving from Egypt to Jerusalem, and then sailing on to the port and city of Rome. Yet by what route do the mirrored earthly pilgrims pass over the sea to Egypt on the first quarter of their circuit? The idol of Crete indicates the way, with the head of humanity turned toward the eternal city in which the Great Circle journey will end, and the shoulders of humanity directed toward an Egyptian port and holy mountain on the pathway of conversion. Broken humanity to be saved can begin its pilgrimage by sailing from the port of Rome by way of Crete to the Egyptian city of Damietta.

Though on most detailed *mappaemundi* Damietta is not marked and the Nile delta is not on a direct line between Crete and Mt. Sinai, it should be noted that early pilgrims concerned with the direction of their eastward sea voyages—and certainly sea captains and sailors—could not have been unconscious of the fact that Damietta, on more specifically drawn Mediterranean maps, lies between Crete and Mt. Sinai. The earliest extant Mediterranean sea charts, dating from the first half of the fourteenth century, are marked by loxodromes or "rhumb lines" showing the movement

20. "Il grande Sion, il Sinai e il piccolo Sion," *Rendiconti della Reale Accademia dei Lincei*, 5th ser. 23 (Roma, 1915): 8–10; Benini's elaborated comments on Mt. Purgatory and related sites in the *Commedia* appear in *Origine, sito, forma e dimensioni del Monte del Purgatorio e dell' Inferno dantesco, Rendiconti della Reale Accademia dei Lincei*, 5th ser. 25 (Roma, 1917): 1037–1055. Both works are found in the Academy's publications under the heading: *Classe di scienze morali, storiche e filologiche*.

of prevailing winds, and the *charta* in the Vatican library collection reveal one such set of "rhumb lines" crossing the central Mediterranean, the eastern half of the Nile delta, and passing very near the marked drawing of Mt. Sinai.[21] God's winds blew the pilgrim ships eastward on a course toward Damietta and the mountain of Moses; in this fashion was the initial part of the Great Circle journey accomplished.

The Thundering Mountain of God

In the *Purgatorio* Dante's trip from this world to the Earthly Paradise is made up a mountain standing at the antipodes opposite Jerusalem with a summit lifted close to the sphere of the moon. Mt. Purgatory rises with terraces for each of the seven deadly sins from a surrounding sea in which Ulysses and his crew once drowned (*Inf.* xxvi, 133–142). It is a construct of steep cliffs (*Purg.* iii, 46–48), winding paths and ridges (*Purg.* vii, 70–72), narrow clefts in the rock (*Purg.* ix, 74–78; xii, 97), and low craggy rocks so large that the poet, bent on the lower slopes under the weight of sin, must clamber up using both hands and feet (*Purg.* iv, 31–33). The summit is always out of sight behind sharply angled slopes (*Purg.* iv, 40–43). Dante, ascending by daylight and resting at night, feels himself growing lighter as he is healed of his sins (*Purg.* xii, 115–136). After seeing angels from Mary (*Purg.* viii, 22–39) and kneeling before the guardian at the gate of Purgatory (*Purg.* ix, 109–111), the poet climbs with ever-increasing ease up steps alternating with terraces. Attention is focused upon individual objects and souls along the way and not upon the mountain as a whole. Dante reaches the Garden of Eden on the summit only after passing through a wall of fire on the top of the stairs (*Purg.* xxvii, 46–57). In the garden the poet looks upon trees, grass, flowers, and a fountain from which flow the rivers of Lethe and Eunoë (*Purg.* xxviii, 121–132).

21. See in particular sailing charts by Pietro Vesconte di Genova, *Codex Palatinus Latin 1362* (ca. 1320), and by Marin Sanudo il Vecchio, *Codex Vaticanus Latin 2972* (ca. 1320). "Rhumb lines" drawn across the Mediterranean toward Mt. Sinai on the earliest extant Mediterranean sea charts, those dating from the fourteenth century, are visible on a number of map reproductions in *Monumenta Cartographica Vaticana*, vol. 1 (Città del Vaticano, 1944), and in A. E. Nordenskiöld's *Periplus, An Essay on the Early History of Charts and Sailing Directions*, trans. Francis A. Bather (Stockholm, 1897). Other Mediterranean sea chart reproductions can be found among the plates accompanying Leo Bagrow's discussion of early sailing maps in *History of Cartography*, rev. and enl. ed. (1964), pp. 61–66.

Mt. Sinai, in the various editions of Fetellus' Guide Book and in the account of Anonymous Pilgrim VI, is interpreted as meaning "bramble" and is listed twelfth among the forty-two Stations of the Exodus extending from the Egyptian city of "Ramesses," said to mean "commotion" or "thundering," to the Holy Land site of "Galgala" on the plains of Moab, a station said to mean "revelation" or "rolling." The mountain stood toward the end of those worldly stations on the Exodus route representing such ideas as "bitterness" (station five), "hatred" (station eight), "discontent" (station ten), and "desolation of the brave" (station eleven). Past Mt. Sinai were Holy Land stations representing "bridle" (station eighteen), "Christ" (station nineteen), "miracle" (station twenty-one), "in the assembly" (station twenty-two), and so on to "revelation" (station forty-two).[22] The rational meanings given to

22. *Description of Jerusalem and the Holy Land*, pp. 14–21. The following is a list of the stations and a condensed summary of their primary interpretations as found in Fetellus: (1) "Ramesses": "commotion or thundering"; (2) "Socoth": "Tabernacles or tents"; (3) "Ethan in the desert": "fortitude or perfection"; (4) "Fyairoth": "mouth of the nobles"; (5) "Mara": "bitterness"; (6) "Helim": no interpretation; (7) "The seventh station again at the Red Sea, some winding of it being met with": no interpretation; (8) "The eighth station in the Wilderness of Sin, which extends as far as Mount Synai": "bramble or hatred"; (9) "Depheca": "pulsation"; (10) "Alus": "discontent"; (11) "Raphidin": "desolation of the brave or bringing back of hands"; (12) "Synai": "bramble"; (13) "The Graves of Lust": no interpretation; (14) "Asseroth": "offense"; (15) "Rethma": "sound or juniper"; (16) "Camoth": "division of a pomegranate"; (17) "Bebna": "in the side"; (18) "Retsa": "bridle"; (19) "Celeta": "church"; (20) "Mount Sepher": "beauty, i.e., Christ"; (21) "Araba": "miracle"; (22) "Maceloth": "in the assembly, i.e., in the church"; (23) "Taath": "fear"; (24) "Thare": "for service or for pasture"; (25) "Methca": "delight"; (26) "Asmona": "haste"; (27) "Afferoth": "bonds or discipline"; (28) "Baneiachan": "sons of necessity or of crashing"; (29) "Gadgad": "messenger, or sharpness, or circumcision"; (30) "Gabatath": "goodness, i.e., Christ"; (31) "Erbrona": "crossing"; (32) "Asiongaber": "to the wood of man"; (33) "The Desert of Sin, which is Cades, or Cades Barne": "holy"; (34) "Mount Or": no interpretation; (35) "Selmona": no interpretation; (36) "Fynon": no interpretation; (37) "Hebar, on the confines of Moab": "heaps of passers-by"; (38) "Oboth": "Mogi or Phitons"; (39) "Dibungat, in which Israel fought against Seon, King of the Amorites, and Og, King of Bason. Seon is interpreted temptation of the eyes; Og, conclusion; Bason, confusion"; (40) "Selmon Deblataim": no interpretation; (41) "Mount Abarim": no interpretation; (42) "The Plains of Moab" on which is located "Galgala": "rolling" or "revelation."

It should be noted that Paolo Amaducci in a little-known work entitled *La fonte della Divina commedia*, 2 vols. (Roviga, 1911) seeks to prove that selected passages in all three canticles of the *Commedia* have their allegorical analogues in what he terms the forty-two "mansions" of the Exodus. Amaducci, however, displays no knowledge of the historical pilgrimage tradition. His case rests on the claim that the *Commedia* is based upon a single primary source, Pier Damiano's seventh-century Latin

those stations that had them—some had none—derived from fanciful etymologies or biblical events and taken together have no clear relationship to ideas about the seven deadly sins or to formal theological or philosophical thought. Sometimes the interpretations and numbers of the stations varied in differing accounts: Anonymous Pilgrim VI, in contrast to Fetellus, reverses the order of stations four and five and gives certain stations slightly different interpretations; John of Wurzburg (1160–1170) mentions only "forty halting places" instead of forty-two.[23] It is sufficient to realize, however, that to pilgrims in Dante's time Mt. Sinai served as a station in a haphazard chain of conceptions linking ideas of evil and confusion, associated with worldly Egypt, to ideas of religion and order, associated with the Holy Land.

Located geographically in the southern corner of the Sinai peninsula between Egypt and the Promised Land, Mt. Sinai like Mt. Purgatory visibly and symbolically united Heaven to earth; by tradition it was on Mt. Sinai that Moses received the Law, Elijah saw God, and "heavenly angels" descended (Fetellus, p. 16). "It is not possible," comments Procopius in a work circulating about A.D. 560, "for a man to pass the night upon the peak, because at night continuous thunderings and other yet more terrible manifestations take place, which overpower men's strength and reason.[24] The lower areas of the mountain and the monastery of St. Catherine at its base, therefore, were said to be inhabited by only the most holy monks. Felix Fabri mentions these monks in his very interesting general account of the mountain: "Sinai is a mount in the country

treatise *De quadragesima, et quadraginta duabus Hebraeorum mansionbus.* Amaducci attempts to relate the allegorical significations for the Exodus stations, as cited in Damiano's work alone, to appropriate segments of the *Commedia.* The relationships drawn are of a general sort and are often overstated; and it seems to me that most of the author's specific assertions are unconvincing. Amaducci ignores references to the Rome pilgrimage in the *Commedia;* he does not conclusively show that Dante knew of Damiano's work; the scholar does not make sufficiently close readings linking the supposed primary source to the poem; and he does not realize that there exist other medieval tracts which sometimes omit allegorical meanings for some stations while providing differing meanings for others. Nevertheless, Amaducci's study represents an early movement toward typological interpretation, and it does have the merit of calling attention to the Exodus motif in the *Commedia.*

23. *Anonymous Pilgrims, I–VIII,* trans. Aubrey Stewart (London, 1894), pp. 40 f.; *Description of the Holy Land by John of Wurzburg,* trans. Aubrey Stewart, notes C. W. Wilson (London, 1896), p. 61.
24. *Of the Buildings of Justinian,* trans. Aubrey Stewart (London, 1896), p. 147.

of Midian above Arabia. It overtops others in height, and its summit seems to reach the heavens. It is worthy of the greatest reverence because of the appearance of the true God in the days of old on one of its peaks, and the wondrous entombment of the most blessed virgin St. Catherine on the other." The pilgrim continues: "There are many mountains in the world from which fire breathes forth—for instance, the volcano Aetna, and Bobius—but their flames are not caused in the same way; for this mount poured forth flames of fire because it was miraculously kindled by God Himself, as we read in Deuteronomy V and Exodus XIX; for we are told that the mount burned with fire as the Lord came down, and the trumpet sounded to the people. . . . For five days the burning fire was everywhere seen by them, yet was nothing burned there, but the grass itself remained green. . . . There are many mountains with caves in them, wherein the heathen used to act superstitiously, and worship idols; but this mount contains caves wherein prophets awaited the oracles of God, and holy monks devoted themselves to the contemplation of things Divine." High praise for the Mt. of Moses is given by Fabri at the end of his statement: "I could tell many tales of the terrors of mountains, which cause men to dread and fear them, whereas Mount Sinai is altogether free from all such; on the contrary, it is so desirable in all respects that it is pleasant to mankind, so much so that men of the highest ranks flock thither from the most distant parts of the world (*Wanderings,* vol. 2, part 2, pp. 585–586).

In making ascents reminiscent of that of Dante and Virgil up Mt. Purgatory, "people of rank from the most distant parts of the world" climbed Mt. Sinai to its summit using paths alternating with about three thousand four hundred stone steps set or carved into the mountain; the paths and steps are still in use today. In two places the steps pass beneath stone arches, also still in existence, constructed at the end of narrow, rock passageways. Just as a guardian sat at the gate of Mt. Purgatory to receive penitent souls, so too at various times beginning at least in the sixth century monks sat at the archways, now called the Gates of Confession and St. Steven, refusing pilgrims permission to ascend until they had confessed their sins.[25]

25. Lina Eckenstein, *A History of Sinai* (London, 1921), pp. 111–112; William Farid Bassili, *Sinai and the Monastery of St. Catherine* (Cairo, 1962), pp. 164–167;

The myth-making potential of stories concerned with the steps and arches can be noted in the accounts of certain pilgrims. Fetellus in the twelfth century emphasized the enormous height of Mt. Sinai by citing the number of steps at "three thousand five hundred" (p. 15). Leonardo Frescobaldi (ca. 1386) stretches the number to "fourteen thousand" (*Visit*, p. 61). Giorgio Gucci enunciates a sounder poetic truth by avowing (ca. 1389) that in "climbing them [the steps], they were infinite" (*Visit*, p. 117). This very same pilgrim learned that the first archway, "or rather a gate, because it was like a gate," was so old that it was "from the hands of Moses"; the second gate was "from the hands of Elias [Elijah]" (pp. 116–117). Reading the details of Gucci's climb, one almost suspects him of having accompanied Virgil and Dante up Mt. Purgatory: "There are three miles of very quick ascent, and you go by a way that is very narrow, and in several places most narrow, with great valleys on either side so that in fear and peril you go, and not otherwise than on foot, and that with fatigue can you go. You find a stairway, on which you ascend the said mount and which was by hand and force made, which stairway several times you leave again and retake. . . ." (p. 117). In stressing the perils of the climb, Florentine Simone Sigoli mentions (ca. 1389) the "many places on the said mountain to which one must cling with hands and feet in order to ascend," and he writes of the "very big crags in height a stone's throw, and up these crags you must climb, . . . and in this there is very great danger, because from one crag to another there are many and deep clefts" (*Visit*, p. 196).

The climb up this most revered mountain, like that up Dante's mountain, was thought spiritually healing to those burdened with sin. In the fourth century, when St. Silvia ascended Mt. Sinai in a manner that even then appears to have been traditional, she and her group started up the mountain which from a distance seemed "to be single, in the form of a ring," [26] accompanied by a "priest

---

Heinz Skrobucha, *Sinai*, pp. 80–89; and O. F. A. Meinardus, *Christian Egypt: Ancient and Modern*, pp. 388, 390.

26. *The Pilgrimage of St. Silvia of Aquitania to the Holy Places*, intro., notes, trans. John H. Bernard (London, 1891), p. 13. St. Silvia's statement about the appearance of Mt. Sinai is not entirely clear, although she seems to be suggesting that Sinai is in the middle of a ring of mountains: "when you enter the ring [of mountains?] there are several, the whole range being called the Mount of God" (p. 13). However, in

and monks who lived there"; along the way the pilgrims "were encouraged by the prayers of the holy men . . ." (*St. Silvia*, p. 13). Pausing on a narrow ridge near "the cave where holy Elijah hid" and "the church which is there," the group offered an oblation and an earnest prayer, and the passage from the book of Kings was read: "for we always especially desired that when we came to any place the corresponding passage from the book should be read" (p. 15). Close to the summit at the traditional spot where Moses is said to have received the Law, St. Silvia states that "the book of Moses was read, and one psalm said which was appropriate to the place . . ." (p. 16). She adds that "on the very summit of the central mountain no one lives permanently; nothing is there but the church and the cave where holy Moses was. Here the whole passage having been read from the book of Moses, and the oblation made in due order, we communicated; and as I was passing out of the church the priests gave us gifts of blessing from the place . . ." (p. 14).

Procopius mentions in the sixth century that pilgrims gain blessings by mounting first to a spot below the Cave of Elijah where stands a small church "dedicated to the Virgin" which "the Emperor Justinian built." Then the pilgrims move on to the summit and find a church of such "venerable dignity" "that none dare to enter it, or even to ascend the mountain unless they have first rendered themselves acceptable by fastings and prayers" (*Buildings*, p. 147). Niccolò of Poggibonsi tells how pilgrims gain a "big indulgence" at the Virgin's Church, a "plenary indulgance" on the summit of Mt. Sinai, and another "plenary indulgence" on the summit of neighboring Horeb, now known as Jebel Catherine (*A Voyage*, pp. 110–113). Thus the temporal punishments of Purga-

---

1695 a line drawing of Mt. Sinai and Mt. Catherine appearing in a French pilgrim book shows the two mountains as ringed with terraces which slope from the summits to the ground. See Monconys' *Journal des Voyages de Monsieur de Monconys' Conseiller du Roy en ses Conseils d'État et Privé et Lieutenant Criminel au Siège Présidial de Lyons* (Paris, 1695), vol. I, p. 403. A reproduction of the drawing appears in Mahfouz Labib, *Pèlerins et Voyageurs au Mont Sinai* (Cairo, 1961), pp. 94–95. The drawing is mentioned because it confirms my personal impression that Mt. Sinai, when viewed from the middle slopes of Mt. Catherine in the late afternoon sunlight, does appear as a lofty, triangular mountain ringed with sloping terraces, an existing visual model for Mt. Purgatory. After the ninth century when pilgrims in large numbers began to climb Mt. Catherine, they would have passed from three to four hours in the late afternoon facing Mt. Sinai during their descent.

tory were remitted through a "processional method" of spiritual
education peculiar also to the *Commedia* and later to be formalized
in Stations-of-the-Cross worship.

At the first stop near the foot of the mountain, pilgrims joy-
fully gazed on Mt. Sinai, sang songs, and embraced the monks in a
way that reflects the souls meeting Dante and Virgil at the base of
Mt. Purgatory (II, 67–78). In the fourth century St. Silvia, when
she first saw Mt. Sinai from a distance, was told by guides that
" 'it is the custom that a prayer be offered by those who come
hither, when first from this place the Mount of God is seen.' So
then we did" (*St. Silvia*, p. 11). About one thousand years later
Niccolò writes of a group of pilgrims at this same place: "from
afar we beheld the precious Mt. Sinai, and out of great joy we fell
to the ground on our knees, with many tears, chanting: *Salve
Regina*" (*A Voyage*, p. 103). The same hymn, sung by souls in
Purgatorio (*Purg.* VII, 82–83), is later chanted by Niccolò's group
along with a prayer on the summit of Mt. St. Catherine (*A Voyage*, p. 113).

Outside the monastery at Mt. Sinai following a dangerous eight-
day passage of the Sinai deserts, Antoninus Martyr records (ca.
560) an emotional meeting with monks and hermits: "singing
psalms, they came to meet us, and falling upon the ground, they
did reverence to us. We also did likewise, shedding tears" (*Holy
Places*, p. 29). And just as Dante moved to greet Casella with an
embrace (*Purg.* II, 80–82), so too did Niccolò and his party greet
the "Greek monks, many of whom came out to see us; and when
we were in their midst, we all embraced with great love . . ."
(*A Voyage*, p. 104).

Near the monastery several days later Niccolò met other pilgrims, "full forty Latin Franks," who clustered about him like
those souls seeking news from Dante and Virgil at Mt. Purgatory's
base (*Purg.* II, 70–73). "For long we talked together," writes
Niccolò, "they asking us about our journey, and we about theirs,
and if it were safe; and so we asked the news of the west, and
especially of Italy, if there had been anything new: and we en-
quired about many other things" (*A Voyage*, p. 116).

The second stop at the valley and Church of St. Mary of the Apparition just below the gates of Mt. Sinai corresponds to that valley
below the gate of Mt. Purgatory where Dante and Virgil make their

first prolonged stop for the night and where two angels from Mary appear. Niccolò describes the climb to the valley over the typical Purgatorial-like terrain of Mt. Sinai: "The mount is rough with a steep grade, and very stony; and ever you climb vertically as if mounting a ladder: and it is a climb of a good two miles. Arriving at the middle of the mount, you find on the way a beautiful church, which stands in a small valley; and this church is called St. Mary of the Apparition, because here was wrought a beautiful miracle, as you shall hear" (p. 109).

In a similar valley on Mt. Purgatory, Dante is aware that it is the hour that pierces "lo novo peregrin d'amore" (*Purg.* VIII, 4). And the poet hears sung the evening hymns "Salve Regina" followed by "Te lucis ante," the last a prayer to the Creator for protection against dreams and phantoms. The prayer is answered when two angels in green garments come "del grembo di Maria" to beat back but not kill the serpent (*Purg.* VIII, 37).

On Mt. Sinai pilgrims such as Niccolò were told that the Virgin appeared with St. Catherine in the valley before the assembled monks and gave evidence of her love for their monastery by miraculously ridding it of "rats and other nasty little beasts" and arranging for its provision (*A Voyage,* pp. 109–110). Pilgrims then worshipped in and around the Church of St. Mary of the Apparition, perhaps again singing "Salve Regina."

The third stop on Mt. Sinai, the two gates before the plain of Elijah, is similar to the gate at the entrance to Mt. Purgatory. "Proceeding on the said mount," writes Niccolò, "you meet to the west two gates, a bowshot apart: and these gates are strong and narrow, vaulted and well fixed in the mountain. Arriving at the gates you find a monastery called St. Elias, the prophet" (p. 110). Niccolò mentions no warders sitting by the gates on the day of his climb, though at various times the monk St. Stephen and other monks were said to have lived on the plateau of Elijah to be near their posts at the gates.[27]

Dante also observes a gate fixed close to the mountain:

> Noi ci appressammo, ed eravamo in parte
> che là dove pareami prima rotto,
> pur come un fesso che muro diparte,
> vidi una porta. . . .

> [*Purg.* IX, 73–76]

27. See footnotes 10 and 25 in this chapter.

[We drew near, and were at a place
where there first appeared to me a break
just like a fissure which divides a wall,
I saw a gate. . . .]

And as a monk might question a palmer at a gate on Mt. Sinai,
the poet is questioned by a porter who sits at the gate carrying the
sword of God's Word in one hand and the keys of pardon and understanding in the other:

"Dite costinci: che volete voi?",
cominciò elli a dire, "ov' è la scorta?
Guardate che 'l venir sù non vi nòi!"

[*Purg.* ix, 85–87]

["Tell, there where you stand, what do you wish?"
he began to say: "where is the escort?
Beware lest coming upward hurt you!"]

Though on the barren, rocky summit of Mt. Sinai pilgrims certainly found no earthly paradise, they did see "speaking pictures"
which, allegorically interpreted like Psalm 114, reminded "true
Hebrews" of the soul's passage to Heaven. Niccolò viewed in the
summit chapel of Moses an *exemplum* in the form of a "painted
board" depicting many of the events with which the palmer now
felt intimately familiar: "how Moses divided the Red Sea with
rod in hand, and how the people of Israel passed over, and how
Pharaoh's army was drowned in the Red Sea; and at the very place
on the Red Sea I have been, which is five days from Babylon; in
this church is represented in order all the history of Moses" (*A
Voyage*, p. 111).

Fatigued and thirsty, pilgrims regularly rested near the end of
the circle beside a church in a garden of repentance, the single
patch of green in the brown valley between Mt. Sinai and Mt. St.
Catherine. It is here that Frescobaldi and his companions "were
honoured: and so they [the monks] do to each one who ascends the
. . . mount (*Visit*, p. 64). Of the twelve tribes of Israel, writes
Frescobaldi, "that part which repented withdrew to this place,
leaving their relatives, who were about three miles from this place;
and for the forgiveness God made them, it [the church] is called
St. Mary of Mercy." Outside the church Frescobaldi found "a
very beautiful garden well planted with the thickest olive trees I
have ever seen; and there are date-trees and figs of Pharaoh,

cedars, oranges, and very fine grapes. And in this garden there are
three very fine fountains with a great supply of water . . . " (p.
62). Niccolò too mentions the "beautiful garden, with many
varieties of apple trees; a stream of running water, in season,
crosses the garden." Niccolò notes that there the monks allowed
them "to eat and drink and sleep . . . " (*A Voyage*, pp. 112–
113).

Admittedly, the garden is very different from the idealized Eden
in which Dante sees "un rio" and a "selva antica," and for reasons
that will later become apparent, parallels need not be pressed. But
to the "honored," though exhausted, pilgrims the garden was a
beautiful haven associated with repentance and mercy and no
doubt would have been long remembered.

It is worth noting that pilgrims regularly received communion
early the next morning, before departing, in the main monastery
Church of the Transfiguration where Christ reigned with two figures at his side sometimes identified as ladies. "In the apse is a
picture of the Saviour," writes Niccolò referring to the dominating
seventh-century mosaic on the rear ceiling and wall, "on the right
is St. Mary, on the left St. Catherine" (*A Voyage*, p. 106). In the
center of the mosaic, which still exists, the Saviour soars toward
Heaven; Moses, Elijah, St. John, St. James, and St. Peter are depicted in various postures below and around Christ; the frame is
composed of round portraits of prophets, apostles and saints. In the
arch of the apse are two adjoining medallion figures which Niccolò
mentions as being on the right and left of Christ.[28]

At the conclusion of a spiritual pilgrimage paralleling that of
the palmers, Dante, meeting Beatrice who serves under Mary, has
been observed to receive spiritual food in Eden while gazing into
Beatrice's eyes and seeing reflected in them the two natures of
Christ symbolized by the Gryphon (*Purg.* XXXI, 118–129). And it
is at this point that Dante, after witnessing a series of visions,
sleeps but soon awakes in a manner likened to the spiritual awak-

---

28. Photographs of the mosaic can be found in Bassili, p. 143, and Georgios Angelou
Soteriou, *Icones du Mont Sinai*, vol. 2 (Athènes, 1958), between pp. 16–17. There
is some confusion about the identity of the figures in the arch of the apse. Bassili
names them as Moses and St. Catherine and asserts that the monks point them out
as Justinian and Theodora (p. 142); Eckenstein states that they are said to be
Constantine and Helena or Justinian and Theodora (*A History of Sinai*, p. 129);
Niccolò gives the identification already quoted.

ening of St. Peter, St. John, St. James, Moses, and Elijah at
Christ's Transfiguration (XXXII, 70–87).

After noting similarities between the poet's otherworldly journey and the palmers' earthly pilgrimages, one can say with some
assurance that those palmers who exultantly returned from their
sojourn "once to Sinai" would have been far less convinced of
Dante's originality in inventing Mt. Purgatory than many modern
Dante scholars and critics. Spiritually uplifted after a passage over
one of Christianity's most important Holy Circles, emotionally
moved to song and tears through participation in a collective religious experience centuries old, the palmers would have appreciated well the tone and content of *Purgatorio,* remembering their
own meeting with Christians at the base of a great purgatorial
mountain, their confession of sins at the mountain's gates, and
their final reception of Christ in the form of communion in the
Church of the Transfiguration. Like Dante, they would have been
led spiritually up the mountain to Christ through the influence of
Mary, who was venerated both in the holiest chapel in the monastery and in the two churches flanking Mt. Sinai's summit.[29] In
A.D. 808 the monastery was named after Mary (*Visit,* 112n.).
Later in the ninth century, it has been pointed out, pilgrims came
to believe that angels had placed the body of St. Catherine upon
a peak of Horeb after her martyrdom. St. Catherine, then, assumed an intermediary position between the Virgin Mary and the
pilgrims, just as Beatrice assumed such a role for Dante. Niccolò
records how during a visionary appearance the Virgin Mary
confirmed St. Catherine's spiritual position telling the monks to
act "for love of me, who am the spiritual mother-in-law of this
lady whom you serve." And turning to St. Catherine she said:
"this is my daughter-in-law; and take it for certain that you shall
not part so soon" (*A Voyage,* p. 110). With such a holy lady as
St. Catherine to serve, Niccolò might well write that when he and
his party first saw her "glorious monastery, . . . we felt as if we

---

29. The churches on the sides of the mountain are, of course, St. Mary of the
Apparition and St. Mary of Mercy. The holiest chapel in the monastery Church of the
Transfiguration, the Chapel of the Burning Bush, is said by Sigoli to enclose the
"exact place where Moses, being on the mount, saw a pillar of fire. . . . They say
that the pillar of fire signifies the Holy Ghost descending from heaven to earth to
take flesh of the Virgin Mary . . ." (*Visit,* p. 195). And Gucci comments upon the
chapel "where God appeared to Moses in the bush, that is, in the fire; and in that it
was preserved without ever being changed, signifies to us how the Virgin without
stain should bring forth" (*Visit,* p. 112).

had arisen from the dead. . . . Straightway we went to the precious tomb," he continues, "wherein was that glorious and blessed body of St. Catherine. From great joy and devotion we all commenced to weep, as those who had found what they desired, and for long we had desired to come to this blessed body" (p. 104).

While for both physical and spiritual reasons Mt. Sinai generally reflects Mt. Purgatory, another mountain was said to have such features as a sheet of flame near the top of the stairs, a garden located on the summit, and streams in the garden flowing from a fountain. These features can be found in charming, secondhand pilgrim tales of an earthly paradise on Mt. Eden or Adam's Peak, tales of a kind Miguel Asín Palacios and others have cited as circulating in the thirteenth century and earlier in an oral and written tradition of Moslem legends.[30] Asín Palacios fails to record, however, that there were pilgrims who, claiming to have heard stories of the paradise from persons living in the East, merged these tales with writings about the Stations-of-the-Exodus route and circulated them in Europe. Fetellus, for example, writes that, because "Mount Eden" is in a distant place somewhere beyond Mount Or, the thirty-fourth station, it is necessary to depend for information upon what "those who live more near to it assert" (Fetellus, p. 19). Fetellus relates only that the Mount "is situated in a sandy district. It is an inaccessible mountain, and of marvelous height, naturally erected like a tower, as if it had been cut away artificially. Its circuit is more than a day's march. On the sides of the mountain trees are rarely seen" (p. 19). Mt. Eden and mountains near it are said to be "cut into from the summit downwards by arches, by caves, by crypts, by cells of diverse dwellings, in which they say that holy hermits and monks dwelt in ancient times" (p. 20). According to Fetellus, the higher parts of Mt. Eden, where "eternal spring" is said to reign (p. 20), are characterized by "the serenity of the air, the redolence of the flowers, the odour of the spices, the variety of precious stones in the rivulets of the fountains, and the shining of the fountains, the affluence of the fruit-bearing trees and the beauty of the fruit, the chatterings and songs of the birds, the shady spaces and their greenness . . . " (p. 19).

Although this account of Mt. Eden is quite vague, the author

30. *Islam and the Divine Comedy*, trans. Harold Sunderland (London, 1926), pp. 113–125. See also chapter II, footnote 4.

calling himself John Maundeville, who less than a year after Dante's death claims to have begun a Holy Land journey,[31] writes in some detail about the location and appearance of the Earthly Paradise. "I was not there," Maundeville modestly admits; "It is far beyond; and I repent not going there, but I was not worthy. But as I have heard say of wise men beyond, I shall tell you with good will" (*Early Travels*, p. 276). Maundeville declares that "beyond the land," beyond "more than five thousand isles," beyond a dark region where "men find nothing but mountains and great rocks" lies the Terrestrial Paradise "towards the east, at the beginning of the earth. But this is not the east that we call our east, on this half where the sun rises to us; for when the sun is east in those parts towards Terrestrial Paradise, it is then midnight in our parts of this half, on account of the roundness of the earth . . . " (pp. 220, 276). Men always go around and down, Maundeville asserts, to reach Paradise; "in going from Scotland or from England, towards Jerusalem, men go always upwards. . . . " "Jerusalem is in the middle of the world; and that may be proved and shown there by a spear which is fixed in the earth at the hour of midday, when it is equinoxial, which gives no shadow on any side" (pp. 220–221).

Maundeville's instructive account of the Earthly Paradise is worth quoting entire:

> Terrestrial Paradise, as wise men say, is the highest place on the earth; and it is so high that it nearly touches the circle of the moon there, as the moon makes her turn. For it is so high that the flood of Noah might not come to it, that would have covered all the earth of the world all about, and above and beneath except Paradise. And this Paradise is enclosed all about with a wall, and men know not whereof it is; for the wall is covered all over with moss, as it seems; and it seems not that the wall is natural stone. And that wall stretches from the south to the north; and it has but one entry, which is closed with burning fire, so that no man that is mortal dare enter. And in the highest place of Paradise, exactly in the middle, is a well that casts out the four streams which run by divers lands.
>
> [*Early Travels*, p. 276]

31. Dante died in September 1321. The writer calling himself Maundeville, according to his own account, set out from England in 1322, traveled through the Holy Land to the regions ruled by "Prester John," and returned to the west in 1356. Shortly thereafter, *The Book of Sir John Maundeville* appeared in French, Latin, and English versions (*Early Travels*, pp. viii, 129).

From this fountain the four streams, which later turn into the Nile, Ganges, Tigris, and Euphrates Rivers, "come down so outrageously from the high places" that they create in the waters below "tempests" and "great waves that no ship may row or sail against. . . . " Maundeville adds that of the "many great lords" with "full great companies" who tried to sail to the Terrestrial Paradise, some died from rowing, some became blind or deaf, and "some perished and were lost in the waves; so that no mortal man may approach to that place without special grace of God . . . " (p. 277). Maundeville's remarks about the drowning of great lords and their companies in waters near Mt. Purgatory thus parallels the account in the *Inferno* of Ulysses' death (*Inf.* xxvi, 91–142).

Although extensive studies of theological, philosophic, literary, and pseudoscientific treatises have disclosed no entirely adequate earthly type for Mt. Purgatory, one finds that from combined elements relating to the Terrestrial Paradise, Mt. Sinai, and the Egypt-to-Jerusalem journey—all in the basically oral pilgrimage tradition—there emerges the unmistakable image of Dante's purgatorial mountain. The details are not always in complete harmony —Maundeville, for example, gives us four streams in Eden; Dante, two; the pilgrims mention two gates on a mount of purgation; Dante, one—yet the individualizing features of Mt. Purgatory are sharply defined in the tradition. From the pilgrim writings one gains a consciousness of pagan and Christian guides; a Terrestrial Paradise on a mount in the east opposite Jerusalem; a thundering mount of Moses allegorically located between earth and Heaven; a summit renowned for divine manifestations and visitations; tempestuous waters in which great lords perish at the base of the mountain; barren slopes fringed by cliffs characterized by large rocks, steep paths, and narrow clefts; a seemingly endless flight of stairs; gateways guarded by figures hovering over kneeling penitents; a sheet of flame before the entrance to Eden; a paradisiacal garden raised almost to the sphere of the moon; and a central fountain from which flow various rivers.

Most significant is the fact that these elements are already fused in the tradition by the underlying assumption that a Christian's longing to travel from Egypt to Jerusalem, to ascend the mount of Moses, and to visit the Terrestrial Paradise is comparable to the soul's longing to pass from earth to Heaven. This symbolic view is reinforced idealogically by a series of stations along the pilgrimage route and spiritually by a system of Holy Land indulgences granting remission of temporal punishment after death. The merged elements of the pilgrimage tradition, united by the central symbolism, produce in rough outline the earthly counterpart for Dante's Mt. Purgatory.

Stations in a Holy City

Those shadowy types mirrored in the bright surfaces of the *Purgatorio* often intermingle in combinations that bewilder. The Terrestrial Paradise on the peak of Mt. Purgatory, as the typology of biblical imitation discloses, casts off an earthly image of Jerusalem, a city crowning the heights of Mt. Sion. Yet this same Mt. Purgatory in the realm beyond death has stairs, gates of confession, and other distinguishing features which, through the typology of worldly imitation, mirror Mt. Sinai on the Exodus route. Why should a single mountain of purgation in the other world shadow both Mt. Sion and Mt. Sinai?

As early as the third century in *De Montibus Sina et Sion*, a work attributed to St. Cyprian, the two mountains of the living were related figurally because they served as the sites of God's great Covenants with man; and by Dante's period biblical commentators through the centuries had elucidated the typological bonds uniting Mt. Sinai and Mt. Sion.[32] Thus medieval Christians came to recognize the climb over the "ring" of stations on Mt. Sinai—where Moses, the foreshadowing type of Christ, received from God the Commandments of the Old Law—as the natural figural prelude to the climactic treading of the Jerusalem "ring" on Mt. Sion—where Christ himself shed his blood to fulfill the Old Law with the New.

Dante, acting out both the Exodus and Redemption on a single mountain beyond life, assumes the part of a pilgrim in this life whose soul is being converted and redeemed on two "rings" of earthly stations: the base and slopes of Mt. Purgatory which throw off reflections of the Exodus stations on Mt. Sinai, and Eden on the peak of Mt. Purgatory which shadows certain redemptive stations

32. A discussion of these typological relationships can be found in Jean Daniélou, *From Shadows to Reality: Studies in the Biblical Typology of the Fathers* (London, 1960), pp. 1–30.

in Jerusalem on the summit of Mt. Sion. Indeed, this figural association of the two mountains in life draws together two strands of Dante scholarship. For while an examination of the pilgrim texts has revealed Mt. Sinai as a model for Mt. Purgatory, a study by Robert L. John has persuasively shown that the Eden of *Purgatorio* is fashioned after sites in that Holy City surmounting Mt. Sion.[33]

33. See John's *Dante und Michelangelo: Das Paradiso Terrestre und die Sixtinische Decke* (Köln, 1959), pp. 18–21, 45–71; and *Dante* (Vienna, 1946).

Pilgrim writings are used to draw a typological relationship between Mt. Sinai and Mt. Purgatory in John G. Demaray's "Pilgrim Text Models for Dante's *Purgatorio*," *Studies in Philology* (Jan., 1969), pp. 1–25; "The Pilgrim Texts and Dante's Three Beasts, *Inferno* I," *Italica* (Winter, 1969), pp. 233–241; and "Patterns of Earthly Pilgrimage in Dante's *Commedia*: Palmers, Romers, and the Great Circle Journey," *Romance Philology* (Nov., 1970), pp. 239–258. Elaborated versions of these three articles appear in the present book.

By referring to traditional patristic writings by Origin, St. Augustine, St. Thomas Aquinas, and others, Carol V. Kaske in "Mount Sinai and Dante's Mount Purgatory," *Dante Studies with the Annual Report of the Dante Society*, ed. Anthony L. Pellegrini (1971), 79 : 1–18, points out the figural link between Mt. Sinai and Mt. Purgatory.

See also Rodolfo Benini's "Il grande Sion, il Sinai e il piccolo Sion," *Rendiconti della Reale Accademia dei Lincei*, 5th ser. 23 : 1–25; *Origine, sito, forma e dimensioni del Monte del Purgatorio e dell' Inferno dantesco, Rendiconti della Reale Accademia dei Lincei*, 5th ser. 25 : 1015–1129; and *Scienza, Religione ed Arte Nell' Astronomia di Dante* (Roma, 1939). Aware that Ortelius and other writers believe in the stupendous height and strange spiritual properties of Mt. Sinai, Benini argues in the cited writings that this mountain, along with the nearby peaks of Horeb and Pharan, together constitute a partly historical, partly mythical "Grand Sion" which rises to the sphere of the moon. Benini adds that astronomical and geographical references in the *Commedia* are often to the "Grand Sion" of the Sinai mountain complex rather than to what he calls "Little Sion" at Jerusalem, and that Mt. Purgatory in Dante's poem is modeled after "Grand Sion." Both Mt. Purgatory and "Grand Sion" are said to be in desert locales, and Benini uses medieval writings to show that a Hell's mouth was thought to be near the Mountain of Moses. Noting that Dante would be inclined to follow the geographical and astronomical notions of Ptolemy, Benini shows that in this ancient system the sun reaches its solstice over the Tropics of Cancer and Capricorn. From passages in the *Commedia*, this commentator next maintains that "Grand Sion" and Mt. Purgatory are each located on one of the Tropics and that the sun at the solstice passes directly over each mountain.

Benini, however, advances no figural readings. And because he does not make use of the body of pilgrim texts, he is unaware that Mt. Sinai is on the Exodus pilgrimage route, that it has special features such as stone stairs and gates, and that a "ring" of pilgrimage stations exist on its pathways. Neither does he realize that early Christians claimed that at the solstice the sun was directly over Mt. Sion at Jerusalem [see, for example, *Arculf's Narrative about the Holy Places, Written by Adamnan* (ca. 670), trans. and notes James Rose MacPherson (London, 1896), p. 16, and passages from *The Book of Sir John Maundeville*, pp. 127–128]. Yet if some early writers believed that the sun at the solstice is over Mt. Sinai while others declared that it was

Allowing for Dante's religious fervor and intellectual curiosity, and also for the medieval penchant for figural imitation of holy sites in art and architecture, it would have been most remarkable had the poet not learned from maps, guide books, biblical commentaries, and other sources the approximate positions of such holy places as the Mount of Olives to the east of Jerusalem, of Golgotha covered by the Church of the Holy Sepulchre in the city's west-central sector, and of the Temple of the Lord in the city's Harem area next to the southern wall. Robert L. John in fact maintains that the poet would have known the exact size of the Temple enclosure, for the Knights Templars in Florence, as in other European cities, constructed their courtyards and local headquarters according to the dimensions of that sacred site's buildings and grounds in Jerusalem. One remembers too that numerous churches in Europe were built as figural representations of the Church of the Holy Sepulchre, and that at Bologna the structures of the fifth-century monastery of St. Stephen were laid out in accord with the locations of key pilgrim stations in Jerusalem, among them, the Church of the Ascension on the Mount of Olives and the Church of the Holy Sepulchre in the city.[34]

Aware that in the poem Eden and Jerusalem are opposite one another on the globe's surface, John asserts that the Terrestrial Paradise, called by Matelda "the nest of the human race" (*Purg.* XXVIII, 78: "l'umana natura per suo nido"), is rendered in most scholarly drawings as a circle; and he notes that on a twelfth-century Knights Templars' map, Jerusalem is depicted as a perfect circle, the form often used for the city on *mappaemundi*. The two streams in Eden are said to shadow a two-forked stream shown on the Templars' map as issuing from the Knights Templars' church and headquarters in Jerusalem's Harem area; and the divine forest of the Terrestrial Paradise, the wooded Harem area that included both the Temple and the Knights Templars' buildings.[35]

over Jerusalem, then astronomical commentary supplements the known figural link between the two mountains and reinforces the view that they are related.

34. Fr. Herbert Thurston, *The Stations of the Cross* (London, 1906), pp. 6–10.

35. The map of Jerusalem is reproduced in John's *Dante und Michelangelo* opposite p. 18; a similar twelfth-century map, depicting the city as a perfect circle with a single stream flowing near the Templars' headquarters in the Harem area, can be found reproduced in *Fetellus* opposite p. 3. Both Robert L. John in *Dante* and *Dante und Michelangelo* and René Guenon in *L'Ésotérisme de Dante*, 3rd ed. (Paris, 1949),

Certain money changers of Florence, John argues, were responsible for Dante's exile from his home city; but in the Harem enclosure Christ, after entering the Holy City, drove such usurers from the Temple. The poet in Eden is said to be in a reflected locale where the Knights Templars' rule of chastity overcomes man's greed and lust; where under the Knights evil persons, and particularly money changers, have no place. And Dante throughout part of the *Commedia* is said by John to wear as a girdle the Knights Templars' "corda" (*Inf.* XVI, 106) of secular and spiritual chastity rather than a Franciscan "capestro" like that encircling Guido da Montefeltro (*Inf.* XXVII, 92). Having arrived in the Jerusalem of the Earthly Paradise before the prescribed limits of his warfare has ended, Dante, in encountering a religious procession that introduces Beatrice and the Gryphon symbolizing Christ, is said to shadow a pilgrim meeting a religious procession within the Temple enclosure.

However conjectural certain details of these readings may be, the general correspondence between Eden and Jerusalem noticed by John, and other critics as well, provides a basis for new insights into the poem's worldly typology. Using the pilgrim texts one discerns how in the Terrestrial Paradise Dante the pilgrim very concretely shadows an earthly Christian involved in a reenactment of the entry by Christ into the Holy City, his Presentation at the Temple in the Harem enclosure, and his Redemption of man on the Cross at Golgotha.

In the *Purgatorio* the figural implications of Beatrice's entry should not be forgotten. It has been pointed out that the poet, while facing east in the divine forest, watches seven "candelabri" float down from above at the head of a heavenly pageant (*Purg.* XXIX, 50); at the same moment heavenly voices chant *"Osanna"* (*Purg.* XXIX, 51), the words sung by the multitude as Christ came into Jerusalem and went to the Temple. When Beatrice at the center of the pageant finally presents herself in a manner compared analogously to the sun rising, the marchers cry *"Benedictus qui venis"*

pp. 9–22, argue that Dante was acquainted with the Knights Templars' buildings and rituals because the poet was a member of this crusading order. Although the evidence of Dante's membership is circumstantial and open to question, the poet was clearly aware of the order's symbolism, as Helmut Hatzfeld avers in "Modern Literary Scholarship as Reflected in Dante Criticism," in *American Critical Essays on The Divine Comedy*, ed. Robert J. Clements (New York and London, 1967), pp. 206–207.

(*Purg.* xxx, 19). For Beatrice has been identified as a type for Christ moving into his city from the Mount of Olives. And Dante has been seen to mirror a pilgrim who stands on Mt. Sion's summit, the Temple enclosure, looking toward the procession.

This "entry scene" in the other world, while reflecting Christ's actions, also shadows very ancient pilgrimage rituals in Jerusalem. Anonymous Pilgrim II during a visit to the Temple describes the "entry" area, the place where the pilgrimage rituals unfolded: "Not far off are shown the Golden Gates, through which the Lord entered Jerusalem when He came from the Mount of Olives riding upon an ass, while the children cried out: 'Hosanna to the Son of David!' " (*Anonymous Pilgrims*, I–VIII, p. 9). Between the Golden Gate and the Temple lies the Court of Solomon; the anonymous author of the *City of Jerusalem* remarks that in crossing the court "towards the rising sun, one goes down some steps to get to the Golden Gate. This is the court which Solomon made." [36]

The pilgrimage ceremonies performed each year at the Golden Gate and the Court of Solomon are outlined by the same author: "No one passed through these gates which were walled-up except twice a year, when the walling was removed, *viz.*, on Palm Sunday —when they went in procession, because Jesus Christ passed there on this day, and was received in procession, and on the day of the Feast of the Holy Cross in September, because the Cross was brought into Jerusalem through these gates, when Heraclius, the Emperor of Rome, made his conquests in Persia, and brought it back through this gate into the city, being met by the procession" (*Jerusalem*, p. 14).

It is the Palm Sunday procession that most closely resembles Eden's holy pageant; Dante beyond life shadows an earthly pilgrim in the Court of Solomon, who faces in the direction of the rising sun, and who watches a stately procession approaching from the east. The earthly pilgrimage type for this pageant, as it was acted out by clerics and pilgrims each year in Jerusalem, was first described by St. Silvia. She explains that a "bishop is escorted like as the Lord was in former time" from the summit of the Mount of Olives, down into the Kedron Valley, and then into the Holy City. "And now when it begins to be the eleventh hour," she writes, "that place from the Gospel is read where the children with

36. *The City of Jerusalem*, trans. and notes C. R. Conder (London, 1896), p. 14.

branches and palms met the Lord, saying: 'Blessed is He that cometh in the Name of the Lord!' And forthwith the bishop arises and all the people, and they go down on foot the whole way from the summit of the Mount of Olives" (*St. Silvia*, p. 39).

In the other world of the poem, the divine pageant halts in Eden, and there Beatrice, the type of Christ, presents herself to the poet. For early readers this holy presentation of a heavenly figure to a living man, though taking place beyond life, would mirror the spiritual encounter of an earthly Christian with Christ in a particular area within the Harem enclosure. The earthly meeting-place would be the domed Temple of the Lord where by tradition the Son was presented, divine beings descended and ascended, and humans saw the hosts of Heaven. Anonymous Pilgrim v speaks of seeing in the Temple a "great and holy rock, whereon He was presented. Here may be seen Jacob's footprints, and here Jacob saw angels ascending and descending" (*Anonymous Pilgrims*, I–VIII, p. 23). Above this rock in the Temple's "choir," according to Anonymous Pilgrim VII, Christians had carved the words: "The King of kings, of Virgin Mother born, was here presented. This is holy ground. Here Jacob saw the ladder; here he built his altar. Well may we hang gifts around" (*Anonymous Pilgrims*, I–VIII, p. 71). The order in which these sites are observed is recounted by Anonymous Pilgrim II: "the first place with which one meets is that of the holy presentation. Hard by it is the place where Jacob slept and saw the ladder, and wrestled with the angel . . . " (*Anonymous Pilgrims*, I–VIII, p. 8).

Through the centuries a hushed murmur reverberated, like the sounds of sea waves, beneath the Temple's concave shell and around the great rock, for within the sacred shrine went on a continuous, whispered interchange between guides and pilgrims of diverse faiths. Christian visitors, going from site to site within the Temple building, doubtless would have heard from Moslem attendants at least fragments of *Isra* and *Miraj* legends, those stories of Mohammed's journey to Heaven and Hell that commentators have cited as sources for the *Commedia*. "In the house of the Dome of the Rock," writes the Moslem Nâsir-i-Khusrau in telling of the Temple, "men are always congregated, pilgrims and worshipers." He notes "that on the night of the *Miraj* the steed Burak was tied up at this spot, until the Prophet—peace and benediction be upon him!—was ready to mount." And Nâsir-i-Khusrau continues, "They say that, on the night of his ascent into heaven, the Prophet—peace and benediction be upon him!—laid his hand thereon to keep it in its place, and there firmly fixed it." [37]

When after Beatrice's entry and presentation Dante has enjoyed a dazzling glimpse of his lady in her chariot, the poet paces behind the chariot as the Gryphon pulls it to the Tree of Life, that tree which was said to have supplied the wood for Christ's Cross. The holy car, surrounded by seven handmaidens, progresses in a semicircle from west to north with the poet following that wheel "which made its orbit in the lesser arc" (*Purg.* xxxii, 30: "che fé l'orbita sua con minore arco"). The chariot and the poet coming to a halt before the tree, Dante next explains that the surrounding forest is empty because of the "fault of her who gave credence to the serpent" (*Purg.* xxxii, 32: "colpa di quella ch'al serpente crese"). He is reminded of the Fall by angels near the tree murmuring "Adamo" (*Purg.* xxxii, 37). Then the tree, crossed by the pole of the chariot, renews itself as does the chariot of the Church and the eagle of Empire. It is in this part of the poem that Beatrice, listening to the chant of her handmaidens, is so moved that she is compared to Mary before the Cross (*Purg.* xxxiii, 4–6); and Dante's lady repeats the words of Christ spoken to the disciples before the Crucifixion: "*Modicum, et non videbitis me; / et iterum, . . . / modicum, et vos videbitis me*" (*Purg.* xxxiii, 10–12).

On medieval maps of "circular" Jerusalem, the Anastasis or Golgotha in the Church of the Holy Sepulchre is marked as a cross to the northwest of line drawings of the Temple. To an early reader surveying such a map, it would be plain that a procession might sweep in a half circle from west to north, following the curve of the city's outer wall, from the Temple of Solomon to the Church of the Holy Sepulchre. In fact, pilgrims walked to and from the Harem area on what is now King David St., which runs east and west, and then turned north to pass through a courtyard into the Church. Fetellus, for instance, orientated to the east, speaks of the Church as being "a little to our left as we go to the Temple," in other words, to the northwest of the Temple (Fetellus, p. 2).

37. Nâsir-i-Khusrau, *Diary of a Journey Through Syria and Palestine* (1047 A.D.), trans. Guy Le Strange (London, 1893), pp. 47–49.

The small procession in the divine forest can thus be seen to shadow the movement of pilgrims to the Church of the Holy Sepulchre in the Holy City; in addition, stations in the Church reminded Christians, not only of Christ's Crucifixion, but also of the Fall and of Mary before the Cross. Fetellus is helpful on these matters; Christians near the entrance to the Church, he asserts, "ascend by sixteen steps, and there is a great rock where the Cross of Christ was erected. Lower is Golgotha, where the blood of Christ trickled down through the middle of the rock, and where there is an altar in honour of the sainted mother of God" (Fetellus, p. 2). The very term "Golgotha," the place of the skull, was thought to take its name from the skull of Adam that was believed to have been buried there after having been miraculously transported from Eden to Jerusalem. Near the place of the skull was an altar, dating from the early Middle Ages, marking the spot where the Virgin Mary supposedly stood during the Crucifixion.

The correlation of Adam, the Tree of Life, and the Crucifixion is evident from an anonymous pilgrim's discussion of the Cross in *The City of Jerusalem*. After commenting that the wood of the Cross came from the Tree of the Knowledge of Good and Evil, the anonymous pilgrim states: "It happened, as they say, when Jesus Christ was put on the cross that the head of Adam was within the wood and when the blood of Jesus Christ flowed from his wounds the head of Adam came forth from the wood and received the blood which is the reason why on all the crucifixes which they make in the land of Jerusalem at the foot of the cross is a head in remembrance of Adam's head" (*Anonymous Pilgrims*, v–viii, pp. 22–23).

Pilgrims in the Church of the Holy Sepulchre were conscious, moreover, of the role of the Empire in the recovery and protection of the true Cross of Christ. The anonymous author of *Guide-Book to Palestine* (ca. 1350), in speaking of the Cross, remarks upon "its glorious discovery in the presence of Helena, the mother of Constantine," the emperor who was responsible for the construction of the original building complex known as the "New Jerusalem." The author also speaks of seeing in the Sepulchre "a stone chair on which St. Helena sat when she caused search to be made for the holy cross of the Lord." [38]

38. *Guide-Book to Palestine*, trans. J. H. Bernard (London, 1894), p. 7.

Day after day, particularly during the Easter season, processions threaded their way through the serpentine lanes of Jerusalem to the Church of the Holy Sepulchre; "On the first day itself, the Lord's day," St. Silvia writes on the eighth day before Easter, "there is a procession to the Great Church—i.e., the Martyrium— and on the second and third day also; so, however, that always when Mass has been celebrated at the Martyrium they come to the Anastasis with hymns. But on the fourth day they go in procession to Olivet, on the fifth day to the Anastasis, on the sixth day to Sion, on the Sabbath in front of the Cross, and on the Lord's day— i.e., the octave—the Great Church, the Martyrium, again" (*St. Silvia*, p. 67). Even the Palm Sunday entry procession ended at the Anastasis. "Although it is late, they have vespers," St. Silvia writes of this ceremony; "then a prayer is said at the Cross, and the people are dismissed" (p. 59). And pilgrims going individually from station to station in the Great Church would, at any time of the year, benefit from numerous indulgences. The author of *Guide-Book to Palestine* claims that veneration before the Cross merits "absolution from pain and guilt," and in the same book "absolution for seven years and seven Lenten seasons" is said to be granted for each act of veneration at the sites of Adam's skull, of Mary's adoration of Christ on the Cross, and of St. Helena's finding of the true Cross (p. 6).

As in the case of the longer Exodus pilgrimage, those holy places and ceremonies comprising the Jerusalem "ring" prompted widespread imitation and so found their way as *figura* into the art and religious practice of the West. The opening of Jerusalem's Golden Gate on Palm Sunday, Fr. Herbert Thurston suggests, appears to have been later shadowed in the opening of the sealed Golden Door of St. Peter's basilica at the start of Jubilee pilgrimages; the annual Palm Sunday procession into the Holy City influenced the Easter-time ritual of the Latin Church; processions to the Cross, as has been observed, were reflected in the West through Stations-of-the-Cross rituals; and the city's holy places themselves were figurally represented in countless architectural and art works. But in many instances, time and distance obscured from western clerics, artists, and laymen the original sources for the *figura*.

Dante's worldly typology in the Eden section of the *Commedia*, whatever its admitted indebtedness to biblical texts and other influences, must also be studied in the perspective of the famed "ring" of stations on Mt. Sion. For on the summit of Mt. Purgatory, Dante's viewing of the heavenly procession that introduces Beatrice to Eden mirrors an earthly Christian's observation of a Palm Sunday procession into the city of Jerusalem. And when the heavenly figures come to a halt, when Beatrice presents herself to Dante as a type of Christ, when the poet confesses his sins to his lady and receives the food of God from her, the shadowed earthly scene of these actions is the Temple of the Lord. Finally, the advance of Dante and other figures, in a northwest arc to the tree from which the Cross was made, shadows an earthly pilgrim's processional approach to the Cross at Golgotha. In the other world, Dante before the tree will be reminded of Empire and Church, the Fall of man, and the piety of Mary; and in the shadowed sense of the poem, the earthly Christian will meditate upon similar holy themes as he venerates stations of the Cross, Adam's skull, Mary's vigil, and St. Helena's holy discovery-place.

Visions of an Eternal Realm

Gazing upward amid the splendor of God's refracted light, Beatrice, in the timeless and eternal Empyrean, calls upon Dante to raise his eyes to the brightening city of Heaven:

> . . . "Mira
> quanto è 'l convento de le bianche stole!
> Vedi nostra città quant' ella gira;
> vedi li nostri scanni sì ripieni,
> che poca gente più ci si disira."
>
> [*Par.* xxx, 128–132]

> [. . . "Behold
> how great the white-robed concourse!
> See how large our city sweeps!
> See our thrones so filled
> that but few are now awaited there."]

The poet, looking up, suddenly sees with a fresh, sharp lucidity; his perceptions are so graphic that it seems as if a veil has been removed from his eyes. For until now, the visual powers of the poet have been somewhat clouded and the deepest reality of the city concealed behind images adequate to Dante's limited sight. Having passed the shore of right love in the Primum Mobile and

soared into the Empyrean, Dante has first observed the city as a
river of light flowing between blossoming banks:

> Di tal fiumana uscian faville vive,
> e d'ogne parte si mettien ne' fiori,
> quasi rubin che oro circunscrive.
>
> [*Par.* xxx, 64–66]

> [From this river issued living sparks,
> and dropped on every side into the blossoms,
> like rubies set in gold.]

The river, the gems, the nearby grasses, Beatrice explains, "are
the shadowy prefaces of their reality" (*Par.* xxx, 78: "son di lor
vero umbriferi prefazi"). The shadowy appearance of these objects, she adds, results from defects in Dante's vision.

Rushing to the river and drinking from it, the poet watches as
the stream takes on a circular form; the flowers and sparks manifest themselves as the two courts of Heaven; and around the courts,
rays of light emanating from God refract from the Primum Mobile
"as a hillside reflects itself in water at / its foot" (*Par.* xxx, 109–
110: "E come clivo in acqua di suo imo / si specchia"). The
great spiral of the visionary city, within which are seen rank
upon rank of the blessed, is identified by Dante in memorable
lines:

> In forma dunque di candida rosa
> mi si mostrava la milizia santa
> che nel suo sangue Cristo fece sposa.
>
> [*Par.* xxxi, 1–3]

> [In the form, then, of a white rose
> the sacred soldiery which Christ with his blood
> made his spouse displayed itself to me.]

The eternal city of the rose, for the poet, is none other than the
bride of Christ, the Apostolic Church of Rome. And there in the
rose's highest, central place above the multitude of the blessed, the
poet espies St. Peter, the Vicar of the Church, enthroned upon
the right hand of the Virgin Mary. To the left of the Virgin, on
that side of the rose occupied by Believers in the Christ who will
come, Dante looks upon Adam and then Moses. And among the
glowing throng below them, the poet picks out the seated figures of
Eve, Rachel, Lucy, Sarah, Rebecca, Judith, Ruth, and St. Anne. To

the right of the Virgin Mary, where in the rose are enthroned Believers in the Christ who has come, St. John is seated on the right hand of St. Peter; beneath the pair is the chair of the angelic Beatrice; and near her seat glimmer the forms of St. Augustine, St. Benedict, St. Francis, St. Luke, and John the Baptist. According to Dante, this luminous "speaking picture" issues a continuous perfume of praise to the Sun that makes eternal spring (*Par.* xxx, 125–126).

The spiritual adventures of Dante in Heaven's endless light stimulate expansive philosophical, theological, and aesthetic interpretations; the highest truths of the poet's vision are here embraced by a symbolism as wide in import as it is ethereal in substance. Even in those regions of light beyond material reality, however, the historicity of the poem's literal sense, the basis for any sustained symbolic reading, can be more precisely established by disclosing how the reaches of Heaven are a figural fulfillment of eternal truths written into God's Book of this material World.

The order of the poet's experiences in coming to and viewing the rose is revealing: Dante leaves the physical universe over Rome, soaring up to the "riva" or shore of love on the Primum Mobile (*Par.* xxiii, 115–117; *Par.* xxvi, 62–63). Flying still higher to the immaterial Empyrean, he surveys a vast river of light filled with angels, seen as sparks, flitting in the currents. The river gathers itself up into the rose of Heaven; and when the poet initially sees the rose in its full glory, he is stupefied and yet inwardly joyful. Dante is likened to a barbarian from the north looking from a distance upon Rome and her mighty works "what / time when the Lateran transcended mortal things" (*Par.* xxxi, 35–36: "quando Laterano / a le cose mortali andò di sopra").

Since Dante's journey in the *Paradiso* has been discerned as a fulfillment of an earthly sea voyage from the Holy Land to Rome, and since the rose has been identified as a type for the eternal city on earth, other possible figural correspondences are suggested by Dante's final movements toward the heavenly city beyond life. It should be remembered that Rome in 1300 was bustling, in Villani's words, with "200,000 pilgrims" who came from "distant and divers countries, both far and near"; [39] many would have

---

39. *Villani's Chronicle*, trans. Rose E. Selfe, ed. Philip H. Wicksteed (London, 1906), p. 320.

stepped ashore at Ostia, the port at the mouth of the River Tiber, and then walked or ridden to the eternal city along river banks teeming with pilgrims. Small craft plying up and down stream and from shore to shore would have been visible. Before St. Peter's Basilica, where crowds were heavy, Christians in their flowing pilgrimage robes packed the bridge at Castel St. Angelo—a second temporary wooden bridge had to be constructed for the pilgrimage of 1350 [40]—and no doubt took to boats in crossing back and forth over the waters. With the Great Circle pilgrimage figure sustained as it is in the *Commedia*, it is possible that Dante's celestial landing and advance along a cosmic river is a transformed and spiritually illuminated reflection of an earthly pilgrim's actions near the River Tiber and in Rome.

What is certain is that Dante's first perusal of the rose in its complete splendor mirrors a barbarian's astonishment at seeing the eternal city and the Lateran from afar. This thrilling first glimpse of the city was the shared experience of visitors in those periods when the Lateran rose above mortal things as the seat of Empire and later of Papacy. "Roma! Roma! Roma!" visitors in 1300 were reported to have shouted as they came within sight of the ancient metropolis,[41] and surely travelers in all ages uttered similar cries or stood silently wondering before the grand panorama. From hills outside the city visitors might see in the west the massive, round bulk of Castel St. Angelo, and near it, the towering and ornamented façade of St. Peter's. Looming eastward of the basilica was the Colosseum and domed Pantheon, and far in the distance to the south hovered the silhouette of St. Paul's Outside the Walls. To the east rose the enclave of buildings mentioned in the *Paradiso:* St. John Lateran consisting of a basilica, assembly hall, and palace.

In lines immediately preceding reference to the Lateran, the

40. Thurston, *The Holy Year of Jubilee*, p. 61.

41. Descriptions of the crowds and quotations from accounts by eyewitnesses are available in Chubb, *Dante and His World*, pp. 23–25; Thurston, *The Holy Year of Jubilee*, pp. 19–20; and Lonsdale Ragg, *Dante and His Italy* (New York and London, 1907), pp. 1–39. The location and appearance of the major buildings and sites in the city appear in the medieval work *Les Merveilles de la Ville de Rome* (Roma, 1650), pp. 9 f. The work was translated into several languages and was circulated widely, in various printed editions, during the late Middle Ages and the Renaissance.

blessed within the rose are depicted as peering at a single point, the threefold light of a star symbolizing the Creator (*Par.* xxxi, 28):

> Questo sicuro e gaudïoso regno,
> frequente in gente antica e in novella,
> viso e amore avea tutto ad un segno.
>
> [*Par.* xxxi, 25–27]

> [This realm, secure and glad,
> thronged with ancient people and new,
> had eyes and love all directed to one mark.]

And within the Lateran in the earthly eternal city, pilgrims gazed at a sacred image of the Creator, it has been revealed, supposedly made by supernatural means. The anonymous author of the fourteenth-century poem the *Stacions of Rome* writes that the icon stands in the "sancta sanctorum" of the Chapel of St. Lawrence:

> Therein is the savior
> To whom men pay great honour
> That which was sent to our lady
> When she was on earth with us
> From her Son who is love.[42]

The Chapel is presented by the author as a place of singular importance: "seven thousand years" indulgence is said to be granted each time a pilgrim worships there, and a soul is said to be released from Purgatory if the Chapel is visited one Wednesday each month throughout the year (*Stacions*, ll. 401–412). So many pardons for sin were to be gained in the Lateran itself, according to the author, that "in al Rome there is no more" (*Stacions*, l. 236).

The poet in the realm beyond next studies the massed souls ranked within the eternal city, though he does not as yet identify any of them. His eyes move up and down, then round in a circle. He sees some countenances radiating love; others smile in the light of spirits near them; the gestures of the figures are observed to be graceful and dignified (*Par.* xxxi, 41–51).

And what does this viewing of the rose most directly reflect upon earth? Is the poet's vision of Heaven to be fitted only within a general pattern of visions on earth seen by such personages as

42. *The Stacions of Rome*, ed. Frederick J. Furnivall (London, 1867), p. 12, ll. 351–355.

Moses, St. Paul, and St. Bernard? One should observe that the eyes of the poet moving up, down, and around are compared to those of a

> . . . peregrin che si ricrea
> nel tempio del suo voto riguardando,
> e spera già ridir com' ello stea.
>
> [*Par.* XXXI, 43–45]

> [. . . pilgrim who is refreshed
> in the temple of his vow when he gazes,
> and already hopes to tell how it is there.]

At this stage in Dante's journey beyond, the time is the Thursday after Easter. The shadowed pilgrim on earth has arrived at the basilica that he has vowed to visit. Standing with a guide in a spacious interior, the pilgrim lifts his eyes to the most blessed icons, altar pieces, and sculptures in a most blessed setting. He observes the appearance of each depicted figure, its location with respect to other figures. And the pilgrim makes a conscious effort to remember the details of these holy sights so that he can later speak of them to his friends at home.

In 1300 the largest and most impressive basilica in Rome, the one that would have been best remembered by visitors, was surely St. Peter's. To approach the five "gates" or doors of the massive structure, Christians, coming from the Lateran during the Jubilee pilgrimage, pushed west through crowds over the Castel St. Angelo bridge, pressed on along a covered colonnade to a central plaza, and there falling to their knees, ascended the main steps to the basilica in this humble posture. Guides were regularly secured in the Atrium near the Porta Guidonea, the "gate" on the far right through which pilgrims entered. Once inside, visitors often saw exposed in the Veronica Chapel, the first chapel on the right, the legendary Veil with its imprint of Christ's features. In the *Stacions of Rome* more indulgences are listed for the Veil of Veronica than for any other single relic in the city; "nine thousand years" pardon for sin was supposedly granted pilgrims from nearby areas for each act of veneration before the Veil, and even greater spiritual rewards were said to be bestowed on those who voyaged to Rome from over the sea: "And those that passest over the sea / Twelve thousand years is granted to thee" (*Stacions*, ll.

66–67). This remarkable indulgence was further increased during Lent: "In lentone is an holy grace / Each pardon is doubled in that place" (*Stacions*, ll. 69–70).

In the Empyrean, Dante's powers of vision grow until the souls of the blessed are individually perceived. First to be identified is St. Bernard, the person who replaces Beatrice as a guide and who wears the same shimmering garments as "le genti gloriose" (*Par.* xxxi, 60). It is at this juncture that Dante is said to stare upon the shining face of the mystic as would a pilgrim upon the Veil of Veronica (*Par.* xxxi, 103–111). The second figure described, this time within the rose, is the Virgin Mary enthroned at the summit of the heavenly city. A number of holy ladies are now named as they are individually seen by Dante below the Queen of Heaven, and each rose petal that divides the ladies from one another is called a "partition-wall whereat / the sacred steps are parted" (*Par.* xxxii, 20–21: "muro / a che si parton le sacre scalee"). After observing and naming still other holy men and women, the poet looks upon St. Peter sitting next to Mary. Dante calls the saint

> . . . quel padre vetusto
> di Santa Chiesa a cui Cristo le chiavi
> raccomandò di questo fior venusto.
>
> [*Par.* xxxii, 124–126]

> [. . . that ancient Father
> of Holy Church to whom Christ entrusted
> the keys to this lovely flower.]

On earth in the Basilica of St. Peter's, pilgrims led by guides, following veneration at the Veronica Chapel, moved to the second chapel on the right where images of the Virgin Mary were exposed. The Christians, then, would turn their eyes from the Veil of Veronica to the Mother of God. Writes the author of the *Stacions of Rome,*

> The alter of the vernicle is on
> Upon the right hand as thou shalt go in
> The second in the honour of our ladie is.
>
> [ll. 37–39]

Amid the array of altars and images within St. Peter's, Christians saw at the extremity of the nave a throne with seats on either hand for the clergy. This nave was reached from the church proper by seven porphyry steps, two of which remain today; and it seems likely that in Dante's period, as in modern times, pilgrims observed in the nave a celebrated bronze statue of St. Peter. The saint is depicted seated, his right hand aloft in blessing, his left holding a key. Although the first historical reference to the statue dates from the fifteenth century, the bronze is generally dated as a fifth-century work, though F. X. Kraus believes that it was cast by Arnolfo di Cambio sometime between 1250 and 1300.[43] But whether or not the statue was on exhibition in 1300, pilgrims in the great basilica, peering at the icons, statutes, and paintings of God's chosen saints, would have been constantly aware that this blessed multitude of the dead was gathered together in commemoration of St. Peter, the first bishop of the church to whom Christ entrusted the keys of Heaven and Hell. Day after day the pilgrims prayed before the altar of St. Peter, each time receiving by tradition twenty-eight years pardon for sins. And day after day they venerated the tomb of the saint and threw gold florins on the floor of his sepulchre.

In the *Paradiso*, what happens in the immaterial expanses over the holy city is a fulfillment of what happened in an eternal city of Empire and Papacy below. Just as Dante arrives on a shore of right love, looks upon a river of light teeming with the blessed, and then sees the celestial city of Heaven, so too earthly pilgrims came ashore at Ostia, moved singly or in groups along the River Tiber, and then caught sight of the towers and domes of the eternal city. And just as Dante travels to St. Peter's gate and then turns his eyes from a face, like that on the Veil of Veronica, to the forms of the Virgin Mary and the hosts of the redeemed, so too earthly pilgrims arrived before St. Peter's Porta Guidonea and soon after moved their eyes from the actual Veil to images of the Virgin Mary and the hosts of Heaven.

In reflecting even briefly on the Great Circle pilgrimage as it is depicted in the *Commedia* and was known to Christians from earliest times, one cannot help but recognize that the identification of life with a great journey or pilgrimage—an identification central to medieval and Renaissance allegory, painting, and

43. The design of the statue, and the dating of it by F. X. Kraus and others, are discussed in Thurston's *The Holy Year of Jubilee*, pp. 157–158.

sculpture—was in its origins far more than a fictional metaphor derived exclusively from the abstractions of artists, philosophers, and churchmen. The identification had deeper and more abiding roots in the concrete experience of western man. To live fully, many Christians felt that they required the spiritual satisfactions of the long pilgrimage. To turn in this life from earth to Heaven, these Christians actually journeyed from worldly Egypt to an eternal city.

Yet with the ending of the crusades, and particularly after the Protestant Reformation, the stations and relics of the Holy Land lost their appeal; and European Christians generally abandoned the practice of long pilgrimage. The desert pathways fell silent. And later western allegorists, following dominant literary conventions and far removed from the sites and times of mass peregrinations, wrote of Everyman's journey in life as a fictional tour amid fictional characters in fictional landscapes.

Not so, Dante Alighieri. The poet in the *Commedia* unforgettably recaptures *in figura* the "real" pilgrimage world once known to myriads of forgotten Christians who long ago roamed the earth's most blessed regions, whose footsteps over the centuries have worn hollows into Mt. Sinai's ancient, stone stairs. On a lofty mountain in a distant "land beyond the sea," many may even have spoken to their guides as does Arnaut Daniel to Dante on the slopes of Mt. Purgatory:

> *"Ieu sui Arnaut, que plor e vau cantan;*
> *consiros vei la passada folor,*
> *e vei jausen lo jorn qu'esper, denan.*
> *Ara vos prec, per aquella valor*
> *que vos guida al som de l'escalina,*
> *sovegnha vos a temps de ma dolor!"*
>
> [*Purg.* xxvi, 142–147]

> [*"I am Arnaut, and now go weeping and singing;*
> *in thought I see my past madness,*
> *and rejoicing I see ahead the day I hope for.*
> *Now I pray you, by that Goodness which guides*
> *you to the summit of the stairs,*
> *be mindful in due time of my pain!"*]

And many pilgrims, toiling upward like Dante beneath desert skies, must have gazed down upon the heaven's blazing stars.

Index of Names and Selected Subjects